THE
ROSE ANNUAL
1956

EDITOR

BERTRAM PARK, O.B.E.

Ch. Mèrite Agricole

Produced by

THE PUBLICATIONS COMMITTEE
of the
NATIONAL ROSE SOCIETY OF GREAT BRITAIN

CONTENTS

CONTENTS

COLOUR PLATES

MONOCHROME PLATES

4

STANDING COMMITTEES FOR 1956

Finance and General Purposes Committee:

G. D. BURCH	A. GIBBS	W. J. W. SANDAY
H. G. CLACY	W. E. HARKNESS	W. H. SUMPSTER
F. FAIRBROTHER, M.SC.	L. HOLLIS	H. WHEATCROFT
	E. ROYALTON KISCH	

Trial Ground Committee:

E. M. ALLEN	W. E. HARKNESS	E. H. MORSE
G. D. BURCH	E. ROYALTON KISCH	MAJ.–GEN. R. F. B. NAYLOR
C. W. GREGORY	E. B. LE GRICE	H. WHEATCROFT
	J. W. MATTOCK	

Co-opted: E. C. PELHAM, B.SC. (Agr.), A. H. LUGG, N.D.H., Herts. Institute of Agriculture

Publications Committee:

MISS A. M. ALDOUS	L. HOLLIS	L. P. ROBERTS
G. D. BURCH	E. ROYALTON KISCH	W. C. THORN
F. FAIRBROTHER, M.SC.	E. B. LE GRICE	MRS. A. WHEATCROFT
	H. A. J. MERRYWEATHER	

Exhibitions Committee:

G. D. BURCH	A. GIBBS	A. E. NEVARD
H. G. CLACY	W. E. HARKNESS	MRS. C. TISDALL
P. FAIRBROTHER, M.SC.	E. ROYALTON KISCH	MRS. A. WHEATCROFT
	J. W. MATTOCK	

The Officers, Past Presidents, the Chairman of each Committee and Hon. Editor are ex-officio members of all Standing Committees.

ARRANGEMENTS 1956

The Exhibitions. By the courtesy of the Royal Horticultural Society, space is being reserved at the Society's Fortnightly Show at Westminster on 1st and 2nd May for a Spring Amateur Competition of roses from under glass. For this co-operation, also for the kindness of the Royal Horticultural Society in permitting free entry of members to the whole of the Show in the two Halls, on presentation of their membership cards, the Council expresses its grateful thanks. The Society's membership card will admit the holder only. Payment for accompanying visitors may be made at the turnstiles.

The Summer Show is to be held in the Royal Horticultural Society's Halls, Westminster, on the 29th and 30th June next; on the first day in both Halls, and in the New Hall only on the second day. The Autumn Show will likewise be held in both Horticultural Halls, Westminster, on the 11th and 12th September; on the first day in both Halls and in the New Hall only on the second day. This is a new departure to hold the Show on two days, and to make it possible it has been necessary to change to mid-week.

The Provincial Show is to be held in conjunction with the Colchester Rose and Horticultural Society in The Castle Park, Colchester (Lower Park) on the

13th and 14th July. This fixture is not included on the Membership Card, as by arrangement with The Colchester Rose and Horticultural Society separate tickets will be issued on application. Members requiring tickets for this Show are requested to apply to The Secretary, National Rose Society, 117 Victoria Street, London, S.W.1, before the 6th July, 1956. (See "Extra Tickets", below.)

Schedules for all Shows will also be forwarded to members on application to the Secretary.

Admission Tickets. The number of tickets to which each member is entitled in 1956 remains the same as in previous years, and is:

To One Guinea Subscribers:

A Membership Card admitting holder to the Society's Shows in London and to several other Shows in the Provinces held under the auspices of local Societies; five transferable tickets for the Summer Show and three for the Autumn Show.

To Half Guinea Subscribers:

A Membership Card similar to that received by the One Guinea Subscriber; one transferable ticket for the Summer Show and one for the Autumn Show.

Extra Tickets. Members may purchase from the Society's Offices extra tickets for the Summer and Autumn Shows at reduced rates: 5s. tickets for 3s. 6d. and 2s. 6d. tickets for 1s. 6d. The prices of public admission to the Shows will be; on the first days 5s., on the second days 2s. 6d.

Two tickets will be issued, on application, to all members for the Provincial Show at The Castle Park, Colchester. Those requiring tickets in excess of this number are requested to make application direct to the Secretary, Mrs. D. Thorn, Pond Farm Cottage, Park Lane, Langham, Colchester, Essex. Prices of tickets are: 13th July, noon until 4 p.m. 5s.; 4 p.m. until 8 p.m., 2s. 6d.; July 14th, 10 a.m. until 3 p.m., 2s. 6d.; 3 p.m. until 6 p.m., 1s. 6d.

N.R.S. Classes at Provincial Shows. Special classes for members of the National Rose Society are included in the schedules of the undermentioned Shows by the courtesy of the respective organizers:

Alderley Edge, July 14th. Hon. Secretary, Mr. L. Chorlton, 106 Church Road, Gatley, Cheshire.

Berwick-upon-Tweed, July 21st. Hon. Secretary, Mr. R. Hankinson, 2 Bowers Crescent, Tweedmouth, Berwick-upon-Tweed.

Bristol, July 4th. Hon. Secretary, Mr. E. R. C. Tizard, Lloyds Bank House, Staple Hill, Bristol.

Edinburgh, August 29th, 30th and 31st. Secretary, Mr. Maurice G. Kidd, W.S., 13 Melville Street, Edinburgh 3.

Formby, July 14th. Hon. Secretary, Mr. S. E. Lytle, 76 Ravenmeols Lane, Formby, Lancs.

Ipswich, July 18th. Hon. Secretary, Mr. Kenneth B. Fisk, 9 Great Colman Street, Ipswich, Suffolk.

Leeds, July 17th and 18th. Secretary, Mr. W. L. Wood, 42 Haddon Avenue, Leeds 4.

Newcastle-upon-Tyne, August 24th and 25th. General Secretary, Mr. R. S. Woolley, 38 Ridgewood Crescent, South Gosforth, or Assistant Show Secretary, Mr. W. H. H. Tyson, Felldale, Durham Road, South Lowfell, Gateshead.

Nottingham, St. Ann's Rose Show, July 14th and 15th. Hon. Secretary, Mr. E. Mills, 77 Flewitt Street, Nottingham.

Southport, August 22nd, 23rd and 24th. Flower Show Secretary, Mr. G. W. Nicholls, Victoria Buildings, Lord Street, Southport, Lancs.

Schedules of any of these Shows can be obtained, on application, from the respective Secretaries.

Admission to Provincial Shows. Arrangements have also been made in 1956 for the free admittance of N.R.S. Members, on the production of their Membership Cards, to the following Shows:

Alderley Edge and Wilmslow Horticultural Society's Show at Harden Park, Wilmslow Road, Alderley Edge, on July 14th, 10.30 a.m. to 7 p.m.

Berwick-upon-Tweed and District Rose Society's Show at The Parochial Hall, Chappel Street, Berwick-upon-Tweed on July 21st, 2 p.m. to 8 p.m.

Bristol and District Group of N.R.S. Members' Show at The Corn Exchange, Bristol, on July 4th, 11.30 a.m. to 7.30 p.m.

Castle Bromwich (R.A.) Horticultural Society's Show at "The Paddock", Hall Road, Castle Bromwich, on August 6th, 1 p.m. to 6.30 p.m.

Formby Horticultural and Agricultural Society's Show at The Park, Duke Street, Formby, on July 14th, 10 a.m. to 8 p.m.

Hitchin Horticultural Society's Show at The Swimming Pool, Fishponds Road, Hitchin, on June 23rd, noon to 7.30 p.m.

Ipswich and East of England Horticultural Society's Show at Christchurch Park, Ipswich, on July 18th, 12.15 p.m. to 8 p.m.

Leeds, The Roundhay (Leeds) Horticultural Society's Show at Roundhay Park, Leeds, on July 17th and 18th, 3 p.m. to 9.30 p.m. and 10 a.m. to 8 p.m.

North of England Rose, Carnation and Sweet Pea Society's Show at Exhibition Park, Newcastle-upon-Tyne, on August 24th and 25th, 1.30 p.m. to 9.30 p.m. and 10 a.m. to 7 p.m.

Nottingham Garden Holders' Association, St. Ann's Rose Society's Show at The Arboretum, Nottingham, on July 14th and 15th, 3 p.m. to 9.30 p.m. and 10.30 a.m. to 8 p.m.

Royal Caledonian Horticultural Society's Show at Waverley Market, Edinburgh on August 29th, 30th and 31st, 1 p.m. to 9 p.m., 10 a.m. to 9 p.m. and 10 a.m. to 6 p.m.

The Council again acknowledges with grateful thanks the generous co-operation of all Societies concerned in the foregoing arrangements. The N.R.S. Membership Card will admit the holder only, but accompanying visitors can gain admittance by payment at entrance. Members are urged to support these Shows and take paying visitors with them. New members and exhibitors will be cordially welcomed by the various Societies.

The Trial Ground. The Trial Ground is situated in the Hertfordshire Institute of Agriculture, Oaklands, St. Albans. The Ground can be reached from London by Green Line bus from Victoria to St. Albans and then by bus to Oaklands which is the stage point, or from St. Pancras Station to St. Albans Station or Kings Cross Station to Hatfield Station and then by bus to Oaklands.

In 1956 the Ground will be open on the following dates

Saturdays: June 30th, July 14th, 28th, August 11th, 25th, September 8th, 22nd.

Wednesdays: July 4th, 18th, August 1st, 15th, 29th, September 12th, 26th.

Members are requested to comply with the following simple rules made for visits during 1956.

RULES FOR VISITORS

1. Admission shall be restricted to members on production of the current Membership Card which will admit the holder and one friend on the dates specified above only, between the hours of 10 a.m. and 5 p.m.

2. Members shall be required to sign the visitors' book.

3. Rose blooms, buds, trees or parts of trees must not in any circumstances be taken from the Trial Ground.

Film, Lantern Slides, Library. Full particulars of the above privileges of membership will gladly be sent to members on application to the Secretary.

Identification of Rose Blooms. Members seeking to identify varieties, the names of which are unknown to them, are asked to write to the expert nearest to their locality and if possible more than one bloom of each variety should be sent—the ideal number is three, showing the different stages of development, the bud, the half-open bloom and the three-parts open bloom. Some wood and foliage would also help, together with a brief description of the habit and approximate age of the variety. If the blooms are placed in water for at least six hours before despatch, they are less likely to drop during transit.

A stamped addressed envelope for reply should be enclosed with the blooms.

W. K. BENTLEY, c/o Walter Bentley & Sons, Rose Nurseries, Loughborough Road, Wanlip, Leics.

D. BIDE, c/o S. Bide & Sons, Alma Nurseries, Farnham, Surrey.

C. J. DILLON, Springfield Nurseries, Woolsington, Kenton, Newcastle-upon-Tyne.

HENRY DREW, Rose Grower, Longworth, Abingdon, Berks.

C. W. GREGORY, c/o C. Gregory & Son Ltd., Chilwell, Nottingham.

W. E. HARKNESS, c/o R. Harkness & Co., The Rose Gardens, Hitchen, Herts.

E. B. LE GRICE, Roseland Nurseries, North Walsham, Norfolk.

A. E. NEVARD, c/o B. R. Cant & Sons Ltd., The Old Rose Gardens, Colchester, Essex.

H. A. J. MERRYWEATHER, c/o H. Merryweather & Sons Ltd., Southwell, Notts.

E. H. MORSE, c/o Henry Morse & Sons, Westfield Nurseries, Brundall, Norwich.

R. V. ROGER, The Nurseries, Pickering, N. Yorks.

E. W. STEDMAN, c/o E. W. Stedman Ltd., The Rose Gardens, Peterborough.

JOHN SANDAY (Roses) Ltd., Almondsbury, Bristol.

A. R. TRESEDER, c/o Stephen Treseder & Son, Ely Nurseries, Ely, Cardiff.

A. & H. WHEATCROFT, c/o Wheatcroft Bros. Ltd., Ruddington, Nottingham.

Extra Copies of Publications. Members may purchase copies post free of *The Rose Annual* for 1956, Price 8s. 6d.; the handbooks *Roses: A Select List and Guide to Pruning*, price 5s.; *The Enemies of the Rose*, price 7s. 6d.; and *Roses: Hints on Planting and General Cultivation*, price 2s. on application to the Secretary.

Badges. A Membership Badge is available on application to the Secretary. Price for Stud or Brooch fitting 3s. 6d. each.

Subscriptions and Resignations. Members are reminded that subscriptions are due and payable on January 1st in each year. Any member wishing to resign must give notice to the Secretary on or before February 1st, after which date the member will be liable for the subscription for the current year.

H. EDLAND, *Secretary*.

'PEACE'

by Mrs. D. Thorn of Colchester
A first prize arrangement at the Summer Show 1955

H.R.H. THE PRINCESS ROYAL, C.I., G.C.V.O., G.B.E., R.R.C., T.D.

THE PRESIDENT'S PAGE

OLIVER MEE

M Y first year as President has been a happy one; active, of course, but always interesting. Attending the Society's business meetings; visiting Flower Shows and Rose Nurseries and responding to invitations from Affiliated Societies involved travelling by rail, motor or plane some 7,000 miles—a "Busman's Holiday"—and I enjoyed every minute of it. As the representative of the National Rose Society I was always given a hearty welcome.

In *The Rose Annual*, 1955, I referred to some of the Society's achievements; to the progress made over the years and to encouraging signs that bespoke promise for the future. In a large measure the promise has been fulfilled. Another successful year has to be recorded: rose growing continued to be increasingly popular and the number of new members joining the Society was well maintained.

We are, of course, indebted to our predecessors for the foundation they laid, but the continued success of the Society can be ascribed to Officers of the Society and members of the Council (attendance at a meeting involves, in some cases, travelling 200 miles or more); to nurserymen who are not on the Council, and to the ordinary members who play a useful part within their respective spheres. And on the credit side there is the high standard of new roses being produced by hybridists. And here I quote the late Dean Hole: "I believe that our sons will see the rose developing its perfections more and more to reverential skill." That prophecy is being fulfilled.

A feature of recent years to note is the rise into favour of the Floribunda Roses. They have secured a high place in public esteem because they grow and bloom well under many different conditions. But the modern Hybrid Tea with its shapely form, high pointed centre, fragrance—yes *fragrance*—and attractive colours retains its adherents.

And this brings to mind the Society's Trial Ground at Oaklands, near St. Albans. The value of the trials undertaken in the interests of the rose growing public has to be known to be appreciated. The tests applied to new roses sent for trial were fully explained in an interesting article by Mr. Edland in *The Rose Annual*, 1955 (page 136), and I need only observe that a variety that satisfies the requirements for the award of a Trial Ground Certificate can reasonably be relied upon to give satisfactory results.

But the highlight of the successful year was the visit of our esteemed Patron, H.R.H. The Princess Royal to the Society's Provincial Show at Leeds. It was a happy occasion. The interest in the exhibits shown by Her Royal Highness and her gracious manner endeared her to all.

Last year I expressed a hope that ere my term as President expired, the membership would reach 50,000. It can be done, and we are well on the way, but your help is desired.

New members may be assured of a welcome, for all who love the rose have many subjects in common.

ROSES AT BUCKINGHAM PALACE AND HAREWOOD HOUSE

THE National Rose Society has been honoured by Her Majesty the Queen graciously accepting a gift of rose-bushes for planting in the grounds of Buckingham Palace.

The new beds are sited near the north border of the lawn on which the Waterloo Urn stands, but sufficiently far from the trees so that the roots do not invade them. The plan is in the form of a large crescent with a centre bed containing about seventy-two bushes of 'Queen Elizabeth' and Peace which were among those selected by Her Majesty. The beds on either side will hold about ninety each in groups according to the variety, and after consultation the following were chosen: *Red:* Ena Harkness, Josephine Bruce, Karl Herbst, Mme Louise Laperrière. *Pink:* Margaret, First Love. *Yellow:* McGredy's Yellow, Spek's Yellow, Ethel Sanday. *Orange:* Lady Belper, Bettina. *Flame:* Mojave.

On examination of the soil it was found to be rather poor so that after double digging and manuring, a top layer of good fibrous loam was also provided by the Society.

The Society has also been honoured by Her Royal Highness the Princess Royal accepting plants for the rose garden at Harewood House, Leeds. These will replace some of the existing beds and the following varieties were selected to the number of 200 in all. Peace, 'Queen Elizabeth', Grand'mère Jenny, Spek's Yellow, Frensham.

ROSES AT BAYFORDBURY

(The National Rose Species Collection)

GORDON ROWLEY

"O, how full of briars is this working-day world!"
Rosalind in *As You Like It*. Act 1.

BAYFORDBURY is one of many eighteenth-century Hertfordshire estates that have changed with the times. These spacious private residences, with their stolid Georgian architecture, their parks and pleasances, their sunken fences and parterres, their pinery, orangery, and ice-box—they have not all survived the change with so little violation to the original landscape. The country seat of the Clinton-Baker family since 1762, Bayfordbury became in 1949 the home of the John Innes Horticultural Institution, founded at Merton in 1910 by private bequest, and long in need of larger premises. As a centre for horticultural research Bayfordbury is well suited, for the 380-acre estate covers a wide range of aspects and soil types, and although only twenty-five miles from London its air is not yet so polluted as to make good cultivation impossible. Furthermore, there is the arboretum, a splendid legacy from six generations of the Baker family who each contributed something to enlarge and maintain the collection.

Such was the interest in all branches of gardening that it is no surprise to find roses given early prominence. In 1846 we read of the setting up of a formal rose garden surrounding a pool and fountain between the stables and kitchen garden. We know little of the original roses grown there, but the collection achieved an honourable mention by William Paul*—no mean compliment in a county renowned for its famous rose gardens. When the Agricultural Research Council decided in 1946 to establish Species Collections as permanent reserves of plant-breeding material, the new home of the John Innes Institution was chosen for the genus *Rosa*, and by April 1951 the Rose Species Collection was complete in broad outline (Fig. 1). But no plant collection is ever complete as long as new seedlings are germinating in the wild, and the search for new material and the discarding of old continues.

* *The Rose Garden*, Edn. VIII, 1881, 29.

GARDEN ROSE HISTORY

The first problem to attract attention, apart from the unending worries of names and identities, concerned the part these species had played in the development of the garden roses of today. A search was begun to discover as many as possible of the "missing links" between, for example, the wild Musk Rose of the Himalayas (R. *moschata*) and its modern descendants like 'Wilhelm' and 'Will Scarlet'. Prying into the past is a thrilling and never-ending sport: it brings disappointments and pleasant surprises. How exciting it was to be able to plant side by side 'La France', the first authentic hybrid tea, 'Cheshunt Hybrid', the first English Hybrid Tea (retrieved by luck from a garden in Gloucestershire) and 'Soleil d'Or', the forerunner of the Pernetianas (Fig. 7). Picture the delight at receiving a plant of 'Madame de Tartas', that famous old Tea Rose of 1859, parent of 'Caroline Testout', and source of so many favourite early Hybrid Teas! This was smuggled through the Iron Curtain by a well-known rosarian who spotted perhaps the only surviving source in the rose collection at Sangerhausen. Here these forgotten beauties can flourish without fear of the extinction which so readily overtakes once-popular roses. The catalogue of resuscitations could be extended, as well as the list of roses still sought in vain: 'Lady Mary Fitzwilliam', 'Lyon Rose', 'Hume's Blush China', 'Park's Yellow China', and so on. The greatest fillip to this search has come from the firm of Messrs. T. Hilling & Co., who presented us with nearly 400 of Mr. G. S. Thomas's collection of Albas, Damasks, Mosses, Chinas, Bourbons, and other shrub roses. Where better to plant these than in the original Bayfordbury rose garden of 1846? (Figs. 5, 6).

The living museum grew and grew, and in 1951 a separate planting was made to show the stages in the development of the modern Floribundas through first the Chinas, Bourbons and Noisettes, then the Portlands, Hybrid Perpetuals and Teas, and later the Hybrid Teas enriched by the Pernetianas and Dwarf Polyanthas (Figs. 2, 7). The side branches of this family tree are devoted to the origin of minor groups like the Scotch Roses, Hybrid Musks, Hybrid Rugosa, and so on.

The first outcome of the study of rose pedigrees has been presented by Miss A. P. Wylie,[1,2] who based her phylogeny on the cytology of modern roses and their predecessors. A continuation of this work, involving numerous hybridizations between the ancestral species in the attempt to retrace the early steps, will take some years before conclusions can be made. It is part of the general rose-breeding programme which aims at finding out how the species can contribute directly or indirectly (i.e. as rootstocks) to the betterment of garden roses. In this connection it is interesting to note how few of the species (as little as 5 per cent) have participated in making the big groups of garden roses. All can be traced back to about seven or eight wild species—often to single clones of species without regard even for their natural variation. Put differently, our shallow genetic pool is long overdue for a high tide to renew its stagnating contents. Many breeders, sensing this, are already busy tapping new sources like *R. macrantha* and *R. multibracteata*, but understanding the nature of a problem goes far toward providing a solution. The rose species offer many features that have been overlooked in the scramble for bigger and brighter blooms: good foliage (*R. bracteata, rubrifolia, fedtschenkoana*), shrubby habit (*R. nutkana, moyesii*), ornate prickles (*R. sericea pteracantha*) or, if you prefer, lack of prickles (*R. blanda*), disease-resistance, hardiness, long life, and so on. And for the seeker after yet further colour novelties, there is the unsolved riddle of the untameable *Hulthemosas*.[3]

As a single example of the introduction of "new blood" let us look at a planting commencing with the wild English sweet-briar, *R. rubiginosa*. By a cross using the pollen of a garden rose, probably a Gallica or Hybrid Perpetual, Lord Penzance produced 'Lucy Ashton' in 1895. Twenty-one years later a seedling from 'Lucy Ashton' gave 'Magnifica', a free-blooming, nearly double, vigorous shrub still retaining characters of the species in its scented foliage. 'Magnifica' has been the means of handing on new characters of hardiness and disease resistance into the modern Hybrid Sweetbriars, beginning with 'Rosenwunder' in 1934, and brought fully up to date in roses like 'Florence Mary Morse', with the Floribunda-type habit, vermilion colour (from 'Baby Chateau') and long flowering period. A more recent line, from Kordes, and promising much for the future is a cross of *R. kordesii* and 'Eos', itself a hybrid between *R. moyesii* and 'Magnifica'. Thus elements of at least five rose species are combined in a single genotype: *R. gallica*, a tetraploid, and *R. rubiginosa*, a pentaploid from Europe: *R. moyesii*, a hexaploid from Western China, and *R. rugosa* and *R. wichuraiana*, diploids from the Japan-Korea area.

OUR NATIVE ROSES

The botanist can learn much from studying collections of wild
species grown side by side, especially if self-pollinated seedlings are
there for comparison. It sets the table for a taxonomic feast far better
than the canned fare of the herbarium. Where *Rosa* is concerned it
makes one wonder at the achievements of past taxonomists like Crépin
and Boulenger who worked on what was by analogy a starvation diet.
The study of fragmentary specimens led to a plethora of names, and to
the invention of numerous "hybrids" to bridge gaps between allied
species. Many of these names can no longer be typified or were
described in too little or too great detail to merit retention. The
alleged hybrids, such as *R.* × *macrantha*, × *malyi* and × *spinulifolia*,
can now be put to the test by a study of their meiosis and pollen
fertility, as well as by trying to remake them from their supposed
parents. The wild roses of Great Britain are especially in need of this
type of study, as most of them belong to the Caninae or dog roses with
a unique subsexual type of breeding mechanism. Reciprocal hybrids
between the same two species look quite unlike each other, and combine different proportions of parental characters. Aneuploids—that is,
deviants from the normal regular multiples of the basic seven chromosomes—frequently occur. Dr. R. Melville of Kew has studied the first
of our controlled Caninae crosses and finds that some approximate to
suspected hybrids he has found in the wild.

ROSE STOCKS

When a nurseryman advertises "Six choice bedding roses for 24s."
this is, strictly, not what he means at all. What he should say is "Twelve
half-roses for 24s.", because each "rose" is compounded of two parts:
a flowering above-ground portion which is privileged to bear the
name wedded to a root system of an entirely different rose—usually
one of the wild species or something not far removed from it. To this
symbiotic relationship of a successful stem on a successful root we owe
much of the extraordinary popularity of roses today. Without it many
choice blooms would have languished in the seed-bed, and distribution
of others would be intolerably slow and expensive. I stress this duality
of garden roses because it is easily overlooked, and leads to anomalies
like selections of garden roses for growing on chalk or light soils or in

dry places: about as sensible as offering a hen lump sugar to make it lay square eggs.

If we probe deeper to find out which rootstocks are best suited to chalk or light soils, or dry, we find a very different story. Little or no work has been done on which the experimenter can rely—certainly nothing compared with the extended survey of fruit stocks undertaken at East Malling. Assessing the merits of different stocks is not a matter of collecting growers' testimonials (of which there are already far too many) but of extensive, long-term field trials in which stocks and scions are compared side by side. But whereabouts can one begin, and which roses should be selected for trial? The forty varieties of stocks at Bayfordbury take no account of the many local races favoured by nurserymen and worked up from supplies in their own area. Multiply this figure by the many thousands of garden roses, all potential customers for borrowed roots, and the number of stock-scion combinations is enormous. In turning to the search for new stocks, new problems arise. First, both seedling and clonally propagated stocks are in common use and each is claimed to have its own merits. The breeding programme differs for both. A seedling stock is required to germinate freely and to breed true for all characters influencing vigour, length of life and compatibility. A stock propagated vegetatively can make use of hybrid vigour, but must root readily from cuttings. Being genetically uniform throughout, clonal stocks are all equally susceptible to attack by fungus or virus diseases. Again, the most promising new stock may prove to be incompatible when budded with some garden roses, and this can be found out only by expensive and time-consuming field trials. Clearly we must not hope for quick results or one panacea to end all budding problems.

The first rose stock trials at Bayfordbury are on a small scale and confined to a simple comparison of widely grown roses. They were planted in the autumn of 1954. The firm of Samuel McGredy & Son presented us with 384 maiden plants consisting of eight hybrid teas budded on eight stocks in all possible combinations. These have been planted on a medium loam soil in four randomized blocks with a guard row round the edges (Fig. 4). Comparisons are made by recording the vegetative performance of each as annual height, number of shoots and weight of prunings, and the floral performance as number and quality of blooms. The last-mentioned character is much harder for the scientist to assay than the poet and painter, whose rich vocabulary unfortunately fails to satisfy the statistician in search of mathematically comparable data. Hardiness, length of life, suckering, incidence of Mildew, Virus, Black Spot and other rose fanciers are also noted for comparison later. What can we hope for from such a trial as this? At most a recommendation in five or six years' time of the best stock for each of the given eight roses if grown under similar conditions, the stock with the best all-round performance, and perhaps a few observations on the relation between plant size and freedom and quality of blooms. The time and length of flowering season may also show differences of importance to growers. Later trials will compare performances on two contrasted soils: a light gravelly loam and a sticky calcareous clay. This is aimed at putting to the test the popular choice of *R. canina* for heavy soils and *R. multiflora* or *rugosa* for light.

Propagation of rose stocks is likewise receiving attention. A stratification technique has been developed for saving a year's wait in *R. canina*,[4] and is worth trying for other refractory cases. The failure to root uniformly from cuttings can be tackled in various ways. For instance, trials were made of hardwood cuttings of many *caninas* from the hedgerows, and seeds taken from the one that gave the highest percentage strike. By selection and hybridization it should be possible to combine free-rooting with thornlessness and other desirable characters of existing stocks. Again, it has been shown[5] that the earlier in the winter months that hardwood rose cuttings are taken the better for rooting: after Christmas, rooting takes place much more erratically. Another approach makes use of hormones to stimulate root formation in hardwood cuttings. From preliminary attempts improved rooting has resulted from the quick-dip method developed at East Malling for fruit stocks,[6] using a 0·05 per cent to 0·15 per cent alcoholic solution of β-indolylbutyric acid. An effort is also being made to raise stocks in stool beds as is usual for fruit.

I have tried to show some of the ways in which a rose species collection can become more than a mere bank of genetic material filed away for posterity, and can be used to tell us more of how roses may be cultivated, classified, and transformed to suit prevailing fashions in garden shrubs and exhibition blooms. It is popularly supposed that scientists are cold-blooded individuals who see no magic in a rainbow once they have explained it in terms of reflection and refraction of

FIG. 1 *Some of the 23 forms of the Japanese* Rosa multiflora

THE NATIONAL ROSE SPECIES COLLECTION AT BAYFORDBURY

FIG. 2 *Hybrid Musks (left) and hybrid wichuraianas (right) in the Genealogical Collection*

FIG. 3   Rosa jundzillii, *an ally of the Dog Rose from Central Europe. It forms a vigorous
shrub covered in large single pink flowers in June*

THE NATIONAL ROSE SPECIES COLLECTION AT BAYFORDBURY

FIG. 4   *Rose stock trials, planted 1954. The performance of each rose is recorded throughout
the season. There are eight different scions on eight stocks here*

light waves. Some may be so, but I can imagine few workers on *Rosa* devoid of a certain pride in their lucky choice of subject, whether the brilliant, shapely double blooms representing perhaps the summit of man's achievement in flower-breeding, or the no less perfect wild, five-petalled rose as Nature bred it. There is indescribable joy in watching one's own hybrid seedlings bloom for the first time—joy that compensates for hours of failure and fruitless effort. Each seedling defiantly disproves that "there's nothing new under the sun". And the pinning down of a single fact more than makes up for the time taken counting and calculating, when life's "bed of roses" seems to contain nothing but the prickles.

REFERENCES

1. WYLIE, A. P., in *J. Roy. Hort. Soc.*, LXXIX, 1954, 555–71; LXXX, 1955, 8–24, 77–87.
2. WYLIE, A. P., in *Amer. Rose Annual*, XXXIX, 1954, 36–66.
3. ROWLEY, G. D., in *The Rose Annual*, 1955, 37–40.
4. ROWLEY, G. D., in *44th Ann. Rep. John Innes Hort. Inst.*, 1953, 27–8.
5. ROWLEY, G. D., in *45th Ann. Rep. John Innes Hort. Inst.*, 1954, 10–11.
6. GARNER, R. J., in "Propagation by Cuttings and Layers", *Imp. Bur. Hort. & Plant Crops, Techn. Bull.* 14, 1944, 80.

The Bayfordbury rose collections are open to the public once yearly under the National Gardens scheme, from whose schedules full particulars can be obtained. Unfortunately it is not possible to receive visitors privately because of the nature of the experiments and lack of staff to act as guides. We grow relatively few modern roses, and inquiries on these are referred to the National Rose Society's Trial Ground at Oaklands, St. Albans.

ROSES AND ROSARIANS

SAM McGREDY

I WILL always remember 1955 as a year of extremes. The weather throughout Europe was number one topic with rosarians, the cruel cold rainy spell being replaced eventually with a typical Cote d'Azur summer. My own mood was one of elation in spring, when the rose seed started to germinate like mustard and cress. Later, I was to crash to the depths of despair when only three out of last year's crop, selected in dull rainy weather, proved of any merit in the continental type heat wave.

The year really opened with the hybridizing season. The first "cross" always seems to stick in my memory and the fragrance of Panorama and Sutter's Gold on that late March morning only whetted my appetite for the months to follow. My first chance to get ahead of the Irish rose year was an invitation to attend the Rome Concours in April. Soon after crossing the Alps I had my first view of a city which has a fascination all its own. The magic of Trevi Fountain and the Coliseum was only equalled by my pleasure at once again seeing roses in full flower, this time among the ruins of ancient Rome. A prolonged drought had had its effect on many varieties but there was still a lot to admire.

I had my first introduction to Circus, which was to sweep Europe and all the Americas in later months. This Swim floribunda with its double Masquerade coloured flowers was unlucky not to win the Rome Gold Medal, which was eventually awarded to the multi-coloured Fanfare from the same raiser. The hybrid tea award went to Climbing Grand'mère Jenny, a very free flowering sport of the famous bush variety. Swim's novelties collected most of the honours, due partly to the fact that they were worked on Shafter, an extremely vigorous stock which seems to like the torrid heat of the Mediterranean area. Wilhelm Kordes told me last year that Rome was famous for its hybrid tea Climbing Sports and consequently I was prepared for the magnificent spectacle of the long archways smothered with blooms in the display garden. Even Climbing Peace, usually shy flowering in this country, was a picture. Amongst the many roses, old and new, Buccaneer and the old Dickson variety Lucie Marie were standing head and shoulders above the rest in the beds. Here, too, were many examples of the vintage Pernet-Ducher period.

I was pleased to meet Major McInroy of the British War Graves Commission in Rome at the Mayor's Banquet. A visit to one of his cemeteries was mixed with a feeling of sorrow and, at the same time, admiration for the immaculately kept lawns and beds of Fashion and Donald Prior. The sacrifices of our forces are being remembered, the whole atmosphere being one of peace and rest.

After an audience granted to the judges with His Holiness the Pope, I was off once more, this time to the French and Italian Rivieras. I cannot say too much for the hospitality extended to me by the Rose King of France, Francis Meilland, and his family. Language barriers seemed to disappear, and the impressive rose breeding station, described in a recent *Rose Annual*, held my interest for most of the evening. There were literally hundreds of novelties under test, and the many admirers of the Meilland roses may be sure that any novelty leaving this firm has undergone very vigorous trials to prove its worth. More will be said of these later on.

Next morning a short train journey across the Italian frontier brought me to the nursery of Mr. Aicardi of Signora fame at San Remo. High up on the hills were block upon block of red hybrid teas being tested for their suitability as cut flowers. I don't think I have ever seen so many different varieties in the same colour range in my life. It was just impossible for me to select in one day the best of many promising novelties. Mr. Aicardi accompanied me in the afternoon to the rose breeding station of Mr. Mansuino and his daughters. From my point of view this place was just a paradise, for apart from the more conventional lines of breeding, a lot of work was being done with various species, notably *R. banksia*, *R. gigantea*, and *R. chinensis* var. *minima*. I saw one group of full grown plants with the same type of double white flowers ranging from six to ten inches in height.

What a sight awaited me on my return home. I arrived on a Saturday morning, and my uncle, Walter Johnston, was standing in a greenhouse of 20,000 seedlings in full flower scratching his head in amazement. Our normal crop under old methods was around 1,000 a year. Without a doubt those beautiful flowers gave me my biggest thrill of the whole year. Some batches of seedlings, notably those of Ena Harkness × Brilliant and Ena Harkness × Friedrich Schwarz parentage were remarkable in quality and form. After Chelsea, I was off again, this time to Bagatelle in Paris. When I arrived I found that the show had been postponed for a week due to bad weather. I think it hardly stopped raining the whole week and in my three or four visits to the test garden I had ample opportunity to see how the different varieties performed under bad conditions.

The ultimate winner was Golden Fleece, a Boerner origination. This Diamond Jubilee × Yellow Sweetheart seedling is a lovely grower with unfading medium yellow flowers.

Circus was second on this occasion, though it came up top again at the Geneva Show the next week. The roses at Geneva were really on top of form. A week's fine weather had made all the difference to the blooms, the whole garden comparing very favourably with our St. Albans. Swim's Fanfare gained second place in the floribunda section, its salmon-rose flowers being produced in great profusion. The same hybridist also gained premier award in the hybrid tea section, with Montezuma, a remarkably vigorous, salmon-rose. Swim can be really proud of his two "top-liners" for 1955—Circus and Montezuma. I think Meilland was a little unlucky at Geneva and Paris. A week earlier his Message, an improved Virgo, would have been well in the running for top honours. As it turned out he had to be content with a Certificate of Merit for Soraya, an Independence coloured hybrid tea. However, this novelty did win the "Most Beautiful Rose of France" award at Lyons. My pick of his seedlings this year is Belle Blonde, an extremely lovely yellow bedder.

Due to the late season I didn't get away to Northern Europe until early August. Consequently with Southport looming up I had to rush, and visited four countries in six days. It is always interesting to visit the Hendricks Nursery in Belgium because in one nursery you can see all the creations from most of Europe's leading hybridists. Most outstanding of all the seedlings was an unnamed very fragrant pink hybrid tea from Meilland. This I believe will be sold in 1956. Cleopatra, the Kordes red and yellow bicolour, was also in great form and my own floribunda Yellowhammer, an award winner at Ghent, looked very happy. Passing through Holland I had my first opportunity to see the famous floribunda rose 'Queen Elizabeth' in quantity. There is no doubt as to the vigour of this variety as grafted plants were already sitting solid in the rows, three feet and more tall. It certainly is a garden rose.

'SIR WINSTON CHURCHILL'

Raised by Alex. Dickson & Sons, Ltd., Newtownards.
Trial Ground No. 868. Reg. No. 368. Trial Ground Certificate.
Gold Medal, Summer Show, 1955.
For description see page 148

On my visit to the Kordes Nursery I ran across what I can only describe as a wonder rose. A cream rose with a reddish pink flush at the edge of each petal, this exhibition quality seedling 5944–51–1 will surely rank alongside Peace, Ena Harkness and Mrs. Sam McGredy as one of the great roses of our time. As Reimer Kordes brought me down a long row of this variety I had no hesitation in saying that it was the best new rose I had seen at any time on any trip to Europe. Cleopatra was again in very good form. The flower is a little short in the centre, but against that it has the ideal bedding habit. Among the flame floribundas Korona, Feuermeer (Sea of Fire), and Atombombe stood out, while Ama, a red floribunda, looked as though it might have the measure of Frensham. Going through the "things to come" I was impressed by the range of Talisman and Sunset, coloured floribundas. Generally speaking, reds and oranges are being overdone by the other hybridists. There were some complex hybrids of Rubiginosa too, which were making good garden plants with really lush foliage.

On the last stretch, my travels brought me to Copenhagen. On arrival at the airport I was greeted by Niels Poulsen and brother-in-law Ken Sorensen with a nice bunch of Virgo roses which had been steeped in blue ink. The blue rose story obviously gets around. During a more restful two days I wandered through the Poulsen rose fields looking at many old friends and some of the future novelties. The baby Peace floribunda Columbine will be a hit with those who like refinement of flower with the cluster flower habit. It seems to have inherited all the good points of its parents Frensham and Danish Gold. Vigour and good foliage are the outstanding features of all the Poulsen seedlings. The Sunday before my return, I acted as godfather to Niels Poulsen's daughter Lise. Her famous mother Inge, and all the other rose names you read every day in the catalogues were present, and it is nice now as I sit at home to be able to associate all the beautiful roses we know so well with personalities who, I may say, are just as charming as the flowers.

Nineteen hundred and fifty-five is now drawing to a close and one overall impression remains. I can think of no more interesting vocation than that of breeding flowers. There seems to be an indefinable bond among rosarians the world over. Nobody seems to be in opposition one to the other; friendship is the keynote. Surely this augers well for the future of the rose.

HOW ROSES LIVE AND GROW

G. J. VON ABRAMS

Research Division, Peterson & Dering, Scappoose, Oregon
(by arrangement with the American Rose Society)

PLANT ANATOMY

IN accordance with the system of our world, it is the nature of the organism to live, to grow and to reproduce itself. It is within this fundamental framework that one must examine the human being, the bacterium—and the rose. In order to accomplish these primary objectives, the rose must do work. The various sorts of work performed by the plant parts. Structure and function are interdependent, and a general concept of structure is prerequisite to an understanding of function.

It has been pointed out that the cell is the unit of structure and function. A mass of cells, organized and specialized to perform a certain function or series of functions, is called a *tissue*. The systematic association of a group of tissues forms an *organ*. Familiar organs of the rose are the root, stem, leaf, the vegetative bud, and the flower and its parts. The root anchors the plants, and places it in intimate relationship with a particular volume of soil. It takes in water and mineral element from this environment, and transports them to the stem. It transports other materials from the stem to the root-tip. The root further serves as a storage depot for various elaborated substances. The stem provides an extension of the transport system, connecting the root with the leaf. It mechanically supports the leaves and flowers and has a lesser importance as a storage organ. The leaf continues the transport system to its outermost layers. This is a most significant fact—the existence in the rose of an active controlled conducting system supplying all parts of the plant and effectively connecting the soil solution surrounding the root-tip with the gaseous environment of the leaf. The ultimate function of the leaf is the synthesis of food, utilizing carbon dioxide from the air, water from the soil and the energy of sunlight impinging upon its broad surface and mediated by the pigment chlorophyll. The function of the flower is reproduction; the formation of seed from which new individuals may develop. If we may digress momentarily to the aesthetic view-point, the function of the rose flower is to inspire rosarians—and even in this way it serves most effectively to perpetuate the rose.

Now we must ask how these functions and others are accomplished. What are the complexities of structure which make them possible? What specialization do cells undergo to form a particular tissue, and what is the organization of tissues to form a particular organ?

The origin of the tissues and organs must be found at points of growth. The rose plant grows in length at the apex of the stem and its branches, and at the apex of each root. This growth consists in the formation of new cells by the division of certain pre-existing ones, and in the increase in size of these daughter cells. The result is as though the growing-point (the apex of root or shoot) were forming new cells behind itself, and simultaneously being pushed outward by the expansion of these cells. Cell division at the growing-point of the stem forms not only new stem tissues, but also the leaves and the vegetative buds from which new branches will develop. Eventually the growing-point of the rose stem forms a flower bud, thus passing from a vegetative to a reproductive phase, and terminating its activity. One or more of the previously formed vegetative buds now becomes active, and a new branch begins its growth.

There is a secondary type of growth in the rose stem and root which causes the increase in diameter. The tissue called the *cambium* occurs in the form of a cylinder, which extends through the entire length of the stem and root. The cells of the cambium divide tangentially, adding new cells both inside and outside the cambium cylinder. As this occurs, the cambium and all outer tissues are forced outward and the diameter progressively increases.

A new cell, whether formed at an apical growing-point or at the cambium, rapidly acquires characteristics typical of the tissue to which it belongs. A diagram of a cross section of a young rose stem is shown in the illustration. Completely sheathing the stem, and indeed the entire primary plant body, is a single layer of cells constituting the tissues called the *epidermis*. The epidermis provides some mechanical protection, but is most important as a barrier against loss of water from the internal tissues. The outer wall of these cells is thickened, and is impregnated with a waxy substance which restrains the passage of water. This waxy substance is not found, however, in root epidermis, since water entering the plant must pass through the root surface. The epidermis of the young rose stem contains a considerable number of chloroplasts. This explains the green coloration of the stem. Other pigments, especially dark red anthocyanins, are frequently present.

The *cortex* is primarily a protective tissue. It includes two types of cells, *collenchyma* and *parenchyma*. Collenchyma cells are elongated and heavy-walled, and they therefore provide mechanical support. Parenchyma cells are thin-walled, and serve as a packing material as well as providing a pathway for the lateral movement of water and materials in solution. In the young rose stem, the outer layers of cortex parenchyma contain many chloroplasts.

The *pericycle* of the rose stem is composed mainly of very long slender cells having pointed ends. The walls are so heavily thickened as to occupy nearly the whole volume of the cell. These cells occur in groups which cap and protect the conducting tissues.

The *phloem* is the outermost of the two conducting tissues. The most important and characteristic cell type of this tissue is elongated and thin-walled, with a living protoplast. These cells form, in effect, a series of tubes running through the entire plant body, from leaf to root tip.

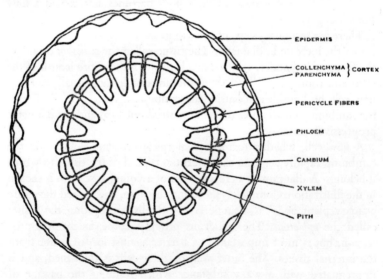

EPIDERMIS

COLLENCHYMA } CORTEX
PARENCHYMA }

PERICYCLE FIBERS

PHLOEM

CAMBIUM

XYLEM

PITH

Diagrammatic cross section of a young stem. Enlarged about 35 times.

The end walls of the cells are perforated, much like a sieve, and through these openings the protoplasm of adjacent cells is connected. The function of this tissue is the transport of foods and other substances, principally in a downward direction.

The other conducting tissue is the *xylem*. The function of the xylem is the transport of water and mineral elements in solution in an upward direction. In contrast to the phloem, the conducting cells of the xylem are not living. However, each conducting cell is in contact, at some point, with a living cell. The walls are greatly thickened, but contain large numbers of perforations, or pits. The most characteristic cell type is greatly elongated, somewhat like a length of pipe with tapering ends. Another type is of very large diameter and much shortened. These cells occur in a long vertical series, with the end walls so extensively perforated as to form an almost uninterrupted tube. Most xylem cells are heavy-walled and elongated, so that they comprise the most important supporting structure of the plant. This function is best pointed out by the observation that wood is composed entirely of xylem. However, conduction is most important, and for the present purpose the xylem may be visualized as a continuous system of pipes and tubes, with connecting perforations, extending throughout the length of the plant body.

Separating phloem and xylem is the *cambium*, the layer of thin-walled highly active cells which, by their division, produce the plant's growth in circumference. The cambium layer produces phloem on its outer face and xylem on its inner face. It is interesting to note that the technique by which roses are propagated is dependent upon the action of this tissue. The cambium of the vegetative bud is placed in contact with the cambium of the rootstock in the process called "budding", and continued cell division in these tissues results in an integral union of the bud and rootstock.

The central axis of the stem is occupied by the pith. The cells of this tissue are large, thin-walled and iso-diametric. They die early in the life of the plant and have no important function.

The anatomy of the root is essentially similar to that of the stem. As pointed out, the conducting tissues are continuous. However, thin-walled pericycle is more extensive than in the stem, and it is in this tissue that branch roots arise. Between the pericycle and the cortex occurs a single layer of cells called the *endodermis*. These cells have a peculiar thickening of the wall, and are thought to function in the control of water movement across the root between the conducting tissues and the cortex. The central axis of the root is occupied by xylem, and no pith occurs.

The leaf is an organ specialized for the manufacture of food. The "veins" of the leaf are in fact strands of conducting tissue—xylem and phloem. These provide water and mineral elements to the leaf cytoplasm, and transport food materials to the stem. The leaf is sheathed in epidermis, and the upper surface in particular is heavily impregnated with a waxy substance which prevents loss of water. The process of food manufacture is dependent upon an intake of gaseous carbon dioxide from the external air. The lower surface of the leaf contains many pores, called stomata, which are bounded by specialized cells able to expand and contract, under physiological control, in such a way as to open and close the pore in the manner of a valve. Through the operation of this mechanism, the leaf is able to effect an exchange of gases with the external atmosphere without suffering a consequent excessive loss of water from its water-saturated internal atmosphere. The internal cells of the leaf, other than the bundles of conducting tissues, are thin-walled, highly active and contain a great number of chloroplasts. These cells do not impinge closely upon one another except at occasional points on their surfaces, but are instead separated by a continuous system of air spaces. This ventilating system is connected with the stomata, and makes possible the contact of each cell with the gaseous atmosphere.

Summary

Structure and function in plant parts are inter-dependent. The plant parts, or organs, such as root, stem, leaf, vegetative, bud and flower, perform certain characteristic types of work. These organs are composed of tissues, which are groups of cells specialized to perform more limited and precise functions.

The organs and tissues are formed at apical growing points, and by an internal secondary growth tissue, the cambium, which produces the growth in circumference of stem and root. For an elementary view of physiology, emphasis is placed upon the conducting tissues, which are continuous through the entire length of the plant body, the gas-exchange system and high chlorophyll concentration of the leaf.

THE SOIL-WATER-ROOT RELATIONSHIP

The rose, like nearly all other living organisms, requires large quantities of water. Water constitutes the major part of the living plant, and in fact may constitute over 90 per cent of the total weight of active protoplasm. It is essential to the living process primarily because of the chemical and physical characteristics which make it an excellent solvent. It is the solvent in which mineral elements are taken into the plant and transferred within the plant. It is the solvent in which foods and other elaborated compounds of the plant are transferred to tissue in which they are utilized or stored. Nearly all chemical reactions and physiological processes of the plant are dependent upon water as a solvent. In addition, water participates directly in the reaction by which foods are manufactured.

Nearly all water available to the plant must be absorbed from the soil by the root system. It is therefore necessary to consider the general nature of soils, and the relationship between soil, water and root. It is not sufficient for the rosarian to think of soil as simply "dirt". Soils are composed of various proportions of rock particles, organic matter, water, air and micro-organisms (bacteria and fungi). Mineral elements and degradation products of organic matter occur in solution in the soil water. Each of these components participates in an endless physical and chemical alteration.

The minute rock particles comprise approximately 90 per cent of the dry weight of an average soil. Classification of a particular soil as clay, loam or sandy loam is based largely on the size of these particles. Dissolution of the rock particles provides a source of mineral elements for plants. Organic matter, the decomposition products of plant and animal residues, contributes enormously to a desirable physical structure of soils. It increases air capacity and water-holding capacity, and provides the physical site for much of the complex soil chemistry. It is an indispensable food source for soil micro-organisms. The importance of the aeration of a soil (specifically oxygen content and carbon dioxide removal) is continually stressed in relation to the growth of rose roots. This is the reason a well-drained soil is desirable. It would be exceedingly difficult to maintain a soil in a condition suitable for the growth of roses, or indeed any other garden plant, without a large population of *micro-organisms*. These minute creatures decompose organic matter, thus releasing the component chemical substances. Certain bacteria are responsible for the chemical transformations of nitrogen and nitrogen compounds which make this essential element available to the plant.

Water occurs in the soil in three principal physical relationships: free water, capillary water and "bound" water. Free water occurs in a soil which is completely water-saturated, all interstices (spaces between particles) being filled. Roses do not survive where this condition is permanent, since the requirement of the root for oxygen is not satisfied. Normally free water percolates downward in response to the force of gravity until the water-table is reached, or until a distribution equilibrium is achieved. When such distribution is complete, a film of capillary water remains upon all particle surfaces. This water film is held against the force of gravity by capillarity. Free water may be distributed in all directions (capillary movement) by this same force. Capillarity is explained by the fact that there is a greater attraction between water molecules and soil particles (or many other materials) than between the water molecules themselves. An object dipped in water comes out wet. The attractive force, water molecule to object, is greater than the attractive force, water molecule to water molecule. (A discussion of these forces would involve the physical chemistry of the molecule.) Similarly, if one end of an open glass tube of extremely small bore is held in a vessel of water, an upward movement of water will occur within the tube, reaching a height considerably above the original level of water in the vessel. This movement continues until the attraction between the water and the inner surface of the glass tube is balanced by the combined forces of the attraction of water to water and the "pull" of gravity upon the column of water. The movement will be greater in a smaller-bored tube, since the attractive force will be as great and the weight of the column of water of equal length will be less. Horizontal movement is of course less restricted by gravity than vertical upward movement. The distribution of water within a blotter provides an excellent demonstration of capillary movement. Water moves similarly in a soil. The size of the soil particles determines the size of the interstices between particles (corresponding to the size of the bore of the glass tube) and therefore limits the distance over which capillary movement may occur. For example, in a sandy soil the particles are relatively large and the spaces between particles large. The weight of a column of water of this size is too great to be lifted or held

'KING MIDAS'
by Arbel M. Aldous.
First Prize in the Decorative Class "to illustrate a theme".
Summer Show, 1955.

by capillary attraction. The greater portion of the water applied to such a soil moves downward by gravity, leaving only a capillary film surrounding each particle.

As water is removed from a soil, by evaporation and by root action, a limited capillary redistribution may occur. As the removal continues, the capillary columns are diminished and eventually reduced to discontinuous films. This water is still available to plants, but probably not as easily available as the water of capillary columns. The common horticultural practice of "mulching" is effective in providing a surface discontinuity in the system of fine capillary "tubes". A mulch replaces a capillary system with a non-capillary one at the surface of the soil, thus limiting water loss caused by surface evaporation.

Most soils contain from 1 to 5 per cent of "bound" water, which is not available to the plant. These water molecules are either held within the colloidal structure of organic matter and clay, or so strongly absorbed electro-chemically to particle surfaces as to be driven off only by very high temperatures.

The ability of the rose plant to satisfy its water requirement does not depend only upon the quantity of available water in the soil. It has been pointed out that after free water has been dispersed by gravity, and capillary equilibrium has been attained, any further reduction of water content reduces capillary movement to insignificance. Even before this degree of dryness has been reached, capillary movement proceeds at a decreased rate. Thus as the absorbing root removes the available water from the soil with which it is in contact, there is no redistribution of water to replenish the supply. The ability of the root to continue to absorb water is dependent upon its ability to move continually to new soil areas—to grow. One root, even though it may grow most vigorously, can contact only a very small volume of soil. The satisfaction of the plant's water requirement, in this respect, depends upon the number of absorbing root tips and their distribution throughout the soil mass. This is a matter of particular interest in the case of rose plants, because they are reproduced commercially upon various types of rootstocks. The number of different species, varieties and strains used for this purpose is very great, and it is important to realize that even closely related strains may differ remarkably in a number of physiological characteristics. The influence of these differences is reflected in the entire plant, and this is a problem which the industry must consider.

For example, the extensive rootstock selection tests being conducted by Peterson & Dering have demonstrated that some strains are superior in their ability to satisfy the water requirement of a number of scion* varieties under conditions approaching a critical water deficit. That does not indicate that the individual root of one strain is able to extract more water from a soil than the root of another strain, nor that a physiological drought-resistance has been imparted to the scion (although this is a possibility) but rather that the superior rootstock has characteristically a large number of active roots and an even distribution of those roots.

The active water-absorbing section of the root occurs just above the growing point and is relatively restricted in length. It corrresponds closely to the region of the root which bears the root-hairs, and, in fact, the root-hairs are themselves responsible for the major volume of water absorbed. The root-hair is an elongate tubular protuberance of the external wall of an epidermal cell, and is thus microscopic. The wall of the hair is essentially like the wall of the epidermal cell, and its effectiveness as an absorbing structure is a result of the vast increase in area of absorbing surface which it provides. Root-hairs are short-lived, but as the growing-point of the root progresses through the soil, new root-hairs are continually formed. Thus great numbers of active root-hairs are progressively in contact with new soil volumes. Older sections of roots (above the section which bears root-hairs) do not absorb water, principally because layers of corky bark tissue are formed by a secondary cambium which arises in the pericycle or phloem.

The water molecule enters the plant through the cell wall of a root-hair or an epidermal cell of the root tip, passes across the cortex and the endodermis, and eventually enters a xylem vessel. Here it becomes a part of the conducting stream which moves upward in a vast series of water columns, supplying the upper parts of the plant. It may be utilized in a chemical reaction, it may serve as a solvent in the downward transport of food through the phloem, it may become a part of the protoplasm or contribute to the fluid of a cell vacuole. It is most probable that it will leave the plant through a leaf stomate in the process of transpiration, for the plant must absorb much more water than it retains.

---

* Scion—the top of the grafted plant, in contrast to the root.

SUMMARY

The large quantity of water essential to the living process must be obtained by plant roots from the soil. Soils are composed of rock particles, organic matter, water, air and micro-organisms, all of which play an important part in the plant's environment. Water occurs in three physical relationships with the soil: free, capillary and "bound". Capillary water is most important to the plant. The ability of the plant to obtain water depends not only upon the availability of water, but also upon root distribution. Most water absorbed by the plant is taken in through the root-hairs, and is then passed across the root to the xylem vessels in which it moves upward to take part in a large number of essential processes.

MULTIFLORA SHOCK ABSORBER

Rosa multiflora is frequently used nowadays in this country as an understock on light soils, especially for floribundas. An entirely new use has now been found for this species.

In the U.S.A., accident investigation by Motor Vehicle Research Inc. has demonstrated that many lives can be saved by the ability of small trees and shrubs to act as crash-barriers, stopping a car at a reasonable distance when it runs off the highway. Experimental tests indicated that *R. multiflora* might provide the answer.

A full-grown planting of this species, 6–8 feet high and 24 feet wide, is claimed to stop a 4,000 lb. vehicle, travelling at 20 to 30 miles an hour, with no apparent injury. It is anticipated that this barrier will be equally effective at speeds up to 50 miles an hour.

R. multiflora is stated to continue to grow after being crushed by the impact of the car. It cannot be "killed out" even when "burnt over".

A crash-barrier of this species has also been planned in England by the Ministry of Transport for the Cromwell Road extension through Chiswick.

N. P. HARVEY

TWO PENNSYLVANIA ROSE GARDENS

CATHERINE E. MEIKLE
HARRISBURG

HERE we are on a quiet, hazy Sunday morning in late summer at the Hershey Rose Garden in south-central Pennsylvania. It is only 9.30 o'clock but already visitors are driving up, cameras in hand. The winding road that brought us up the hill has deposited us in a spot advantageous for viewing the "Chocolate Town", as Hershey is called. The chocolate bar manufactured here has taken the Hershey name to the far corners of the earth.

The model community built by Mr. Milton S. Hershey for his employees includes not only the customary bank, post office, department store and hospital but many other facilities that have geared the town for large-scale entertainment. Four golf courses, an outdoor stadium seating 15,000, and an indoor sports arena attract sports lovers from a wide area. The swimming-pool and ballroom, as well as numerous amusement features in the 1,000-acre park, make Hershey a popular spot for summer outings. The community building on the main street houses the town library, a theatre and cafeteria.

The large institution that we passed on our way to the rose garden is the Milton Hershey School, established in 1909 to provide a home and education for needy orphans. Mr. Hershey endowed the school and lived to see it grow to a capacity of 1,200 boys. It gives the opportunity for learning twelve trades, as well as college preparatory and business courses. Here are classrooms, shops and gymnasium but no dormitories, for the school is operated on the farm-home plan. Groups of twenty to thirty boys live as a family, with a married couple acting as father and mother, in large, red-brick homes on the farms that provide the milk for the Hershey chocolate factory.

Farther up our road, at the crest of the hill, stands the luxurious Hotel Hershey. Its Spanish-type architecture and restful patio-lobby are distinctive. It commands a magnificent view of the Lebanon Valley, with acres of rich farmland encircled by gentle hills.

It was in April 1936 that construction of the rose garden began, on a south-eastern slope of largely shale soil. A semi-formal garden was

'RED WONDER' (flor.)

about ⅔ natural size

Better Times × poly. seedling.
Raised by G. de Ruiter, Holland.
Trial Ground No. 325. Reg. No. 339. Trial Ground Certificate.
For description see page 143, "Rose Annual" 1955

planned, for the enjoyment of the public. Over 12,000 bushes were planted that autumn, but several additions since then have brought the present total to something like 42,000 plants. Fortunately the site allowed expansion, and the garden plan was flexible.

The location of the garden makes possible many beautiful vistas. From the summerhouse near the top of the slope one looks down on the circular reflecting pool. This is an artificial lake that was constructed in an eroded gully. On it are swans and ducks; ramblers and polyanthas grow on its banks. Around the pool are located oblong rose-beds, of varying sizes, with generally only one variety to a bed.

Farther down, the slope is terraced. Grass walks four to six feet wide allow the streams of visitors to pass from one section to another. Pergolas covered with New Dawn are placed in the lowest part of the hill-side. At the gift shop in a comfortable grove of trees may be purchased potted rose plants and a variety of gift items. Extensive rose-beds lie east of the reflecting pool. Beyond the summerhouse, spring-flowering bulbs and summer bedding plants have been added to the display of roses.

Responsible for the design, construction and supervision of the Hershey Rose Garden is Mr. Harry L. Erdman, Director of Horti-culture for the Hershey Estates and a former treasurer and president of the American Rose Society. Not only new varieties but also old and "middle-aged" ones are grown here. As replacements are needed, the newest varieties find their way into the garden. Many evergreens, sheared into columns and pyramids, stand like guards over the roses. Some clipped hedges and shrub borders are a welcome note here and there, and along some of the driveways are set iron posts connected with heavy chains on which Paul's Scarlet Climber is trained.

A warm August morning is not the time to expect any rose garden to be at its best, you may say. True—especially just after a record-breaking hot spell, followed by equally record-breaking rains. But let's walk through the garden anyway, noting which varieties have best survived the bad weather. Anything that looks good now really *must* be good!

First of all, here's a large bed of Warrawee and high plants of Red Radiance, clothed with foliage down to the ground. Mrs. Sam McGredy looks quite good, and the President Eisenhower is still better —very bushy and healthy.

Down in the terraced section there's a planting of something pink, tall and wonderful. Closer inspection proves it to be 'Queen Elizabeth'. Naturally, we are delighted to see this new prize-winning floribunda making such a fine showing. Perhaps the sweet, bright pink flowers were larger earlier in the summer, but now they are about three inches across, borne on sturdy canes that branch out at the top. Near by is Buccaneer, a splendid bright yellow, not so high as 'Queen Elizabeth' but very good nevertheless.

And in contrast to these new roses, here is an outstanding "old-timer", Duchess of Wellington, with excellent healthy looking foliage although the flowers are thin in comparison with many others. Another standby is Betty Prior, of which there is a thick planting.

A stone wall holding the bank across this lower part of the garden serves as the background for a row of hybrid perpetuals, species and other old roses. Here is *Rosa gallica*, laden with fat orange fruits and famous old Frau Karl Druschki with some snowy bloom centred with soft melon-coloured stamens. Isn't there just a whisper of fragrance too, or is this wishful thinking? Among others in this gallery of rose ancestors are thrifty bushes of Mme Albert Barbier, Ulrich Brunner, Mme Hardy, Lucy Ashton, and Salet.

Going back to modern roses, here is a gay colour that makes a person stop: Fashion. The plants are low but good. And how lovely Helen Traubel is! The flowers are still large, this late in the season. Maman Turbat is a mass of pink, covering the ground. Over here along the driveway is an extremely tall border of Henry Nevard. It must be six feet high. Some deep crimson blooms are showing.

Another old rose, National Flower Guild, is doing well at Hershey. Plants are full of foliage. Condesa de Sástago, too, is well-branched. Capistrano and Mission Bells are impressive, especially the latter, with very fine colour.

Can white ever be described as "smashing"? If so, Blanche Mallerin fits the word, for it is fully as eye-catching as any scarlet. Good News is another that does very well here; there are two splendid beds of it.

Now let's stroll down through this less planted area. If the rose garden is extended, no doubt this is the direction it will take. Here are wide grassy stretches, punctuated with evergreens, deciduous trees and huge shrubs. We notice handsome specimens of various cedars and junipers and thriving hedges of mahonia, viburnum, halesia and euonymus.

And what is this picket-fenced area with its boxwood-edged rose-beds? A plaque marks it as the original rose garden of Mr. and Mrs. Milton S. Hershey, planted in 1908 at their home (now the Hershey Country Club) and transplanted in 1942 to its present location. It gives a pleasant personal touch to this immense garden.

A bit beyond is still another rose planting, which includes several new varieties. Among those that have made an encouraging start are blazing Wildfire, Grand'mère Jenny, Konrad Adenauer, dazzling Red Favourite and Montezuma.

Circling back to our starting place, we stop long enough to admire the summer bedding plants now in full bloom. Among them are asters, zinnias, marigolds, lantana, cannas, phlox, salvia and gaillardia. A fine abelia hedge grows along one side, balanced by azaleas on the other.

And so we take a final lingering glance at the Hershey Rose Garden, the largest in America.

Twelve miles west of Hershey, in Harrisburg, the capital of Pennsylvania, are the Breeze Hill Gardens. This two and a half acre property was the home of the late Dr. J. Horace McFarland, with whom many members of the National Rose Society undoubtedly had correspondence. In his capacity as editor of the Annual of the American Rose Society for almost thirty years, Dr. McFarland tried to keep in touch with rose progress in every country.

There is nothing elaborate or ostentatious about Breeze Hill. Here the emphasis is on the plant material. This was not intended to be a public garden nor a botanical garden, but a demonstration of the use and culture of worth-while plants under ordinary growing conditions. It is a group of small gardens rather than one large layout. The object was to have a continually changing series of growing pictures, presenting a succession of bloom all through the year, from the witch-hazel of January to the Christmas rose of December.

Dr. McFarland was a fortunate man in that he was able to combine his vocation of printing with his avocation of horticulture, particularly rose culture. As the Mt. Pleasant Press, which he headed until his death in 1948 at the age of eighty-nine, turned more and more to the speciality of horticultural printing, the necessity of having good photographs of plants on hand became more urgent. So it was that Breeze

Hill Gardens developed into the outdoor laboratory of the Mt. Pleasant Press, where so many pictures of growing things have been taken that it has been called "the most photographed garden in the United States". Seedsmen and nurserymen with new plants to test and eventually sell have sent specimens to Breeze Hill for growing and photographing, so that later accurate pictures would be available for sales purposes. Roses, about 3,000 bushes in over 800 varieties, lead the parade of beauty.

Both practical and far-sighted, Dr. McFarland was able to visualize the possibilities of the rose as a home-garden plant. In 1916, when he assumed the editorship of the *American Rose Annual*, rose-growing was a hobby for only the rich man. More than any other person, Dr. McFarland brought roses to the small backyard. By publishing true accounts of successful ventures made by ordinary gardeners into the mysteries of rose culture, he proved that rose-growing is possible for anyone who tries. Energetic and very public-spirited, he lectured widely on civic improvement, conservation and related subjects. He wrote several books and many magazine articles, largely about roses. Four varieties were named in his honour: Editor McFarland, The Doctor, Horace McFarland, and Breeze Hill.

The Breeze Hill property, 500 feet above sea-level, was bought by Dr. McFarland in 1909—"a two and a half acre plot attached to an abandoned vineyard". He called it his "piece of pie" because of its wedge shape, almost a quarter-circle. In the heavy clay shale were growing pear-trees, persimmons, some hemlocks, pines, horse-chestnuts old roses and lilacs, and neglected grape vines. A venerable sycamore, known to have been a large tree in 1819, has been carefully preserved, so that it still is the monarch of all things growing at Breeze Hill.

Major changes were accomplished through the years, and more and more the emphasis was on roses. Dr. Walter Van Fleet and many other hybridizers sent their fledglings to Breeze Hill for testing. The garden came to have an important influence on the growing and marketing of roses in the United States. Peat moss mulch, autumn planting of roses, and Black Spot control were tested and proved here, and the day-by-day observations made by Dr. McFarland provided the basis for the editing of the *American Rose Annual*.

In 1928 the rose garden proper was laid out. It is oval in shape, with

FIG. 5   *Moss and French Roses in the Old Rose Garden.   Their flowering period is from June to early July*

THE NATIONAL ROSE SPECIES COLLECTION AT BAYFORDBURY

FIG. 6   *The Bourbon roses are past their first flush of bloom, but will return in profusion in the autumn.   They show strongly the influence of the China roses in their foliage, perfume and recurrent flowering*

THE NATIONAL ROSE SPECIES COLLECTION AT BAYFORDBURY

FIG. 7 *Early Hybrid Tea roses in the Genealogical Collection: "La France", the first, introduced by Guillot in 1867, is in the foreground, right*

AT HERSHEY THE HOTEL OVERLOOKS THE ROSE GARDEN

a grass plot in the centre, bisected both ways by grass walks. In each of these quarters rose-beds are located, curved to match the outer side of the plot and edged with dwarf boxwood. Beyond the hybrid teas which occupy these centre beds are pillars connected by interlacing arches on which climbing roses grow. The space in front of the climbers is devoted to polyanthas and floribundas, and between the climbers are hybrid perpetuals and some shrub roses. The varieties planted here are those that have been well tested and have proved satisfactory. Test beds are located in a different section.

This main rose garden is a little gem, large enough to produce an unforgettable picture of great beauty and yet small enough to be viewed in entirety from any of its grass walks. One of the approaches to it is planted on both sides with a tall hedge of Frau Karl Druschki. When this blooms in early June, one wonders if any bride could have a lovelier aisle or a more promising prospect ahead!

Just beyond this formal rose garden is a magnificent taxus specimen clipped into an imposing pyramid. The path beside it leads to the rock garden, a quarter-circle of weathered limestone boulders adroitly laid out on a natural western slope. The rocks are mostly covered with all manner of small creeping plants, and a tiny waterfall has been carefully constructed so that it makes a tinkling sound. Among the more conspicuous plant material here are a pair of holly trees, cotoneasters and azaleas. A large *Pinus Bungeana* overlooks the rock garden.

The next of the series of gardens at Breeze Hill surrounds an oval water-lily pool. A few steps lead up to it from the rock-garden area. Azaleas are planted around the pool; in spring these are faced with narcissus and pansies. More hollies and a large group of viburnums are features of this garden. A low stone wall on two sides has chinks for delightful small plants.

Shallow steps again lead up from this section to the next—a peony garden, centred by a sundial in a grass plot. Lilies and summer bedding plants are also used in some of the boxwood-edged beds. On one side is a clipped yew hedge against which daffodils dance in early spring; opposite is a banked planting of azaleas and, in the far shade, rhododendrons. On the fourth side stands a rustic summerhouse covered with Mary Wallace roses.

Beyond these small formal gardens lies a long grass walk with a four-foot border on each side, made lovely in spring by flowering trees and early bulbs and in summer by thriving perennials. Other noteworthy plants in this far corner of the property are a fine kolk-witzia, numerous large magnolia trees, a border of tree peonies and some crepe-myrtle, which is rather unusual this far north. In one section, species and other old roses have been allowed to grow at will. Not far away is a fifteen-foot specimen of the dawn redwood, that Oriental tree with such an interesting history of survival and re-establishment in the western world.

All along the curved outer side of the Breeze Hill lot are the rose test plots, in a series of parallel beds. Here are the roses of very recent introduction, plus many unnamed ones sent for trial purposes. Sur-rounding them are climbing roses on arches. New varieties are easily compared and evaluated here, and over the years hundreds of them have been grown and photographed.

Breeze Hill, the garden with a special purpose, still feels the influence of Dr. McFarland. Who can say that his spirit is not hovering here?

MISCELLANY

A. NORMAN
DEPUTY PRESIDENT

For the amateur rose exhibitor, the Summer Show must have been one of the most satisfactory for many years. The day preceding was perfect for cutting blooms, no rain, no wind and what sunshine there was was just pleasantly warm. The Show day itself was one that the exhibitor hopes for but seldom gets—cold, with the possibility of rain that did not amount to much.

It must have been a matter of satisfaction to many members who have in the past left a cheerful fireside in the winter months to sally forth to instruct, by lectures, those less knowledgeable, to see the results of their efforts in the quality of the roses shown by amateurs in the smaller classes.

I wonder when Ena Harkness will cease getting bigger and bigger. When it was first raised it was quite a small rose with no pretensions to get among the box giants. Some of the blooms shown were among the largest in the Show. Had Red Ensign increased by the same amount the blooms would be about nine inches across.

The blue rose is a great source of interest, which reminds me of a comment by a Council member—"Who wants a blue rose?" Truly the unfamiliar of the present is the commonplace of the future, and in the same way in which the brilliant orange roses have been accepted, so will the blue rose when it comes. After all, orange roses are quite new to our gardens, while blue roses are certainly not.

Looking at some of the old Gallica roses which I brought back with me from Ireland, one cannot but notice that there is much more blue in their make-up than red, and yet this was the type of rose once grown. Whether there is any desire for a blue rose or not, I am personally quite prepared to take the risk of raising a Cambridge blue Virgo, even if I had to keep it to myself!

I was very pleased to see a nice bowl of my old favourite Mrs. Henry Bowles at the Summer Show. Although I should not be prepared to say they were as good as the blooms we used to see twenty-five years ago, they were, nevertheless, very good. What a remarkable variety it was. When cutting for a show one hardly had to inspect the blooms closely for nearly every one was without a blemish.

Very few of the old standbys are being grown at the present time, Mrs. Charles Lamplough is not often seen, and as far as one can see has not been superseded. Red roses were always an exhibitor's problem in days gone by—Earl Haig, Lord Allenby, George Dickson, W. E. Chaplin, none of which could one be sure of at Show time. Now we have as many good reds as one can do with.

Quite a number of members each year bring roses for naming at our Advisory Bureau. The wisdom of Solomon is often extolled, but I doubt if he had the problems that we get so often. Poor wilted blooms, pest-ridden foliage on hair-pin-like stems. Were they really good examples of their particular variety it would be difficult in many cases, but with such poor material it is wellnigh impossible to determine their name.

A large number of them are ramblers. When these roses were being raised round about the 1900's they came in shoals. The late Dr. A. H. Williams, himself a lover of this type of rose, told me that he grew nearly every one as they were introduced, but was beaten in the end by the quantity put into commerce. How few have remained. Emily Gray, of his own raising, but not Blushing Lucy which also gained a Trial Ground Certificate, which is a pity. It does seem that we want some new ones, and there is the possibility that with varieties we have to serve as male parents some very delightful ramblers could be raised.

Unfortunately there is no doubt that they do not pay to raise from a purely commercial point of view. In raising the hybrid teas and floribundas one can see what one has got by their blooms four months or so after sowing. With ramblers no flowers will be seen the first year, and quite unlikely the second, and not until after their long, strong growth will it be possible to appraise their value. When I raised Crimson Shower it was one of fifty plants, and I well remember the large amount of garden room they required. And yet here is a field for the amateur to whom final financial considerations are of little importance, and who possesses a fair amount of patience, to try his hand. All that is required is a plant of R. *wichuraiana* as a seed parent, and the crossing can be done in the open garden. Although the species is a late bloomer it ripens seed regularly.

I wonder if anyone has discovered a satisfactory method of tying the growths of roses budded on Rugosa standard stocks. Every year the same thing happens, a wild, gusty day in June and several growths are found to have been blown out of the stocks. Dwarf roses are of little trouble as the stake is firmly fixed in the soil, and there is only the growth from one bud to tie. The best, it would seem, we can do in the case of standards is to tie the stake to the stem of the stock and then tie the growth to it as well as one can; but after having done one's best, casualties still happen. Perhaps the only way would be to cut them back to about nine inches or so, which would have the effect of making the growth less vulnerable to the wind. Such a procedure would certainly require a deal of courage to say nothing of the loss of potential show blooms.

I was shown some special budding tape which, it was claimed, would expand with the increased growth of the stocks. I cannot see this being taken up by commercial growers of roses, for constriction of the stock is the least of their worries. What is required is something that will make the tying in of buds less irksome and quicker.

Mr. Gregory of Chilwell tells me he has a yellow sport of Lady Belper. It is very curious how these sports always seem to come after a certain lapse of time—usually between five and ten years after the introduction of the parent variety. I noticed a splash of red on one of my plants of that variety, and found it was a bloom that had half the petals red, but all on one side of the flower. It is quite useless, but I budded it merely out of curiosity as to what it will do. The fact that roses sport at the same time thousands of miles apart is quite easy to understand, for wherever they may be, they are all part of the original seedling. Flaming Sunset in Canada and Cheshire. Hoover in America and Great Britain. Mrs. Sam McGredy was very much given to sporting, but the prize must surely go to Talisman with nearly thirty registered sports.

It is a matter for conjecture as to whether soil conditions play any part in sportiveness, for whereas Mr. Harkness on his good rose soil at Hitchin has never had one sport, the late Mr. Ley on Bagshot sand at Windlesham had several, two of them being climbing sports—Else Poulsen and Mabel Morse.

I wonder if anyone has been troubled with encroaching roots of the elm. I have two whose trunks are about eighteen inches in diameter. At one time I was at a loss to understand why a number of roses failed in two beds, and when taking them up in the autumn I discovered that the roots of the elms had travelled through them and in each case the roses were making poor growth in their track. The farthest point reached by the elm roots was just twenty-eight paces, a distance that one would believe to be quite beyond the influence of encroaching tree roots. The only remedy short of cutting down the trees, which is out of the question for several reasons, is to cut through the roots each year. It is not wholly satisfactory, but it is the best one can do.

Now that the summer is well advanced one can see the effect of the damage done to the plants by the severity of the past winter. On the whole, recovery has been much better than I hoped. Of those that have suffered the least—Peace, Dorothy Anderson, Diamond Jubilee, Lady Belper, Virgo, Eden Rose, Rex Anderson, Karl Herbst, Monique, and all the floribundas. The greatest losses of plants were—Crimson Glory, Show Girl, Charlotte Armstrong, Barbara Richards, Phyllis Gold, Fred Howard. Dormant buds (on Rugosa standards) of both Charlotte Armstrong and Crimson Glory were killed, in spite of the fact that they were budded early and knitted well into the stocks. The same thing happened to the dormant buds of Crimson Glory in the winter of 1947.

On looking at the list of the floribundas in the rose analysis one cannot help noticing the great advance since the end of the war. No less than thirteen varieties have been added, and with the great improvements made in this type of rose, the position of the pre-war varieties will be precarious in the extreme. Those with single flowers on the trusses tend to be less popular, and in many instances this is understandable as many of those with few petals have stamens which darken with age, and mar the whole effect. This is most noticeable where Souvenir de Claudius Pernet (or its descendants) has been used as a pollen parent.

Judging by the vast numbers of floribundas on trial at Oaklands, it seems that the list in the analysis will have to be lengthened to include all the desirable varieties. I can also see some very wordy discussions as to which group some of the new ones should be placed in, with 'Queen Elizabeth' heading the list.

The vagaries of the English weather is proverbial, but this month it has acted in an extraordinary way. On the morning of August 7th in my daughter's garden at Wonersh, in Surrey, a sharp frost was experienced which blackened tomatoes and French marigolds. I have read somewhere that August was the one month when frosts were not recorded. Just over a fortnight later at Southport a temperature of 101°F. was reached in the Show tent! Naturally, the roses were the first things to show the effects of the tropical heat, which they did by displaying their innermost charms—in many cases long before the judges had made their awards.

On looking round some of the nurseries the effect of the long absence of rain (many of them did not even get a thunder shower), except for the size of the blooms, the plants had made quite average growth, and with the well ripened growth there should be fewer failures during the winter. It was very noticeable how fine were the blooms of Karl Herbst. After the very disappointing performance of last year it will come again into favour.

THE PARC DE LA GRANGE ROSE GARDEN AT GENEVA

ERIC BOIS

Late Director of the Parks and Promenades Department of the City of Geneva.
President of the Committee of the International New Roses Competition of Geneva.

THE City of Geneva glories in possessing one of the finest and most important Rose Gardens in Europe and embankments planted exclusively with rose bushes. In fact, the plantations of rose bushes on the Quai Gustave Ador, one mile long, which leads to the Rose Garden, are important and number 13,000 rose bushes which, in June–July, produce an incomparable display. They are planted in beds in the broad and long lawns on the banks of the Lake of Geneva and constitute a truly unique adornment. The beds are arranged lengthwise, on each side of the lawns and a number of them are planted with a row of standard roses in the centre. The rose-trees are grouped in one-colour shades so as to obtain an important decorative effect, and enhance the value of each variety. This display of roses draws thousands of visitors every day: although there is no protection of any kind, it may be said that never has any damage been committed.

The inception of the plantation goes back to 1936; the last rose-trees were planted in 1939 and all are still in a perfect state of vegetation. It even seems that they are finer each year. This result is certainly due to sensible pruning, to meticulous care, to regular treatment and to the use of suitable organic manure.

With regard to the Rose Garden, situated in the Parc de la Grange, it occupies an area of 12,000 square metres and contains 12,000 rose-bushes. It spreads over three terraces overlooked by an Italian pergola covered with ramblers and wistarias.

The lower terrace is planted solely with polyanthas, ramblers on pylons or festoons, and weeping standards.

The flower patterns contain only one variety each and the beds around the periphery are reserved for collections of twelve plants in each variety.

The two upper terraces are given over to the hybrid tea type and planted in accordance with the same plan as the lower terrace, that is to

THE HERSHEY ROSE GARDEN

looking towards the gift shop among the trees

AT BREEZE HILL

The Frau Karl Druschki hedge

The central terrace

THE ROSE GARDEN AT THE PARC LA GRANGE
GENEVA

General view from the upper terrace

say, the smaller collections are on the outer surround and the massed beds are single-coloured and distributed in such a way that the tones of the flowers harmonize pleasantly. Various standard roses are planted at certain spots, as well as a large number of Albertine and Paul's Scarlet weeping standards.

At the centre, large ornamental ponds and a bubbling fountain. Opposite the pergola, a large ornamental pond overlooked by a fine statue of a young man. The Rose Garden itself stands out against a background of large trees. There is only one circular path in orange gravel. All the other paths are in grey-blue stone, laid in the grass against which the roses stand out well.

When the roses are at the height of their first bloom, it is almost impossible to move about because of the crowds of people, but, throughout the season, there is a very large public and one can see unceasingly people noting the names of the varieties they prefer, all being clearly indicated on discreet, but very legible labels.

Some beds are reserved for interesting novelties, and as soon as a superior variety is found it takes the place of one that is deteriorating.

This Rose Garden was created and planted in 1945-6. From then on there was noted among nurserymen and rose-growers a considerable increase in the sales of rose-bushes, and this increase has continued regularly. The Rose Garden has thus considerably contributed to the extension of the planting of rose-trees in the gardens of our country.

Let me add that the plantations of roses in large quantities not only produce an incomparable decorative effect, but perfume the air at certain times of the day. These ornamental plantings contain about 150 rose varieties, all selected from among the best, both old and new. It is not always easy to find those planted twenty years ago, in the rose-growers' catalogues, and therefore the Parks Department of the City of Geneva has been compelled to do their own grafting in their nurseries. But, when it happens that too large a number of rose bushes deteriorate, as may happen sometimes, it is then necessary to change the whole variety. This does not matter, provided the harmony of colours is respected, as these plantations are intended to please the eye and not to constitute a conservatory of varieties.

To conclude, let me say a few words about the Concours International de Roses Nouvelles de Genève, which took place for the eighth time in 1955.

So as to avoid any risk of theft of new varieties, the rose-trees of the competition are planted in the enclosed nursery of the Parc de la Grange and can only be visited with a permit. This competition has assumed considerable importance, growers placing their complete trust in it. In 1955, 115 varieties competed, submitted by thirty exhibitors from ten countries and for 1956 these numbers will be even larger. This great success comes certainly from the way in which points are allotted, each member of the adjudicating committee entering his decision personally on his sheet.

The rose-trees, which are kept growing for two years before being judged by the International Adjudicating Committee, are pointed several times by a permanent Adjudicating Committee of specialists from Geneva and finally by the International Adjudicating Committee, which includes the greatest names in rose specialists in the world. Those who submit new varieties cannot be members of the Adjudicating Committee and are only authorized to enter the competition area when all the judges have handed in their notes.

I do not propose to give a list of the varieties planted in Geneva, as I do not think it would interest the reader. However, if anyone should wish it, I shall be pleased to send the list.

And to conclude, let me point out that apart from these mass plantations, several thousand rose-bushes are still used in ornamental beds in the numerous public gardens of Geneva, City of Parks.

The initiative for the creation of the Rose Garden was taken by M. Eric Bois, at the time Director of the Parks and Promenades Department of the City of Geneva. The plan is the work of M. A. Auberson, landscape architect in the same department.

LADY MARY FITZWILLIAM

JAMES ALEXANDER GAMBLE
TALL TIMBERS, MARYLAND

HIDDEN away among the lists containing over 16,000 improved rose varieties recorded since 1800, are the really great few; those that have largely made this flower what it is today. For roses with their exquisite colour tints and textures, beauty, fragrance and charm, now add loveliness to memorable moments and are established as the world's most widely beloved flower.

These few really great "Mothers of Roses" down the long stretch of some one hundred and fifty years have, it seems to me, earned a special place of honour in our rose thinking. They richly deserve to be searched out and the contribution of each to the better roses we now have be made more generally known to those who enjoy this flower. It would seem desirable also that all these be preserved for posterity in such a way as to prevent their further disappearance. And unless this is done soon, some of those still here will be lost and become only names to the rose folks who come after.

The writer, exploring the recently published American rose lexicon, *Modern Roses IV*, came to know that over 1,300 of the 3,575 varieties with listed parentage in that volume trace directly or indirectly to one English bred rose, Lady Mary Fitzwilliam. Undoubtedly, among those 3,575 there are still other varieties that also trace to her. It could well be also that among the 2,275 varieties for which no parentage is given there are a substantial number also related to this rose. From this survey came the realization that from the rose improvement standpoint, Lady Mary Fitzwilliam has no equal. The more than 1,300 varieties in whole or in part of her breeding comprise over 37 per cent of the roses having recorded pedigrees.

They trace largely to Lady Mary Fitzwilliam through four of her seedlings, Antoine Rivoire, Mrs. W. J. Grant, Mme Caroline Testout, and Kaiserin Auguste Viktoria; some 860 to the first mentioned, 506 to the second, 204 to the third and twenty-six to the Kaiserin, or a total of over 1,600 tracings to these 1,300 plus varieties. Many varieties in this most numerous of all rose families are related to both Antoine

Rivoire and Mrs. W. J. Grant and in a lesser number of cases, to Mme Caroline Testout as well. It is noted also that Lady Mary Fitzwilliam was the pollen parent of each of these now famous seedlings.

Mme Caroline Testout and Antoine Rivoire were produced in France by Pernet-Ducher in 1890 and 1895, Mrs. W. J. Grant in Ireland by Alexander Dickson and Sons in 1895, and Kaiserin Auguste Viktoria by Peter Lambert in Germany in 1891.

Most of the breeding from these varieties before 1900 occurred in France, Germany and Ireland. Soon after 1900, however, Americans began to have a part in rose production from them. It seems unfortunate that only a few of the many seedlings of Lady Mary Fitzwilliam are listed.

Lady Mary Fitzwilliam

Lady Mary Fitzwilliam herself was born in England in 1846, the granddaughter of the Duke of Ormonde. In 1877 she became the daughter-in-law of the sixth Earl Fitzwilliam and soon thereafter was named Lady-in-Waiting to the Duchess of Saxe-Coburg, of which House Edward VII was a member. Royal permission and special warrant was received in 1882 by Henry Shepard, hybridizer of this rose, to name it after this great English lady. While she died in 1929, her rose, through its descendants, continues to carry the remembrance of her into increasing millions of homes and gardens throughout the world.

Antoine Rivoire was the President of the Horticultural Society of Lyons, France. Mildred Grant was the wife of W. J. Grant, a noted exhibitor of roses at National Rose Shows in England. Both Mr. and Mrs. Grant were personal friends of Alexander Dickson who bred the rose which he named Mrs. W. J. Grant. Mme Caroline Testout was a French seamstress with an establishment in London.

Kaiserin Auguste Viktoria, born the Duchess of Olga, became the mother of the six sons and one daughter of the German Kaiser. She was an ardent supporter of Sangerhausen, the state rose garden of that country, and was much loved by the German people. When visited by the writer in 1935, Sangerhausen had among its over 6,000 rose varieties, plants of Lady Mary Fitzwilliam and of most of the other

'BEAUTÉ'

about ⅔ natural size

Raised by Charles Mallerin, France.
Trial Ground No. 666. Reg. No. 534. Trial Ground Certificate.
Certificate of Merit, Autumn Show, 1954.
For description see page 141, "Rose Annual" 1955.
The blooms photographed for the "Rose Annual" 1955 were unfortunately not representative of the variety.

so-called rose "breaks" which contributed so much to rose improvement since La Reine in 1843.

Little did Lady Mary Fitzwilliam, Antoine Rivoire, Mildred Grant, Caroline Testout or the Duchess of Olga realize that, in lending their names and prestige to these five varieties, roses subsequently bred from them would find their way into so many millions of homes and gardens and that the number of such would continue to increase long after they and their immediate families had gone from the earth.

COLOUR IN THE LADY MARY FITZWILLIAM FAMILY

The head of this rose family, Lady Mary Fitzwilliam, was a flesh-coloured, two-toned pink. Her seed parent, Devoniensis, was cream coloured and her pollen parent Victor Verdier, of the La Reine family, was bright rose. Antoine Rivoire, rosy flushed and shaded carmine, had a copper-coloured seed parent. Mrs. W. J. Grant, imperial pink, had a two-toned pink seed parent. Mme Caroline Testout, a two-toned pink, had a rich rose-coloured seed parent. Kaiserin Auguste Viktoria had a rose-coloured seed parent. Of the varieties which trace to Lady Mary Fitzwilliam whose colours are recorded, some thirty per cent are pink, twenty-eight per cent are red, twenty per cent bi-coloured, fourteen per cent yellow, and eight per cent white. From the amount of pink in their forebears, one would have expected to find an even higher percentage of pink varieties. The roses which appear to have done most in transmitting the pink shades include Ophelia, Mrs. George Shawyer, Killarney, Premier, Columbia, Mme Butterfly, Rapture, Lady Sylvia and Radiance.

Red

There seems to be a surprising number of red varieties in this family line. The varieties which have done most to transmit this colour include Liberty, Richmond, Hadley, Hoosier Beauty, Étoile de Hollande, Christopher Stone, Mrs. Charles E. Russell, and that fortunate combination of Ophelia and Liberty breeding resulting in Sensation which in turn, crossed with a seedling of Mme Caroline Testout, got Cathrine Kordes, seed parent of Crimson Glory.

Later, through the hybridizing talent of Dr. W. E. Lammerts of California, Crimson Glory became the pollen parent of Charlotte Armstrong. Drs. Lammerts and Swim, using the latter as seed or as a

pollen parent produced such outstanding modern garden roses as
Applause, Chrysler Imperial, First Love, Helen Traubel, Mirandy,
Nocturne, Rose of Freedom, Sutter's Gold, Tallyho, and others.

Blend Colour

The high percentage of varieties of blended colours in the Fitzwilliam family is not surprising because of the large number of out-
crosses to Souv. de Claudius Pernet. Ophelia seems also to have transmitted a great deal of blend pigment. The breeding of Talisman,
President Herbert Hoover and Joanna Hill appear in the genetic background of many of the more recently produced blended coloured
roses. To a less extent in earlier productions the same is true of Phari-
saer, a seedling of Mrs. W. J. Grant.

Yellow

That Ophelia also contained and transmitted much yellow colour is
indicated by her progeny Golden Ophelia, Mrs. Calvin Coolidge,
Souvenir, Mrs. Franklin D. Roosevelt, Yellow Gloria, Joanna Hill,
Roselandia, Fontanelle, Token, and Golden Rapture among others.

White

The eight per cent of the some 1,300 varieties which are white in
colour came largely through Mme Caroline Testout, her daughter
Frau Karl Druschki, and to a less degree through Kaiserin Auguste
Viktoria. Of the observed white varieties in the Lady Mary Fitzwilliam family, most were by Frau Karl Druschki. In crossing she was
largely used as the seed parent. In the eleven cases where used as the
pollen parent, only four of the resulting seedlings produced were
white; others were pink, yellow, and dazzling red, i.e. Fern Kemp, and
Commandeur Jules Gravereaux. It is of special interest to note that
perhaps every one of the white rose varieties recorded with parentage
trace to Lady Mary Fitzwilliam.

FRAGRANCE

Ever since roses came on the earth, fragrance seemingly has been
their most intrinsic possession. As has been written, "without fragrance,
the most beautiful rose is incomplete". The many fragrances in the

rose lift up the spirits of those who have them to enjoy and has endeared this flower to millions. Fragrance is also the character which has helped to spur the efforts of rose improvers to make this flower even more beautiful and desirable ever since that art began. Rose varieties without it, however lovely otherwise, do not usually stay long in most gardens; hence the pressure on modern rose hybridizers to introduce only rose productions that are preferably very fragrant.

Some 1,000, or over seventy-seven per cent of the varieties tracing to Lady Mary Fitzwilliam are reported as having some fragrance. Broken down, the count shows 16·2 per cent as possessing a slight fragrance, 43·7 per cent as fragrant and 18·2 per cent as very fragrant. No fragrance is recorded for the rest of this family. Some of these, however, are reported as fragrant in other listings. This fact suggests that *Modern Roses IV* is still incomplete from the fragrance reporting standpoint. Paying even more attention to fragrance appears very important to the best future of this flower. A wealth of fragrant varieties are especially found among the descendants of the Ophelia and Liberty divisions of the Fitzwilliam family. The former in particular seems to justify the widely held belief among students of this flower that, as a class, they lead in fragrance.

The writer also observed that over 300 of the varieties which trace to Lady Mary Fitzwilliam are reported as having no fragrance. As already indicated it is believed some of these are in reality fragrant, i.e. of the many recorded sports of Ophelia, over half have no fragrance reported. Other members of the Ophelia group that have also sported roses with no reported fragrance, include Talisman, Joanna Hill, Better Times, Columbia, and some twenty others.

It is unfortunately true that too many varieties without scent have actually occurred in the Fitzwilliam family. A study discloses that these largely resulted from Mme Caroline Testout and her daughter Frau Karl Druschki, especially when they were crossed with non-fragrant varieties such as Phyllis Gold, and Ville de Paris. Nearly one hundred of the recorded varieties without fragrance are closely related to Frau Karl Druschki.

The above is not to say that Frau Karl Druschki did not help get varieties that were fragrant, i.e. White Clouds by herself and Kaiserin Auguste Viktoria, and Voie Lactée by herself and Julien Potin. These are very fragrant. However, in most cases where Frau Karl Druschki helped to produce roses having a very pronounced fragrance, this usually occurred when she was mated to varieties possessing heavy fragrance, such as Chateau de Clos Vougeot, General MacArthur and others.

It is observed generally that in the production of non-fragrant varieties, one, and in some cases both, of the parents used were without scent. In contrast, when non-fragrant parents were used in crossing to the Fitzwilliam family, thirty-six of the resulting seedlings were recorded either as fragrant or very fragrant.

For over seventy years now the rose varieties resulting from Lady Mary Fitzwilliam, this English bred rose, have shown increasing beauty of bloom throughout the growing season, and are, in the main, highly fragrant and, most important, several of them have bred better roses than themselves. The fact that the progeny of Lady Mary Fitzwilliam so thoroughly dominate roses reveals her to be the foremost contributor to modern roses in our time.

THE LADY MARY FITZWILLIAM FAMILY

The tables which follow bring into focus the relationship of Lady Mary Fitzwilliam to the rose varieties of the different colours now popular in home gardens.

Due credit is here recorded to each of the varieties of other breeding that were used in the crosses of the many who trace to Lady Mary Fitzwilliam

White Varieties

Related to Lady Mary Fitzwilliam through

NAME	Antoine Rivoire	Mrs. W. J. Grant	Mme Caroline Testout	Kaiserin Auguste Viktoria	RECORDED FRAGRANCE
Blanche Mallerin	X	—	—	X	—
Kaiserin Auguste Viktoria	—	—	—	X	F.
Mme Jules Bouché	—	X	—	—	F.
Mrs. H. M. Eddie	—	—	X	—	F.
Neige Parfum	X	—	—	—	F.
Pedralbes	—	—	X	—	S.
Snow Bird	—	—	X	X	V.F.
White Briarcliff	—	—	—	X	F.
White Wings	X	—	—	—	F.

S. indicates slight fragrance, F., fragrant, V.F., very fragrant.

'MESSAGE'

about ¾ natural size

(Peace (Mme A. Meilland) × Virgo) × Virgo.
Raised by Francis Meilland, France.

Pink Varieties

Related to Lady Mary Fitzwilliam through

NAME	Antoine Rivoire	Mrs. W. J. Grant	Mme Caroline Testout	RECORDED FRAGRANCE
AnnaMarie	X	—	—	V.F.
Babe Ruth	X	—	—	F.
Briarcliff	X	X	—	F.
Curly Pink	X	X	X	F.
Dainty Bess	X	—	—	—
Dolly Darling	X	X	X	F.
Editor McFarland	—	X	—	V.F.
Ernie Pyle	X	—	—	V.F.
First Love	X	X	X	F.
Hedda Hopper	—	X	—	F.
Juno	X	X	X	S.
Katherine T. Marshall	X	X	X	S.
Lady Ashtown	—	X	—	S.
Mary Margaret McBride	X	—	—	—
Melody	X	—	—	F.
Miss Rowena Thom	—	X	—	V.F.
Mme Butterfly	X	—	—	V.F.
Mrs. Charles Bell	—	X	—	—
Ophelia	X	—	—	S.
Pink Dawn	X	—	—	V.F.
Killarney	—	X	—	V.F.
Pink Satin	X	X	—	F.
President Macia	X	X	—	F.
Radiance	—	X	—	V.F.
Rapture	X	—	—	—
Santa Anita	X	—	—	—
Shangri-La	X	—	—	V.F.
Show Girl	X	X	X	F.
Sterling	X	—	—	F.
Suzan Lotthé	X	—	—	F.
Symphonie	X	—	—	V.F.
The Doctor	X	X	—	V.F.
Vanity Fair	X	—	—	V.F.
Yours Truly	X	—	—	V.F.

S. indicates slight fragrance, F., fragrant, V.F., very fragrant.

Red Varieties

Related to Lady Mary Fitzwilliam through

NAME	Antoine Rivoire	Mrs. W. J. Grant	Mme Caroline Testout	RECORDED FRAGRANCE
American Flagship	X	X	X	S.
Applause	X	X	X	S.
Better Times	X	X	—	S.

Red Varieties—*continued*

Related to Lady Mary Fitzwilliam through

NAME	Antoine Rivoire	Mrs. W. J. Grant	Mme Caroline Testout	RECORDED FRAGRANCE
Bravo	X	X	X	F.
California Centennial	X	—	—	S.
Cedric Adams	X	X	X	F.
Charlotte Armstrong	X	X	X	F.
Christopher Stone	—	X	—	V.F.
Crimson Glory	X	X	X	V.F.
Crimson King	X	X	X	V.F.
Dick Wilcox	X	X	X	F.
Ena Harkness	X	X	X	V.F.
Étoile de Hollande	—	X	—	V.F.
Fandango	X	X	X	F.
Grace Moore	X	X	X	F.
Happiness	X	X	—	S.
Heart's Desire	X	X	X	V.F.
Henry Field	X	X	X	F.
Mirandy	X	X	X	V.F.
Nigger Boy	—	—	X	V.F.
Nocturne	X	X	X	F.
Poinsettia	X	—	—	S.
Queen O' the Lakes	X	X	X	F.
Red Duchess	X	X	X	F.
Red Radiance	—	X	—	V.F.
Rome Glory	X	X	—	V.F.
Rose of Freedom	X	X	X	V.F.
San Fernando	X	X	X	V.F.
Tallyho	X	X	X	—
Texas Centennial	X	X	—	—
Valiant	X	—	X	F.
Velvetier	X	X	X	F.
Volcano	X	—	—	V.F.
Will Rogers	X	X	X	V.F.
Zulu Queen	X	—	—	F.

S. indicates slight fragrance, F., fragrant, V.F., very fragrant.

Yellow Varieties

Related to Lady Mary Fitzwilliam through

NAME	Antoine Rivoire	Mrs. W. J. Grant	Mme Caroline Testout	RECORDED FRAGRANCE
Debonair	X	—	—	F.
Eclipse	X	—	—	F.
Joanna Hill	X	—	—	F.
Mme Chiang Kai-shek	X	—	—	—
Mrs. E. P. Thom	—	X	—	F.
Mrs. P. S. du Pont	X	—	—	F.
Narzisse	X	—	—	—
San Luis Rey	—	—	X	F.

F. indicates fragrant.

Blend Coloured Varieties

Related to Lady Mary Fitzwilliam through

NAME	Antoine Rivoire	Mrs. W. J. Grant	Mme Caroline Testout	RECORDED FRAGRANCE
Allure	X	X	X	S.
Brandywine	X	—	—	S.
Butterscotch	X	—	—	S.
California	—	X	—	F.
Commando	X	—	—	F.
Comtesse Vandal	X	—	—	F.
Contrast	X	—	—	—
Copper Luster	X	X	—	S.
Edith Wilkie	X	—	—	S.
Enchantment	X	—	—	S.
Forty-niner	X	X	X	S.
Girona	X	—	—	F.
Gloaming	X	—	—	F.
Good News	X	X	—	F.
Gordon Eddie	X	—	—	F.
Hill Top	X	—	—	—
Huntsman	X	X	X	F.
Mark Sullivan	X	—	—	—
Max Krause	X	—	—	F.
Miss America	X	—	X	F.
Miss Clipper	X	—	—	F.
Mission Bells	—	X	—	F.
Mme Cochet-Cochet	X	—	—	F.
Mme Henri Guillot	X	—	—	S.
Multnomah	X	X	X	S.
Olive Percival	X	X	—	V.F.
Paramount	X	X	X	S.
Peace	X	—	—	F.
Pearl Harbor	—	X	—	F.
Pearl S. Buck	X	—	—	F.
President Herbert Hoover	X	X	—	V.F.
Ramon Bach	X	—	—	V.F.
San Gabriel	X	—	—	F.
Saturnia	X	X	—	F.
Serenade	X	—	—	S.
Sierra Glow	X	X	X	V.F.
Signora	X	X	—	F.
Stockton Beauty	X	X	X	F.
Sutter's Gold	X	X	X	V.F.
Sweet Sixteen	X	X	—	V.F.
Taffeta	X	X	—	F.
Talisman	X	—	—	F.

S. indicates slight fragrance, F., fragrant, V.F., very fragrant.

PARIS–GENEVA–BADEN–LONDON

LOUISE BECHTEL
MOUNT KISCO, NEW YORK

SINCE the war, we two American rose lovers have often renewed our impressions of English and European rose-growing. In 1955 we planned to sail at a time when we could, at long last, see some of the great concours held in the spring, and talk with rose hybridizers in some countries we did not know well. This report will keep to the concours we attended. It is by the member of our team who is the more willing to put down general impressions, leaving the technical details to others.

First on our schedule came the concours at Bagatelle, possibly the most formidable, certainly the most dramatic and formal judging event of all. Here we watched a very large jury, including a number of lady amateurs, in operation. We milled about in the background among many famous "originators", some of whom calmed their nerves with photography, watching the jury move from bed to bed, *en masse*, or scurry one by one to fill out their individual point-sheets. Finally, one winner was announced on the spot, an American hybridizer who leaped, beaming, behind his bush of floribundas to be photographed. The jury hurried to the Orangerie for further decisions. Over all was a proper air of tenseness and drama. Distinguished officials wore formal clothes, the French ladies wore wonderful hats; but none of us lived up to the formal beauty of that famous garden. Except for those few hours, it was opened to the public as usual. The concours was announced in the press, and the public invited to vote for their favourite new rose in boxes set up in the garden.

Equally formal and picturesque was the superb lunch given by the City of Paris to the jury and its friends, high up in the Tour Eiffel. After what can only be called beautiful food and very special wines, park and city officials spoke briefly, and the awards were announced. Here we met rosarians from Japan, Spain, Portugal, Holland, Belgium, Denmark, as well as friends from Britain, France, and America. The event matched the supremacy of the flower being celebrated, and happily honoured the audience which had come from so many lands. Here we met such great hybridizers as Spek of Holland, Sam McGredy of Ireland, Francis Meilland and Jean Gaujard, of France, and Niels Poulsen from Denmark, for the first time taking the place of his famous father. Here, too, was André Vilmorin and his sister, the witty poet and novelist, Louise Vilmorin. We even met a famous couturier, and a great French botanist. Our host, for this event, that ever-kind and wise French nurseryman, Henri Nonin, later gave the jury a cocktail party in an old house on the left bank, in an apartment beautifully decorated with great sprays of some of his climbing roses.

Through it all, this amateur was wondering greatly how so many varied opinions could be co-ordinated so quickly; how much the personal taste of each judge counted; and how much matters of pure luck, as to weather, normal date of bloom, and other factors, had affected the fate of the many fine roses that were out of the running.

The Geneva concours was a contrast in many ways. The trial grounds are behind locked gates, in the nursery of the Parc La Grange, on a hot, steepish slope which surely gives the roses a stern trial. The jury, much smaller (no ladies, no amateurs), seemed to work on a more serious, more individual scheme. Some of us on the sidelines were the same as at Bagatelle. The hot hours of work were followed by a charming formal reception in the distinguished old mansion nearby.

This concours is the climax of much publicized rose weeks that centre in the beautiful rose garden of the Parc La Grange, so intelligently designed, and so different from Bagatelle, with its pool and fountain, its strange big modern trellis, and its background of the blue lake and the dramatic Jet d'Eau. Here are superb, permanent rose plantings, where we saw many old friends, but also many European roses not known in America. During the rose weeks, it is illuminated at night, and there one night we saw a ballet performed among the roses, a truly magical event. Other programmes given in this park, to celebrate the rose, included a fashion show, an opera, and concerts by famous orchestras. Also, the city publishes a beautiful souvenir work about roses.

Already, we were finding out that, at different concours, the same rose may perform differently. This was even clearer when we went to Baden-Baden, arriving the day before the actual meeting. But we met several of the officials, and examined the trial ground. As at Geneva, it is not in or near the big public rose garden, but on a distant, hot hill-top, in a separate nursery. By mid-July, it had achieved a blaze of bloom, with several entries looking glorious which at the former trials had looked poorly. Here again one recognized at once, in spite of the use of numbers instead of names, the multiple entries of the three Meillands, the new colours developed by Kordes, Tantau and Poulsen, the plants from such American firms as Armstrong and "Jackson and Porkins", as a French newspaper called them.

Meanwhile, we had also seen the huge rose show at the Bundes-garten-Schau at Kassel, a fascinating exhibit from all German nurseries. Spread through the great area of the old Orangerie, were tables upon tables of massed blooms, many arranged in huge low circular bowls. As background decorations, there were ornamental grasses, del-phiniums, and other tall perennials. All tables were spread with cuttings of evergreens, on which big chunks of ice were regularly renewed. A great audience filed through continuously, paying a small entrance fee, many of them checking catalogues or taking photographs.

One could go from these superb cut-flowers out to the fabulous hill-side rose garden, whose paths wander on from formal beds of hybrid teas near the entrance, up the terraces among hybrid polyanthas and park roses, on to a section under the thrilling "Sessel Bahn" (ski lift to you) where old roses and species are grouped. At night, the whole city gathered on the higher terraces to look down on a poetic "illumina-tion" consisting of myriads of low wax candles, set like clusters of fallen stars over the lawns of this four-hundred-acre park.

How different from any other rose shows are those of the English. Once again the summer show of the N.R.S. at Westminster was superb to our eyes, though the English themselves thought it suffered from the late spring. A month later we saw again fine rose displays at a fortnightly show. The British appear to be outstanding as rose-growers, besides having eminent hybridizers. At the Vincent Square Show, in both halls, when this demonstrative, talkative American was over-heard, she was rewarded by responses that prove how deeply the gardening public *feels* about roses. Sample remarks: "There she is! She is right at the end of my garden where I can watch her from my dining-room window!" "I wear him all season in my button hole. You'll find him better in the next aisle." "Do you really grow old roses in America? Tell me which you like best, I must have some." A Royal Air Force Captain begged an exhibitor to give me an old rose I was admiring greatly.

It is the combination of superb blooms shown by nurserymen, plus the cross-section offered as blooms successful with amateurs, that makes the London shows so exceptional. Besides, there is that wall against which the newest hybridizations are shown; and this year, there were three fine displays of the "old" and species roses. Also, in these shows, one sees so many older hybrid-teas still popular, a fact reflected in the English catalogues, with lists so much larger than any American catalogues now offer. Also, the public can meet at Vincent Square many of the heads of nurseries, who there cement long friendships with their customers. There was no formal function that we knew of, but in that crowded dining-room so fortunately provided below stairs, or in the little Press dining-room, we could talk with famous "rose men" or with amateurs perhaps more famous than we knew, even some from India.

At the heart of the British judging system you have that superb trial ground near St. Albans, with its long-experienced, devoted keeper. A visit there, a talk with him, an explanation of his record-keeping, shows why the medals and certificates of the N.R.S. are so highly valued both by continental growers and Americans. This is really the English "Concours", whose awards are based not on the votes of a huge jury, most of whom look at the plant once, but on records plus the notes of a few specialists, a system which seems to me the fairest of any.

In England, a far greater number of amateurs than anywhere else have real rose gardens of their own. Some of the public gardens and the gardens of big houses now kept by the National Trust, are disappointing today, due to lack of money and labour, but even there, one finds very old rose plantings cherished and often still flourishing. One can only envy and wonder at a nation of so many good gardeners, a land where horticulture has such a special tradition.

Alas that America is probably too big for any hope to achieve there such single shows or concours as those we saw abroad, representing the rose growing of whole nations plus entries from other nations. There are only two things I can dare to say we do better: flower-arrangement and publicity. The "decorative" classes at English shows are rather horrible to eyes trained by long-looking at the works of the ladies of the Garden Club of America, an organization to which there is no British or continental parallel. Also, our garden shows, particularly those in New York, are given much better newspaper and magazine coverage. The weekly garden sections (with news of shows and of awards) and the special garden issues of our larger newspapers have no parallels abroad.

Our journey included five countries. It was doubly illuminating, because, in talking around the subjects of roses, horticulture, the education of gardeners and hybridizers of the future, our discussions informed us as to so many other matters in each country. Such sharing of thoughts and facts with men distinguished in their fields is more revealing than any reading, and we are more than grateful to all who made it possible.

THE ROSARIAN'S BOOKSHELF

Old Garden Roses. By Sacheverell Sitwell and James Russell, with paintings by Charles Raymond. In six parts in a numbered limited edition at from £7 7s. per part, each containing 8 paintings, reproduced facsimile by collotype in 8 colours. 17 in. × 12¼ in., 52 pp.

Part I with beautiful coloured illustrations by Charles Raymond, forms a valuable contribution to the study of the origin, history and evolution of many old garden roses. It will find its place in libraries alongside the works of Redouté, Lindley and Bunyard and will be welcomed by many enthusiastic collectors of old garden roses. The writers have also made a strong appeal to the younger generation to gain a practical knowledge of their varied qualities with a strong emphasis on perfume. In so many gardens privet and laurel are extensively used as screens or hedges, but the authors have stressed the pleasure that can be derived by utilizing many of the old shrub roses for the purpose. Mention is made of Zephirine Drouhin, a hybrid Bourbon, introduced in 1868, this rose is quite thornless with beautiful carmine pink flowers and very fragrant. It will provide an ideal hedge 6 to 8 feet high with a very long flowering period.

Sentiment will make a strong appeal to many of the older generation who remember some of the roses described by the authors in their grandfathers or parents' gardens, and how often one hears the criticism: "Roses are not what they were—they have no fragrance." The statement by the authors that modern roses have very little, if any, scent is a strange distortion of the facts. There is a very much higher proportion of fragrant roses in our gardens today than there were in the nineteenth century. It must be admitted, however, that some are almost scentless but the perfection of form, the beautiful and endless variation of colour compensates to a very large extent to the lack of that elusive quality—scent. The devotion and enthusiasm of the authors to old garden roses is almost infectious and many readers after studying this volume will have grave doubts as to the merits of privet and laurel. Should this materialize, the authors will be amply rewarded.

W. H. SUMPSTER

'LA JOLLA'

about ¾ natural size

Charlotte Armstrong × Contrast.
Raised by Herbert Swim, Armstrong Nurseries, California.
Trial Ground No. 303. Reg. No. U.S.A. Trial Ground Certificate.
Certificate of Merit, Summer Show, 1955.
For description see page 146

STRAINS PRODUCED IN ROSE
HYBRIDIZING

E. B. LE GRICE

PROGRESS in hybridizing is made two ways. The quick way, where by chance two good parents are brought together and happen to produce their best at the first crossing. This result is usually what might be termed unhampered promiscuity and such hybrid results give vigour and unusual progeny. But for one such result there will be thousands of failures and, more important, the following hybridizing of successive generations will produce inferior results. Mr. A. Dickson, writing on the hybridization of roses in *The Rose Annual* 1909, describes the thirty years' work which was even then producing the Alex. Dickson type. His finest strain up to that time, which owed its origin to the famous Lady Mary Fitzwilliam, began with Mrs. W. J. Grant; the influence of this has been felt in many roses of today.

It is this initial strain production which takes time, even generations to build up, although now that some of the laws in genetics are known the strain may be built up more quickly.

In my article I would like to consider such strains as they relate to countries rather than individuals, although in each case a keen hybridist will always be seeking for and experimenting with fresh blood, either to strengthen his present strain or to evolve a new one.

Here it might clarify the issue if we sought a definition of a strain. A strain is the production of a succession of varieties, bearing common characteristics of colour, habit, growth, foliage, etc., reproduced in successive generations but modified to improve the general qualities of the rose.

A famous strain was that of Liberty, which has influenced most reds of today and at the moment Masquerade looks like producing a numerous strain of great popularity.

Beginning with some of the smaller countries which have had a great influence on roses of today we consider Denmark. People speak of the Poulsen type of roses, a tribute to the raiser of Else, Kirsten, and Karen Poulsen. One might think of the Poulsen strain as being more limited to Poulsen's Pink, Supreme and Irene of Denmark. Here, certain characteristics are reproduced, type of foliage, size of bloom head, and the spacing and placing of the flowers. No one knowing the strain would doubt the origin of any of these varieties. Here the two main objectives desired have been attained, floriferousness and hardiness.

Turning to Holland we find that the main interest for many years has been the production of roses for forcing. Now that the main means of transport is by air, this factor has had a great influence upon the hybridizer. Briefly the object has been to produce a small to medium sized flower, the colour of which is bright and visible from the young, pointed bud. Number of petals is of less importance than their thickness and durability of texture. The stem must be thin but wiry, the foliage of medium size and widely spaced. The flowers should be carried singly to avoid disbudding. Given these advantages a larger number of rose blooms can be packed into a smaller space and will weigh far less than the average hybrid tea flower. Looking at the varieties raised in Haps— the Verschurens and Verschuren-Pechtolds—one is interested to see how generations of specialization have produced strains which carry these factors. Tawny Gold of Leenders has also proved useful for this purpose. It is more difficult to speak of strains as far as De Ruiter is concerned. He has produced many varieties showing versatility and originality. From these some strains emerge. The Herald strain from De Ruiter's Herald to Border King. His dwarf "compacta" strain named after the seven dwarfs, even if of limited practical use, has yet been an undoubted hybridist's triumph. Other strains have emerged, the Pygmy strain of dwarf hybrid tea. The miniature type of Roulettii, which under the original work of Jan de Vink has proved to be of great popularity and wide range.

One hesitates to assess the work in France which has changed so rapidly since the advent of Peace. The ideal of the slightly rounded, globular bud with brilliance of colour has almost disappeared and two types appear to be more general. Both are characterized by length of stem at the sacrifice of freedom of flower but the latter failing is being improved. A whole succession of forcing varieties are appearing. Primarily for forcing they have a useful future outside as well. Beauté, Bayadère, Henri Mallerin are typical roses of this strain. The Peace strain has lead to a more heavily foliaged type with larger, fuller flower.

Too shy for forcing they are welcomed in the garden for their vigorous hardiness and size of flower. There is a third type, a hardy strain in which freedom of flower is a first consideration. Of these, Virgo and Michèle Meilland are fair examples. All these three strains are having an important bearing on rose production throughout the world. A noted strain of floribundas has come with Alain followed by many fine varieties such as Moulin Rouge and Tonnerre.

If one hesitates to assess the work in France it seems temerity to seek to do so in Germany where originality has produced so many new types that only an article from Mr. Kordes himself could clarify the issue.

However, certain strains are apparent. Undoubtedly the one with the widest commercial influence has been the Crimson Glory strain. This variety is still prominent as a parent for hybridizing, and despite the drawback of a weak flower neck and temperamental growth is still giving outstanding progeny. Crimson King, Lillie Dauber, possessing better characteristics of stem have failed in other ways but Baden-Baden, etc., are showing that this red strain has still a great future both for outside and for forcing.

Of the lovely strain of climbers at the Trial Grounds much might be said. They themselves would repay much study. Breaks such as these, Kordesii, Elmshorn, and the hybrid musks of Eva strain. The hybrid spinosissima, the Frühlingsgold strain, all are outstanding, although few, except Eva, will appear to have a lasting effect on world hybridizing at the moment.

The shrub roses with their triangular umbels of flower have brought a new conception to landscape gardening and though such vigour is overwhelming in the small English garden there are uses for these sturdy bushes in parks.

Side by side with this bewildering mass of choice material produced by Mr. Kordes one finds the work of Mr. Tantau whose vigorous type of floribundas, noted for their large and brilliant flower heads, their healthy growth and their continuity of flower should be a promise of even better roses to come. Reliability and dependability with variety of colour describes this strain.

Turning to America we are struck by the enormous advance which has been made under the encouragement of patenting. The name of Boerner, associated with Messrs. Jackson and Perkins, has introduced new and striking shades mainly in the floribunda type. Of these, the Pinocchio strain (the original emanating from Kordes) including Lavender Pinocchio, probably culminate in Fashion, which itself has given rise to countless progeny, few of which will survive the handicap of its inherent weakness for disease.

Mention has been made of Masquerade which has lured every hybridist into its mesh. Again a multitude of seedlings await appraisement after trial before their value can be known. One more strain originated by Dr. W. G. Lammerts which is having a definite trend on hybridizing is the Charlotte Armstrong strain, a production of great freedom of flower, branching habit, beauty of growth and vigorous health. The flowers may be thin but the petals are thick and of good texture and many a good rose will probably be evolved from what is still a young strain. In America we have all the advantages which skill and knowledge, backed by financial aid can give.

This article as it lengthens warns me that the British contribution, which in the past has been very great and will be so again, must probably await assessment in more competent hands. Brevity in this case does not imply lack of material to be discussed but fear of the Editor's blue pencil.

Briefly, one turns to the firm of McGredy, where the ideal of an English rose of show bench perfection has ever been the aim and often the achievement. Probably no firm has so affected the standards sought for in the ideal rose as has the firm of McGredy. The form of Peace as a bloom is really a tribute to the English raisers, whose ideal of a rose has apparently found universal acceptance.

Of the firm of Dickson, perhaps more than any other, it may be said that strain with their roses was all important. During the last thirty-five years (a small part of their long history as hybridizers) I have watched with interest the emergence of their various strains from time to time. Referring once more to Mr. Dickson's article in 1909 he says: "We aimed at producing a type having vigour of growth, freedom and continuity of bloom, the flowers full and perfectly formed with unusually long petals at the same time growing on bushes, the foliage of which is luxurious and handsome." One has only to think of Shot Silk, Canary, Lucie Marie and a host of other worth-while roses to see that his aim has been achieved.

Another hybridist whose distinct strain has produced some fine roses

'BELLE BLONDE'

Raised by Francis Meilland, France.

about ¾ natural size

is Mr. Herbert Robinson. Beginning with the Gold Medal variety Phyllis Gold, we have had a succession of yellows followed by Gay Crusader and Doreen, all noted for their spreading, vigorous habit, and numerous flowers on one stem.

It would be a serious omission to the contribution made in the raising of roses to omit the most characteristic and probably unique strain of single roses which our climate demands and brings to perfection. As far back as Irish Elegance, Irish Fireflame and Isobel, these lovely roses have claimed the hybridist's attention, to be followed by Mr. Archer with his lovely Dainty Bess and his floribundas, Cheerio, Fairy Cluster, and so on. It is this appeal of the single rose which has been continued in my own Dainty Maid and Charming Maid. While economics forbid the production of single roses which only appeal to the English public, sentiment demands that this special product for our own climate should continue to appear.

In this all too brief summary of the trend of roses today much has been omitted. Variety of growth, colour and shape will alter but many of the present strains will reappear in future years, bearing the fruit of patient research of past generations.

ROSES TO BE

MR. AND MRS. WALTER D. BROWNELL

RHODE ISLAND, U.S.A.

ALL rose hybridists realize that for a new rose variety to become popular it must be better by some standard than its predecessors. Important improvements require time and much patience. Very few hybridists have chosen the same procedure and each have their own objectives.

Mrs. Brownell and the author have been co-workers in rose research for fifty years, for soon after the turn of the century, at our summer home on Rhode Island bordering the ocean, we planned a small rose garden. Although this had no particular intimacy with rose hybridizing, yet that is where the work began and the reason was because the plants lost their foliage in August and died in the winter.

Great is the confidence of youth and from this sprang the thought that something could be done about it, especially due to the fact that Mendels' paper with the outline of heredity, and the results from cross-breeding had been rediscovered to start a solid foundation in genetics.

For the first decade or two our effort at rose betterment had scarcely become more than a hobby, we adopted our objectives not so much of our own choosing as by the wish of others. By setting out to learn what gardeners most wanted, it was found that about nine out of ten preferred the rose to all other flowers, but others almost in equal number declined to suffer the disappointments in growing them. They wished to have longer lived and sturdier bushes capable of surviving cold winters, to be immune to Black Spot and other fungus diseases and to have continuously blooming climbers. Longevity seemed to us to hang on survival through environmental conditions, which could be controlled by definite resistance to moderate sub-zero temperatures and immunity from certain fungus infections.

These things could be obtained by inheritance of restraining traits from ancestors that possessed them; and as to the third objective, namely, truly ever-blooming climbers, Nature herself must be depended upon for an evolutionary miracle. We shall shortly see why hybridizing has failed in this and just how Nature has recently succeeded.

We are amazed to look back over the last thirty years at the quantity of work that has been done. There have been some fifty varieties produced by the writer and his wife in this joint research, but as to there being a "masterpiece" among them the report is failure, but we look upon them as perhaps some of the forerunners of the future garden rose.

We dreamed of roses of normal colour, form and size growing in the shrubbery and holding their own with other forms and species planted there or growing as ever-blooming specimen plants on lawns and comparing in size with bushes of lilac, hydrangea, or forsythia.

The early part of the research for rose betterment consisted mostly of hit and miss breeding and in the study of appropriate material. The first ten years were devoted in part to the search for a suitable species. After considerable time in travel, with roses chiefly in mind, we found a solution in a book from England. It was in that monumental work by Ellen Willmott, *The Genus Rosa*; the species *Rosa wichuraiana*. She tells us of the great value of this species with its fungus resisting foliage, its deep colour and glossy texture, its resistance to winter injury, the delicious fragrance of its flowers and its potential future for the production of its hybrids. We decided that *Rosa wichuraiana* had the most to offer. All of the Brownell rose varieties are selected hybrids of this species and its descendants, and we call them sub-zero because they inherit its resistance unprotected to sub-zero cold, to 15°F. below zero, and with some earthing up, have the ability to live through 35°F. below and colder. In addition this species can transmit its non-susceptibility to Black Spot to some of its descendents. This with its hybrids has served over the years to cross with some of the most beautiful hybrid teas, and accounts for the introduction of seven-leafleted leaves in our sub-zero hybrid teas and floribundas.

After some length of time, it became evident that cold and disease resistance could be bred into seedlings of the hybrid tea type.

After many generations of breeding, winter resistance equal to that of *R. wichuraiana* was obtained in appropriate breeding plants so that some tested and selected varieties proved adequate. But the problem of non-susceptibility to Black Spot has proved a very difficult one. It means that a plant must be produced that will withstand Black Spot without dusting or spraying even if planted in the middle of a bed of susceptible plants all of which are infected.

Another approach of importance was the matter of colour control.

A large proportion of the rose species from which come all later roses are red and pink, averaging about 15 per cent on the blue side of our spectrum. As roses fade, they usually turn more blue. This blueing is considered a faded colour, and is unpopular. It therefore became advisable, to produce breeding plants more nearly spectrum red. This was done by combining with yellow.

To fortify this new race with a greater degree of vigour and cumulative growth the early hybrid tea roses came into being through hardy climbers. This was important, because it brought breeding plants that bore hybrid tea type to grow by cumulative growth, after cold winters, nearly twice as large as formerly and with double the quantity of blooms.

We obtained assistance from Professor J. B. S. Haldane, the eminent biological chemist, mathematician and geneticist; Dr. C. D. Darlington, the author of books on cytology and genetics; and E. W. Earlenson, who classified Genus Rosa by the expression of its chromosomes. Professor Herbert Walter of Brown University, author of genetic textbooks, gave us a special course in genetics.

If three unit factors, or character determiners, are involved in a cross, you may require sixty-four seedlings on the average to obtain the objective. If there are ten factors, it may require a million seedlings. Therefore, when breeding for a new race it is desirable to breed for one desired characteristic at a time.

From the time of the pollination to the introduction of a desirable variety, it usually requires six or seven years. That time is spent in seed germination through the first winter, propagating five to ten plants in the second year, in the third year one hundred plants, in the fourth year a thousand plants, the fifth year ten thousand plants, in the sixth year harvesting, and in the seventh year distribution. After all this the nurseryman has a quantity of plants, of a selected variety, ready to picture in a catalogue and to distribute.

Let us follow one seedling variety from its pollination to its first propagation by budding. Girls do this work, their scissors slashing off the unopened petals, removing the anthers, covering with cellophane bags and snapping on a rubber band. This they each do, perhaps five hundred times a day, for weeks and weeks. Thus the blossoms are prepared for the pollen application two days later with pollen from another flower. In the autumn the seed pods are gathered, held for a few weeks in a refrigerator to after ripen, then the seeds are removed and returned to cold. About January 1st they are planted in flats and taken to the greenhouse. The seeds begin to germinate in six weeks, and as they start to grow they are lifted and potted. By May seedlings should be large enough to be planted outside.

We may expect one or two for introduction out of 20,000. The seedlings do not all bloom at the same time, and they must be scouted for selections almost daily through the summer. Rose seedlings change materially as they develop. One that seems promising at first, later becomes very uninteresting, while one scarcely noticed the first year becomes glorious a year or two later.

Then, too, that all-important label must be attached to each seedling. This is a double labelling system that identifies the two parents, and completes the hereditary line back to the original species ancestors. This is of great importance, because errors might lead us a long way up a blind alley. Years of later effort may be based on a very few crosses. Under our system one variety for introduction is about the average from a year's crop of 20,000 hybridized seedlings, and very little of the work can be fully delegated to others.

Now let us take a short look backward at garden roses. All species roses grow from seed true to type; hybrids inherit from two different parents, so they and their seedlings, are never fully alike. Cultivated roses, until a century or two ago, were all once bloomers. When the ever-blooming type came to the U.S.A. from China the foundation was laid for the first great evolutionary step in the development of garden roses. These facts, so well known, are mentioned only, to denote a portion of the material on which progress in rose betterment lies.

As a result of the coming of "everbloom" there are probably more than 5,000 named varieties of hybrids produced by ancestral crossing of the ever-bloom type with the once bloom. Many of the flowers of present rose varieties are as beautiful as a rose can be. But why are not the plants more sturdy? The answer to this is well known. When a selection is made from many seedlings produced by crossing two parents one may be beautiful and weak, another strong and not so handsome.

Perhaps the hybridist selects one seedling variety from a long list of hybridized seedlings for its lovely flower, regardless of its sturdiness. Repeating this for several generations, it is clear that by successive selections we may have obtained a variety with flowers of much grandeur, but on a plant of much physical weakness. That is just what has happened with the greater part of the rose breeding procedure of the past and quite naturally so, because for more than one hundred years that work has been done with limited resources. To have selected for both bloom, and sturdiness, would have required many times the labour and expense. Later rose breeding has been on a loftier scale, so that many recent varieties show improvement in both flower and sturdiness of plant.

To appreciate fully the rose types of the future, it is important first to realize the fact that nothing can be *added* by breeding two plants together. The resultant seedlings will only inherit a rearrangement, or recombination of the characteristics of the two parents. On this point it is well known that there are but two types of flowering or floral expression in Rosa; what we call the "once bloom climber" and the "everbloom bush". The distinction is most important. Some would define the once bloom as bloom stems that grow from wood grown a previous year which do not usually repeat. Everbloom might be explained as all growth being bloom stems, setting one or more flowers after about six to twelve leaves. We call the latter hybrid teas, polyanthas, floribundas and otherwise.

It is also important to note that in the cross of once bloom climber with everbloom bush only one or the other obtains in the offspring but not both. That is to say, if we cross everbloom hybrid tea with once bloom climber, some seedlings will be once bloom climbers and some everbloom bushes. This may be because there is no locus, or place in the cromatid, thread or chain of character determiners for both.

You wish to grow your favourite rose, and gather the blooms all the season on tall bushes that require no special attention, or to see on the roof of the garage climbers actually flowering as do hybrid teas. This cannot happen by hybridizing and it cannot happen by environment. It can only happen through variations, that is to say, changes in the character determiners of growth and performances of the variety.

Variations or sports. What is a variation or sport? The plants are composed of innumerable cells. The centre or nucleus of each contains the character determiners, and those are the things that the hybridist breeds. Of course, he does it by applying the male pollen to the female part that grows the seed.

Thus it is that the seedling receives only a combination of characters from the two parents, one that supplied the seed, and the other the pollen; nothing new can be added by this breeding process. Recombination may produce a very interesting rose variety, and as we have seen each such offspring will be different from its sister. But it cannot produce variations or sports to develop the future everblooming roses we are after.

Whether we call these new types Variations, Sports, or Mutations, they come into being usually by a change in a cell, adopting not active but usually latent characters, latent in the plant itself (not a recessive) but derived from an ancestral plant.

These sports may develop various unusual performances and expressions including colour, form or type of growth. Such sports are, first, only one change in only one cell of a plant. By self division, that is repeated again and again for thousands of times a branch or stem is thereby formed that can be grafted, and grown by regrafting, into unlimited numbers of that same new variety that has been produced as a variation.

Some of the possible bloom forms, through variations or sports (but not through hybridizing) are as follows, and we can put them in our dream:

(1) Forms consisting of varieties with canes of different lengths, that bloom at their terminal the same season that such canes grow.

(2) Forms consisting of varieties with canes that bloom at the end, and part way down the canes, in racemes the same year they are planted.

(3) Forms consisting of varieties with canes that grow flowering bloom stems and hybrid tea branches and canes that bloom therefrom all the same year.

(4) Forms consisting of everblooming varieties with canes, stems, and branches that develop into a bush, like the shrubbery in the border, limited in growth to six to eight feet.

Will the climbers bloom the first year? Yes, selected varieties of all of these types, including the climbers, will first bloom from the base, like hybrid teas, and can bloom as freely as any hybrid tea; and as to all of these, let me assure you that there can be no limit to the size, colour, form and fragrance of the blooms, within the range of modern roses.

The new things in *Rosa*, of which we are today dreaming, cannot be produced by fertilization, or in fact by any sort of environment, or by hybridizing.

We have a Mary Wallace by our kitchen sink, known to be of constitutional once bloom, that nearly all summer has two or three blooms showing. These are due to environment that causes a repetition of the once bloom. Such repeats on other varieties may prove to be a constitutional change.

The scientists have recently made great advances in discovering the causes, and influences of various environmental materials, things that increase and decrease the bloom quantity and constancy. But these influences are separate and apart from the constitutional factors of once bloom and everbloom, even though some of them may be produced by constitutional factors. This is a difference the plant breeder must keep clearly in mind, lest he may spend months and years to little or no purpose.

So do not let anyone tell you that any fertilizer, or other environment, can create for us the roses we want for the future, nor by plant breeding alone; but only as Nature shall consider the time propitious to so help man's efforts; something she has not chosen to do heretofore. You still might ask, If these things are possible, why have not the new types we have so long wished, been produced previously? Because Nature in the wild has never brought and held the things together in the manner most desired. She may have produced many new combinations and variations that have died unseen because man was not there with the pollen brush and the knowledge to detect and formulate new breeding plants.

We have had only in mind mutations, or sports of climbers (tallness) that sport to take on the hybrid tea "everbloom" traits, and bloom throughout the season as freely as any hybrid tea; and at the same time retain the variable tallness of the climbers. Or more briefly our dream is not of climbers that can be produced by these hybrid teas changing to climbers, because that will not give us what we want; but of climbers taking on the completeness of the everbloom of hybrid teas, and at the same time retaining the fullness of climbing. You will also consider that the plants in our dream retain the winter hardiness of hardy climbers.

In conclusion. We, the Brownells, have done but little in producing beautiful roses. We have merely set the stage during a number of decades. Nature has been very kind. She has made this dream a reality. She has given us ten varieties of hybrid teas non-susceptible to Black Spot. She has permitted us to introduce fifty varieties all of the sub-zero resistance. She has produced, in our breeding grounds, thousands of varieties of the new race, with tallness and sturdiness combined with "everbloom"; including all of the everblooming types mentioned in the "dream", in many of their stages of development.

It often takes many years for a new rose type to be well known and become popular. This will be true in many countries where once bloom climbers, that do not bloom the first year planted, are usually grown. Some time in the future the preference will be for climbing roses that bloom the first year planted, like hybrid teas, and set blooms on all stems and canes as they mature the same year those stems and canes grow.

THE ROSARIAN'S BOOKSHELF

Poulsen on the Rose. By Svend Poulsen. 160 pp. illustrated with 12 coloured plates. (MacGibbon and Kee, Ltd.) 12s. 6d.

This book, referred to as a revision of Mr. Poulsen's book first published in Denmark in 1941, left me a little confused in my endeavour to do full justice to such a well-known authority on the rose. Concise and containing an abundance of information, most certainly, therefore exceedingly useful as a book of easy reference but without quite the subtle variation that might well have added considerably to its literary qualities. The reference in detail concerning species and early cultivated varieties together with the chapter devoted to propagation is obviously the work of one with much experience, as we know to be the case, and the enthusiast will find much of instructional interest readily to hand.

I found matters concerning cultivation dealt with in a concise fashion. Possibly more pages could well have been devoted to this subject, but the impression gained was of a desire to cover a wide field for consumption both in this country and in Denmark. It is necessary for the British reader to bear this in mind. Pruning is also dealt with in the same chapter, but I found the references somewhat disjointed and conflicting with many of our own practices. True, suggestions may be good ground for experiment, and one cannot lightly contradict an author of such wide experience, nevertheless I wish a little more time had been given towards the clarifying of such an important matter. Possibly I am too dogmatic to accept the suggestion that roses planted in "Herbaceous Borders" in company with Larkspur, etc., is a good way of getting better colour effect. Most of us may prefer to see our roses keeping their own beautiful company. The colour plates may fairly be described as having no influence on the merits of a publication packed full of information, and even if on occasions we find ourselves in disagreement, the book is an aid to good growing and to a better understanding of the rose.

W. J. W. SANDAY

RESEARCH ON BLACK SPOT DISEASE

FREEMAN A. WEISS

(EXTRACT FROM THE POTOMAC ROSE SOCIETY'S BULLETIN)

D R. EMSWELLER reports on the first results of the work of Mr. W. R. Jenkins on rose research, working at the University of Maryland under a fellowship of the American Rose Society.

Mr. Jenkins is concerned with the problem of finding natural resistance or even immunity to Black Spot disease somewhere among all the kinds of roses. This does not mean the testing of existing cultivated roses for resistance to this disease. We already know or can infer, that most if not all our hybrid-teas, floribundas and shrub roses are inherently susceptible to this disease because the species of roses which were their forebears are all susceptible. Mr. Jenkins wants to find a natural species possessing complete immunity (even though it may not be much of a rose otherwise) that can transmit this character to hybrids with improved varieties, and thus synthesize a new race of cultivated roses that will not have to be sprayed—or at least not for the control of Black Spot. This is a long-term project of course, and Mr. Jenkins is only concerned with the initial phases.

He has found a rose species, *R. bracteata*, from China, that is essentially immune to all the races of Black Spot fungus which he has thus far encountered. He employed a laboratory test for determining Black Spot resistance that gives the fungus the most favourable conditions for infection that are possible. The tests were repeated hundreds of times and, with present methods, will give more dependable results in a few hours in the laboratory than are ordinarily obtainable by field-testing for several seasons. Only *R. bracteata*, among the many species (but by no means all that exist) of roses attained this high rating, although a number of species showed different degrees of resistance.

Mr. Jenkins also found that races of the Black Spot fungus exist that differ in their capacity to attack different varieties of roses. Some are only weakly parasitic, others are highly virulent, and some are weak on certain varieties but severe on others. This fact explains some of the contradictory results which have been noted in field tests of Black Spot resistance and control, and demolishes the idea long held by rose breeders that all Black Spot is the same and that tests made in one part of the country would be applicable to all other parts. Mr. Jenkins is now determining means of classifying the different races of Black Spot —an important matter, since they look essentially alike even under the microscope, and must be distinguished by their parasitic behaviour.

A very meritorious piece of work, reflecting credit not only on Mr. Jenkins but on his advisers and the sponsors of the project. It is also an example of the valuable results which can be expected from systematic research on all phases of rose culture, such as is projected by the Rose Foundation of the American Rose Society as rapidly as rose nurserymen, florists and the general rose-loving public will supply the funds.

We are much impressed with this approach to the problem of producing really better, and not just slightly different, roses than the method Dr. Emsweller saw practised in England, where rose varieties under test were given no protection from disease or pests in the fatuous hope that by purely natural selection strains will be developed that are more resistant to adversity. This, to be sure, is Nature's own method, but Nature is very profligate with time in her experiments. Albeit we have been assured that "there will always be an England"; perhaps the British rose-breeders will better ensure that their time does not somehow run out, by starting their survival tests with material that has proved to have some resistance at the outset.

Communicated by DAVID Y. WHITTET

From the *Annals of Penicuik*

"In 1373, David of Penicuik, for good advice rendered to him, granted to his cousin, William of Creichtoune, Lord of that Ilk, his whole lands of Burntstoune and Welchtoune, with their pertinents, lying in his lands and lordship of Penicuik. These lands to be held by the said William of Creichtoune and Thomas of Creichtoune his brother. The *reddendo* or condition of holding the property, was a red rose, payable to the superior if asked for, on the ground of Burnstoune, at the feast of the Nativity of St. John the Baptist.

"This charter was confirmed by King Robert II at Scone on 29th March, 1373, in the third year of his reign."

"MY MASTERPIECE"

MATH. TANTAU

UETERSEN, HOLSTEIN

FORTY-NINE years ago, in 1906, the firm of Math. Tantau was born; in that year the senior principal, Math. Tantau, began his life's work. A mixed nursery business was the foundation on which the now world-famous enterprise was built. Before many years had passed it was the roses which gave this business its special character. Very shortly after the First World War, all plants which had till then been cultivated were abandoned, and the business went over to special rose culture. Very careful and detailed work was devoted to building up the business into the firm of Tantau as it exists today.

Though this progress was much obstructed by the bitter confusions of the post-war years that followed the First World War, the inflation, which reduced the German currency to all but complete worthlessness, and in particular, by the intervention of natural disasters which very nearly spelt the ruin of the enterprise. Nevertheless, the firm of Math. Tantau never relinquished its goal and persevered in extending the cultures. During the First World War, the senior principal announced himself no longer satisfied with the mere growing of roses; he wished to do more than this, and accordingly turned his attention to cross-breeding them. Already by 1919 such progress had been made that his first creations could be introduced on the market. At that time they were still small-blooming polyanthas, the strains called Beauty of Holstein and Stadtrat Meyn. Many other polyanthas and hybrid teas followed. But the senior principal was indefatigable in his efforts. He had an aim in view, which proved to be correct and important. In the year 1928 the first hybrid polyantha Johanna Tantau was introduced. All the breeding work of the following years pursued this aim of producing large-blooming polyanthas, and a considerable number of new strains were registered. But alas, the work of the firm was again to be interrupted. In 1939, a fateful year for the whole world, when once more the Horsemen of the Apocalypse stormed over the globe, the Second World War broke out, with all its terrible devastating effects and consequences. It seemed as if rose culture must finally succumb. Land and greenhouses had to be put to other uses.

In addition, there was the lack of staff to contend with, and manifold other difficulties. But despite all these problems, the firm of Math. Tantau did not give up, but continued tirelessly with its work, under the most onerous circumstances, keeping its aim constantly in mind.

Meanwhile there came more and more inquiries and an ever-increasing request for large-blooming roses flowering all the year round. The triumphal progress of the hybrid polyanthas or floribundas had begun, and soon reached proportions exceeding the wildest hopes. Everywhere the floribundas find the most extensive use in large parks, in gardens, in cemeteries. It is nowadays scarcely possible to imagine a park unadorned with floribundas and without Tantau varieties in it. This great success is in large measure due to the products of Tantau breeding. There is not a rose nursery in Germany at the present day which does not cultivate Fanal or Käthe Duvigneau, to name only two, and these varieties are met with everywhere. The path we took was the right one, and we shall continue to lay increasing emphasis on this type of breeding. The demand for hybrid teas is on the decline and it may not be long before they are relegated to a subordinate position as bedding roses in Germany

One of our principal new varieties, for example, is Schweizer Grüss (called in England Red Favourite), a variety which is not unfamiliar in any part of the Federal Republic today. We have never heard a word of complaint against this variety; everyone sings its praises to the skies. Its outstanding qualities have raised it decidedly to the status of a world-wide rose. With this much-sought-after low-growing floribunda our firm was able to fulfil a long-felt wish of many rose lovers. The plant has an erect habit of growth, an entirely even height, and is hardy enough to survive the winter. The yew-green foliage is strikingly healthy. The uniquely beautiful blood-red colour of the flowers, with its velvety sheen and without any trace of a bluish glimmer in it, is so intense, and at the same time so warmly glowing that the eye is at once drawn to rest upon it with delight. Red Favourite will always keep its unblemished beauty, for its immaculate hue suffers no changes. It is unaffected by weather, strong sun, or steady rain. The separate bloom, large and semi-double, is a joy in itself, but the wonderfully free flowering of this variety exalts it to a rose of the first quality. There can scarcely be a soul who would pass by this flower without lingering in admiration. Yet this variety in the meantime is no longer in a class of its own. Our new introduction, the Hobby rose, an offspring of Red Favourite, does not lag behind it in any particular. Its colour is an unusually pure dark pink with a salmon hue shining through it of enchanting beauty, its growth, fullness of bloom, hardiness, free flowering, and foliage, are so perfect as to leave but little to be desired.

The aims we have at present in view are now directed towards still further enlarging the blooms of floribundas while nevertheless preserving their full freedom of flowering, to a greater degree than we have so far been able to attain. In this regard we are able to be fully confident, for considerable progress in breeding possibilities has already been achieved which will probably very soon be made available to the public. These new additions will yet further strengthen the advance of the floribunda varieties, while the hybrid teas will fall to an increasing extent into the background.

As has been proved already, Tantau varieties also thrive and flourish well in England. Quite a number of our roses have already been tested in the Trial Grounds at St. Albans and several have been awarded a Trial Ground Certificate after testing there. It would give us real pleasure if our varieties and new strains should in the future also meet with the same success, and we hope moreover that our floribunda roses will gradually find a welcome in English parks and gardens.

ARE WE GETTING TOO MANY NEW ROSES?

N. P. HARVEY

M OST people would, I suppose, maintain quite firmly, that there are far too many new roses. Such a statement is, of course, only a half-truth and like most generalizations it is usually made without attempting to get down to fundamentals.

The old Greek saying, "Variety is pleasing", may sound trite to modern ears but is surely one of the basic keys to human aspirations. Man accepts a measure of standardization or uniformity in some directions but when it comes to the choice of flowers for his garden, the books he wishes to read or the music he enjoys, he prefers a rich variety.

If we demand variety, then we must surely welcome novelty. There are, I submit, two reasons behind the desire for novelty or newness. The first is the fundamental instinct of the human race to perpetuate the species and in so doing the individual hopes that he or she will transmit something personal to the offspring. The artist, the sculptor, the painter, the author, the composer, in fact, any person who creates something new, has precisely the same feelings. One of the best definitions of art is "the communication of experience".

The man who breeds a new variety of rose, or other plant, is also expressing a fundamental human aspiration. You can, I suppose, retort that a perpetual search for novelty sometimes leads to mediocrity but the principle is unquestionably right even if the results are in certain instances disappointing. So much for those who sneer at hybridizers and imagine that all "intelligent" people should concentrate entirely on old-fashioned roses and species. Do these men and women of myopic vision suggest that music stopped after Beethoven, and that Walton or Britten are unworthy of encouragement?

The second reason behind the continuous desire for novelty is that most people like to enjoy the creations of others. The *public* wants new roses and especially varieties that are in some way different. Recently one nurseryman who had 30,000 surplus trees of older varieties at the

end of the season, stated that the same quantity of the newer introductions would have sold without difficulty. Another, no less important, reason for the wealth of new varieties is strictly utilitarian or
functional, as the architect would say. With very few exceptions, most
varieties of plants, including roses, tend to deteriorate in time when
propagated vegetatively, unless they are close to the original species.
In recent years, Dame Edith Helen and Mrs. Henry Bowles have
begun to go downhill.

If we agree that new varieties are desirable on both aesthetic and
utilitarian grounds, can it be said that there are too many? Ever since
man started to raise new roses, complaints have been made that there
were numerous varieties not sufficiently distinct to warrant naming.
There is, of course, an easy but insidious way round this difficulty.
Why not allow the experts to decide for you? Let a Committee meet
periodically to determine which are the best fifty or one hundred roses
and prohibit the nurserymen from growing any other varieties.
Heaven forbid! May I remind you that politicians on both sides of the
fence seem increasingly anxious to tell the man-in-the-street what
is good for him? (It was a Labour M.P. who stated that "The gentleman
in Whitehall really does know best" and a Conservative Chancellor
of the Exchequer who informed us that he had hesitated about releasing
more of the Post-War Credits because Service Gratuities had not
always been wisely spent!) Let us ensure that this never happens in the
rose world.

Certain roses are obviously outstanding and both experts and
amateurs would be practically unanimous about this. Peace, Grand'-
mère Jenny, Ena Harkness and Frensham immediately come to mind
though a few people find Peace too variable for their taste. When we
come to those varieties which, though still good, fall below the highest
standards, individual opinions and experiences will differ. Some
varieties will only give their best performance in dry areas, others in
cool districts. Preferences as regards colour, form and habit will vary
considerably.

No Committee or other body of men and women, however
knowledgeable and well meaning, has the right, in a democratic
country, to order us what clothes to wear, which books to read or
which roses to grow in our gardens. We only tolerate censorship of
books when it involves the banning of American horror comics or

'SWEET REPOSE' (flor.)

Geheimrat Duisberg × poly. seedling.
Raised by G. de Ruiter, Holland.
Trial Ground No. 323. Reg. No. 376. Trial Ground Certificate.
Gold Medal, Autumn Show, 1955.
For description see page 148

obviously pornographic publications likely to corrupt youthful minds. Freedom to publish is, of course, abused, but the advantages of frank criticism of men and events more than outweigh any abuses.

If we argue on these lines, it follows that rose varieties termed bad cannot be disallowed by authority. To me a rose which has a fine scent but is an indifferent grower and subject to disease, is a bad variety. Others may prefer to grow such a variety for scent alone, ignoring obvious weaknesses. They have every right to cultivate the rose of their own choice and it would be immoral to prevent them.

If we object to drastic prohibition, how then can we secure better roses? The answer should be clear to anyone who has followed my argument. *By permission, recommendation and suggestion.* The issue of a Trial Ground Certificate denotes that the successful variety has given good results with reasonable attention and should satisfy the average amateur. These Certificates undoubtedly help to eliminate the second-rate varieties, though it must be remembered that some roses which fail to make the grade at Oaklands succeed elsewhere. Golden Revelry, Pink Spiral, Royalist, and Tzigane are examples.

There were over 200 new varieties in the Trial Ground last year. Only a small proportion gained Certificates, inferring that some raisers do not pre-select sufficiently thoroughly. Is it unfair to suggest that valuable ground is thereby wasted? The standards of 1955 are surely in advance of 1939 and the number of worth-while varieties is greater.

The scope for the hybridizer seems limitless. Out of approximately 120 rose species less than twenty have been used by breeders and the colour range in the main groups, i.e. hybrid teas, floribundas, ramblers, climbers and miniatures, is still limited, if one considers the eventual possibilities. There are no pure scarlets or pillar-box reds, and no blues in any group. Bicolours and multicolours are few in the floribundas.

How many red hybrid teas possess really strong flower stems? Crimson King and Chrysler Imperial can be cited, but hardly any other reds. Again, nearly every red, except Karl Herbst, is susceptible to Mildew and the majority (save perhaps Josephine Bruce and Mme Louise Laperrière) have a tendency to blue in hot weather.

Bicolours which retain their colour in heat are badly needed, though Gay Crusader and Tzigane point the way. Virgo remains the only white hybrid tea which is undamaged by rain.

Improvements in form, foliage and other characteristics are equally desirable and it is impossible to visualize stagnation. No real attempt has yet been made to improve the relatively poor lasting qualities of most varieties, whether on the tree or when cut.

The complaint that too many varieties are marketed which are very similar in colour is probably true, but it is often forgotten that no variety is really exactly like another. Even where colours apparently correspond, there will always be differences in foliage, habit of growth and form of flower.

The market obviously cannot absorb all the worth-while new roses, accordingly some fall by the wayside, just as certain books are over-looked and join the publishers' remainder lists, notwithstanding individual excellence. We must hope that public taste, guided by expert opinion, will continue to reject the second-rate, thereby focusing attention on the best and raising the general standard even higher.

Our heartiest congratulations to Domenico Aicardi of San Remo on his investiture by the President of the Italian Republic as Cavaliere al Merito de Lavaro. He is world-famous as the raiser of new roses, including those well-known varieties Signora and Glory of Rome.

OBSERVATIONS ON THE SHAFTER
STOCK (DR. HUEY)

ANDRÉ LEROY

*From a lecture given by M. André Leroy at the Annual Congress of the French
Rose Society at Angers, 1954, and first published in Les Amis des Roses.*

THE origin of the discussions on the Shafter stock (Dr. Huey) go
back to 1946, the date of the sending to the International Concours of New Roses at Bagatelle of trees budded on this stock presented by the firm of Armstrong Nurseries, of California, U.S.A.
(H. Swim, Raiser).

Since receiving the rose-trees, on March 1st, 1946, we have observed
their exceptional vigour, characterized by very thick wood, and neck
from 8 to 10 cm. in circumference.

In the spring of 1947 their growth was very different to that of all
the other rose-trees in the rose garden, and all to their advantage. The
numerous young shoots developed with strength and a rapidity rarely
equalled by our very good French varieties. In June the French raisers
present at the conference were astonished by this growth; M. Mallerin
was sure that this vigour could only come from the stock. The name
of Shafter was mentioned. The propagation of the stocks at the end of
the conference after uprooting the trees, and the study of young plants
confirmed that it was the Shafter stock (Dr. Huey).

SHAFTER. It is a horticultural variety that the Americans class in the
group of climbers with large flowers. It is a hybrid of Wichuraiana
(Ethel × Grüss an Teplitz), very vigorous; the branches of a current
season's growth can reach 4–5 metres in length. The leaves are composed of five or seven leaflets. The leaves with five leaflets are normally
predominant. The flowers are semi-double, dark red and 5–6 cm. in
diameter.

Shafter has a very long period of growth.

During these observations there was a general opinion against this
new stock. Several arguments arose, and here is the analysis.

First Argument:

Roses budded on Shafter would not live in France.

On this point here are the records made at Bagatelle in the spring of

1954 on the American rose-trees, budded on Shafter by Armstrong Nurseries.

Trial 1952–53 (Mojave). We still have the five original plants in a very good state of growth.

Trial 1951–52 (La Jolla)–(Buccaneer). We still have the five original plants of each in a very good state of growth.

Trial 1950–51 (Helen Traubel)–(Chief Seattle), (Fred Howard). We still have the five original plants of each in a very good state of growth.

Trial 1949–50 (Beacon)–(First Love). We still have the five original plants of each in a very good state of growth.

Trial 1948–49 (No presentation).

Trial 1947–48 (Sutter's Gold)–(Fandango), (Juno). We still have two trees in a very good state of growth, the three missing trees of each were sacrificed for study.

Trial 1946–47 (Taffeta)–(Pinkie)–(Applause).* We still have the five original trees of each in a very good state of growth.

One could ask if the stock is susceptible to French winters. The answer is obvious because the American rose-trees resisted minimum temperatures observed below at the meteorological post at Bagatelle since 1946.

LOWEST TEMPERATURES

1946. Dec. 21, 9.5°F. with similar temperature for 9 days.
1947. Jan 29, 9.5°F. with similar temperature for 5 days.
1948. Feb. 25, 14.4°F. with similar temperature for 6 days.
1950. Jan. 21, 16°F. with similar temperature for 6 days.
1954. Feb. 2, 5.9°F. with similar temperature for 15 days.

Second Argument:

Roses budded on Shafter would be less free flowering than others during the first year of planting.

This statement contradicts the facts. Here are in fact the comparisons between the number of flowers of Armstrong-Swim varieties, grafted on Shafter, and the number of flowers from French varieties, the best in the corresponding trials (grafted on Canina or Polyantha) after weekly countings. (Flowers produced during the two years of growth.)

* The old plants in this group have been replaced this winter.

CONCOURS 1946–7

Armstrong Varieties		French Varieties	
Applause:	219 fl.	Dr Valois:	199 fl.
Forty-niner:	111 fl.	Minerve:	113 fl.
Taffeta:	125 fl.	Charles Mallerin:	49 fl.
Janetha		Haisha:	89 fl.
Armstrong:	107 fl.	Français	
Pinkie		(H. Poly):	464 fl.
(Poly):	1,515 fl.		

CONCOURS 1947–8

Sutter's Gold:	127 fl.	Mme Vincent	
Fandango:	92 fl.	Auriol:	99 fl.
Juno:	117 fl.	Alaska:	67 fl.
Allure:	96 fl.	San Diégo:	101 fl.
		Annie Brandt:	84 fl.

CONCOURS 1949–50

First Love:	294 fl.	Mme L.	
Beacon:	184 fl.	Laperrière:	242 fl.
Bravo:	150 fl.	Altesse:	130 fl.
		Châtelet:	187 fl.
		Eden Rose:	87 fl.

CONCOURS 1950–1

Helen Traubel:	209 fl.	Confidence:	239 fl.
Chief Seattle:	146 fl.	Tzigane:	144 fl.
Fred Howard:	120 fl.	Mascotte:	18 fl.

CONCOURS 1951–2

La Jolla:	202 fl.	Naples:	136 fl.
Buccaneer:	257 fl.	Baiser:	198 fl.

CONCOURS 1952–4

Mojave:	169 fl.	Bettina:	161 fl.
		Pastorella:	132 fl.

The comparison from the point of view of freedom of flowering is all to the advantage of the roses budded on Dr. Huey.

Third Argument:

The acceptance at the trials of roses budded on Shafter risks a deception of the public because they admire the roses in the competition, then on buying them they receive less vigorous plants grafted on Multiflora or on Canina.

From this criticism we find:

(1) That the most vigorous rose-trees are those budded on Shafter.
(2) That the French nurserymen are not actually able to provide the public with rose-trees grafted on this stock.

In view of this situation, because we know that the value of Shafter is undeniable, it would be better to study, to acclimatize, and propagate it in quantity, and not to consider it as undesirable.

Fourth Argument:

The Shafter is not utilized commercially, because it is difficult to multiply except in the south of France; two years' culture is needed to prepare the subject and two other years to form the rose-tree, therefore more expense incurred than on those on Canina.

A—*Multiplication of the subject.*

Following the trials made at Bagatelle by Mr. Jupillat, head gardener, it is found that one can obtain the plants sufficiently strong to sell commercially in a time that does not exceed that for the same production of Canina. Propagation can be made in the following way:

CUTTINGS. Second fortnight in June (simple cuttings and on a heel) portions from the branches around 25 cm., taken from the lateral branches coming from the big wood shoots of the previous year. Set out in light soil and in a half shaded position. The cuttings are rooted in the autumn with a 95 per cent take, protected with a covering of oak leaves during the winter. The rooted cuttings are not moved until April, and are then put out in the ground where they are to be budded in August or September of the same year.

Observations: In order to study their resistance to the cold during the winter, no protection at all was given these last years. The cuttings had resisted the winters of 1950–1–2–3 very well (see minimum temperatures above).

In comparison, the winters 1953–4 were not as good as other years (minimum 5.9°F. in our shelter and from 2.3°F. in the open air). Results in spring: 30 per cent of the cuttings completely frozen and the rest more or less frozen on the upper part. It is wise therefore to prepare a light covering at the beginning of the winter in the nursery; leaves or frames.

B—*Time necessary for the production of a plant.*

All the trees budded in August–September on Shafter, produced roses as strong the following year as those budded on Canina.

'SORAYA'
Raised by Louisette Meilland, France.

CONCLUSION

We must remember that the roses under observation were particularly well looked after. An adaptation to large-scale culture remains to be done, they require a complete study elsewhere.

The remaining rooted cuttings after the winter 1953–4 were given to M. Michard, of the Vilmorin Establishment in the following March and planted on a large scale. They did not take very well because, without doubt, they were set out too early (extremely cold spring and the young subjects were somewhat damaged by the frost). But the transplanting was done very carefully at Bagatelle and without one loss.

Large-scale trials have begun again with stronger plants (protected in winter) and planted up a little later.

NOTE

At the time of putting in the cuttings, it is best to take the precaution of removing the basal eyes to avoid the development of suckers later on. It is also noted that all the old plants in the rose garden at Bagatelle and originating from Armstrong & Co. never suckered.

Finally it is interesting to point out that the resistance of Shafter to the effects of chalky soil appears less than that of Canina. It is, nevertheless, clearly more resistant to lime-induced chlorosis than Multiflora. It seems that it prefers a light, sandy clay soil rather than a heavy, cold one.

A ROSE BY ANY OTHER NAME

G. D. ROWLEY

in *"Journal of the John Innes Association"*

THERE are many ways of describing a rose: you can eulogize it in blank verse, serenade it by moonlight, or define it in best botanical dog-latin—*"Receptacula ovoidea, apicem versus contracta . . ."* and so forth.

Nurserymen's catalogues provide many an answer to the problem of how to give a word-picture of the Queen of Flowers. Some are strictly factual:

> "Produces large, soft, pale rose double flowers with freedom."

Others are less restrained:

> "Scintillating blossoms dyed in the raspberry-lake of ripe pomegranate juice cascade over slender sea-green bushes, porphyry-barked, mulberry bemossed."

Believe it or not, both these refer to the same rose, the old Moss Zenobia! The latter comes from the 1953 Shrub Rose List of Manor Cottage Nurseries, Abingdon, which abounds in quotable excerpts as, for instance:

> " Du Maitre d'Ecole. A gorgeous belle bearing largesse of massive, balmy cabbages, cyclamen-pink and amethyst lustred copper and bronze, waning to the soft mauve of wisteria tassels."

Beauty, we are so often reminded, exists in the eye of the beholder, yet what wonders the rose-tinted spectacles can work for some! Not even Mr. G. S. Thomas, that ardent champion of old garden roses, can raise much enthusiasm for the Boursault group, which he reluctantly dismisses as "Thornless and scentless roses; generally speaking, of little value." Yet don your tinted glasses and you will see them in another catalogues as:

> "Regency charmers of alpine × china breed, all graceful, scandent, thornless shrubs with satiny melon-green leaves and big

bouquets of middling-sized, ruched flowers; the Blush has clusters of rose du Bari clove-carnations languishing a peachy bloom."

Often a rose is praised for different characters by different writers, each striving in his own way to overcome the "sales resistance" of his readers. Consider the old hybrid perpetual variety Reine des Violettes. Mansfield (1947) starts the ball rolling by concentrating on its colour:

"It has been claimed to be the 'blue' rose, and is probably the nearest approach that has yet been attained to an object which is quite undesirable."

Ellwanger finds it merely "Muddy", but another catalogue falls for it neck and crop:

"One of the rare souvenirs we yet own of the mid-Victorian furore for rich, ripe puces, amaranthes and heliotropes, it is a bold bush of flashing jade bestrewn with richly-perfumed blossoms of amethyst irised purple." Etc., etc., etc.

Several writers prefer to keep off the controversial subject of colour, commending it instead as a "Vigorous, rustic shrub", "Very freely flowering", or for its "Glossy, disease-resistant foliage". MacFarland (1947) tries a new approach; shock tactics:

"Raised from Pope Pius IX. Large, full, deep violet-red."

And I am sure that by no means exhausts the possibilities for this one variety alone.

Turning from the raspberry-lakes and balmy cabbages to consider poetry, we are surprised to find it relatively restrained and a good deal more utilitarian than in years gone by. Books on roses such as Dean Hole's had a couplet or two on every other page; nowadays the practice has gone out of favour. Modern poets sing the praises of the rose in a more down-to-earth manner:

> " If you're anxious to learn about roses,
>   And want your blooms to be 'mighty',
>   You don't have to go to college;
>   Join the American Rose Society.

There's an abundance of art in this hobby,
The rose in its beauty and piety.
The organization best qualified to aid you
Is the American Rose Society."
           !   !   !

Incidentally, if you feel impelled to read the remaining five verses of
this epic, we recommend taking the hint in line four and consult H. H.
Allen in the June 1953 issue of their magazine.

Modern roses also get their ecstatic descriptions by enthusiastic
nurserymen. From the beautifully illustrated French catalogue produced by "Universal Rose Selections" comes this description of
Antheor (translated).

ANTHEOR (F. Meilland) 1948.
"Lovers of the Mediterranean, those who knew the 'veritable
folly of light combined with the folly of water', of which P. Valéry
speaks, will wish to recapture their rapturous memories in this flower,
which opens elegantly to reveal its 35 reddish-apricot petals
illuminated with Nankin yellow. The bud is long, elegant, well
wrapped. A habit with erect growth, of precocious flowering and
rapidly growing, predestines the variety to forcing and use as a cut
flower. Lovers of the sun who are eternally exiled far from the deep
blue skies, at the mention of this name, 'Antheor', will conjure up
their images of steep red rocks, blue sea, lonely creeks, and through
this colouring tinge their imaginings with an aura of tangible
beauty!"

What a disappointment to find this same rose dismissed in one line in
an English catalogue.

"Antheor. Apricot, shaded rose pink. A perfect button-hole rose."

'POULSEN'S SUPREME' (flor.)

Raised by Svend Poulsen, Denmark.
Trial Ground Certificate, 1950. Certificate of Merit, 1952.

'SALMON PERFECTION' (flor.)

Raised by G. de Ruiter, Holland.
Trial Ground Certificate, 1951. Certificate of Merit, 1952.
We regret that this plate was incorrectly titled in the *Rose Annual*, 1955.

Then the poet who inspired the description of the first named over-flows again for Tahiti (translated):

TAHITI (F. Meilland) 1947.
   Certificate in the 1947 competition "La Plus Belle Rose de France".
   "Where have these enormous flowers drawn the ardent life that pulsates in them? Are not such exuberance of bloom and such astounding excess of beauty the fruit of exotic saps? At the sight of this amber yellow following the chrome yellow of the buds, then enriched wherever exposed to the sun with a suffusion of carmine lacquer, we evoke the happy isle in the shimmering infinite of the Pacific. Oh Tahiti, thou who sendest forth thy palms to meet the waves, thou who art caressed by the breath of the trade winds, thou who art engarlanded with dance and flower, thou wilt not deny the magnificent vaporous appearance of this rose, nor its exceptional vigour, nor its astounding abundance of bloom!"

But an English catalogue can rise no higher than:

   "Tahiti. Amber flushed with crimson, colour deepens with age."

After all, perhaps it is better to see your selected varieties growing in the nursery fields before you order them.

                                                                B. P.

HOW I GROW MY ROSES

R. F. B. NAYLOR, C.B., D.S.O.
BARNET, HERTS.

HAVING served nearly forty years as an officer in the Regular Army my efforts at rose-growing have been, to say the least, spasmodic. However, whenever I was able to visit my home I was in a rose atmosphere as both my parents were enthusiastic rose-growers. When I retired in 1946 I settled at my present home which is in a good district for roses. I found as a near neighbour that great rosarian, J. N. Hart, and I have benefited much from his unrivalled experience.

My soil varies considerably but for the most part it has a clay sub-soil and light to medium loam top-soil. I have two distinct rose gardens, both having been planted with roses for upwards of fifty years. In addition I have two rose hedges planted in virgin soil. There are in all about 600 roses of all sorts and in addition I have a few maidens each year budded on Canina—these are used for replacements. I grow my roses primarily for display, but having been persuaded three years ago to enter for the National Rose Show, I now grow a proportion for exhibition blooms.

As the rose beds are of long standing most of my planting is in the nature of spot replacements. Where this is the case I dig a hole two spits deep, fork up the sub-soil, put some turf at the bottom with a good covering of farm manure—this is then mixed with fresh soil obtained from somewhere else in the garden. The roses are planted in a mixture of fresh soil and peat with a handful of bonemeal, the whole being well trodden in.

If I am replanting a complete bed the same procedure is carried out, but in this case I only replace the top spit with new soil if the existing soil is too unsuitable. This latter proved to be the case on my Frensham hedge. First year cut-backs receive no more manure until they have been planted for twelve months. In the case of established bushes I give a double handful of bonemeal and one handful superphosphate per bush in April. At this time all beds are also mulched with a good layer of spent hops which have been stacked for some months—the longer the better. I fork this in lightly the following winter. The only drawback to this excellent mulch is that the birds love it, and in their hunt for worms are apt to scatter it over the adjacent lawn or paths. I find it provides an excellent humus, and with the bonemeal and super-phosphate gives excellent results. In late July established plants have a watering with weak manure.

I am not wedded to any particular school as to the season for pruning. In the late autumn heavy heads or trusses are removed so as to lessen the chance of root disturbance by the winter gales. When I consider the sap is well down, which may be any time from December to March, I carry out my pruning. In general I go in for medium to long pruning on the principle of the stronger the growth the lighter the pruning. In 1954 one of my bushes of Peace was six feet high and had seventy-five blooms out or in full bud at the same time on its second bloom, and my bed of The Doctor is four feet six inches high and gives excellent exhibition blooms; both these varieties are long pruned. Whenever I may have pruned I go over the bushes again, when danger of hard frosts is past, and cut out any wood damaged by frost since pruning. At any time of year I cut out wood which looks unhealthy or is producing very weak growth. In the case of my rose hedges (Frensham and Penelope) my object has been to grow them four feet six inches to five feet high. To attain this I pruned normally the first year after planting. Subsequently I pruned very lightly until the desired height was attained. Since then if they are getting too crowded or coarse I cut out old wood as new growth replaces it.

I spray as and when necessary with Sybol or Bouisol White Oil, and for thrips I use D.D.T. One last point, when cutting roses for the house I take care not to cut too high a proportion with long stems, on the principle that one should leave more leaves on the bush than one removes. I apply the same principle of course when cutting off dead heads.

To end what on reading it through seems pretty "textbook": What do I consider is the most important thing in growing roses? Take great trouble in their initial planting, and give them as good a start in your garden as you possibly can. No amount of after-care can compensate a bush which has been carelessly planted.

E. R. C. TIZARD

BRISTOL

How he prayed and how he fasted,
How he lived, and toiled and suffered.

I HAVE to thank Longfellow for the conclusion on the manner in which my roses are grown. It is the simplest précis of what I am about to write and it will save the time of those who have no desire to read further.

In the early days of the last war I had to change my residence and found myself with a small garden that was ugly, untidy, and unseminared. The soil was a mixture of about three parts ashes from the countless fires of a cold banking establishment, one part broken china of late bedroom and early tea period, and one part dirt of a dusty and characterless appearance. There was nothing large about this garden except an apple-tree, which occupied most of it, and a privet hedge which housed every undesirable insect. They were removed. That is a simple statement of a complicated task. Imported soil and peat, supplemented by the products of a nearby stable, improved conditions and removed, to some extent, the rose-trees planted from signifying that "brief life is here our portion". Rose-trees were difficult to obtain in those days and I had to be satisfied with old trees moved from another garden. And they flourished. They gave a great deal of pleasure during a time when joy was at a discount. From that response began a confirmed devotion and a realization that roses could be grown in adverse conditions provided there was a determination to improve matters.

My small garden was eventually filled with rose-trees and the problem of continuation arose. I approached a friend, who offered me some ground he did not use. His expression on showing me the plot was a clear indication of his conviction that a mental home was more in keeping with my acceptance. I stood to my chin in grass, docks, nettles, thistles and the finest horse-radish I have ever seen. It had a good ground covering of coltsfoot, couch, dandelion, and bindweed. Sufficient ground was cleared to plant about fifty trees and two hundred briars. Each year another portion was cleared for the purpose of transplanting maiden trees and the planting of more briars. Therein lies the full joy of:

> *Still achieving, still pursuing,*
> *Learn to labour and to wait.*

Being surrounded by weed, keeping the cultivated land clean is an endless and arduous task. The time given to this has been reduced by the use of a suitable flame-gun. The preparation of new ground has been hastened by spraying with a selective weed-killer. With limited time available for the cultivation of roses it is impossible to advance beyond the immediate requirements for planting and more drastic methods cannot be employed. I am still left with the problem of the grass, mainly couch. This is burnt off and a rotavator brought into use which brings many of the roots to the surface to be raked off. After this has been repeated the work of digging has lost its dread.

This ground has produced good rose-trees and consequently good roses. I am quite orthodox in the manner of cultivation. I use as much cow manure as the credit squeeze will allow, as a top dressing in the spring. All the trees do not benefit in this way but they get their turn and in the meantime get a dressing of peat. They all receive at intervals, after pruning until early in July, an application of a fertilizer based on the N.R.S. formula. They are never watered and have to suffice with the "gentle rain from heaven". They have survived the conditions of the past summer remarkably well. I am not free from disease and Black Spot has been a source of worry in recent years. It is not so apparent in this dry season. To combat this trouble I spray with copper sulphate during January and, after pruning, with a colloidal copper mixture. During the winter I endeavour to tidy up the trees in preparation for the hard pruning that most of them receive when that task is commenced about mid-March. I plant my rows two feet six inches apart but in future I intend to plant them three feet apart and floribundas will receive proportionate consideration. My main interest at the present is growing roses in nursery fashion and not in laying out rose-beds.

The way I grow my roses is not the one I would select but if you cannot choose the means that are most desirable, you are fortunate to be given the opportunity to strive. If, in the process, you encourage a prolapsed intervertebral disc, sciatica and the use of a walking-stick but are not deterred, you are with those who:

> *Say not the struggle nought availeth,*
> *The labour and the wounds are vain.*

B. W. W. SAMPSON
BROOKMAN'S PARK, HERTS.

I STARTED rose-growing seriously when I moved into my present house in South Hertfordshire, which was new in 1937. The garden was meadowland which consisted of about ten inches of heavy loam with a clay subsoil, containing some stones. The site is about 400 feet above sea-level which is higher than most of the surrounding country-side. It, therefore, usually misses the late spring and early winter frosts. In preparing the rose-beds care was taken not to bring any of the sub-soil to the surface, but I did endeavour to loosen the clay by the use of a fork, without actually turning it over. The old turf was chopped up and buried at the bottom of the top spit. Bonemeal was used generously, and the ground was allowed to settle for several weeks before planting my first batch of roses in early November. I was very fortunate in purchasing my first roses from a Hertfordshire rose specialist, from whom I obtained excellent advice about varieties, and a strong recommendation to join the National Rose Society, which was done immediately.

Originally there was no intention of exhibiting, but I found they did so well on this soil that I was encouraged to do so, first of all locally and then at the national shows. This called for a little more specialized treatment. All the rose-beds are now raised about five inches which allows them to drain more easily, and thus the roses never have their roots in stagnant water. My own experience is that more losses are sustained through waterlogged soils than from any other cause. A certain amount of loam is always kept under cover, this is mixed with peat, sand and some bonemeal and is used at planting time to cover the roots. Sometimes it is necessary to replace one or two roses in an established bed. In this case I take out at least two bucketfuls of the old soil and replace it with fresh loam to which rotted manure or compost has been added. This, together with the above-mentioned planting mixture, gives the roses a very good start.

I prune early in March, being very careful to collect all prunings and dead leaves, which are consigned to the bonfire. The beds are then given a dressing of four parts meat and bonemeal, two parts super-phosphate, and one part sulphate of potash, and forked over lightly. Each year one-third of the beds are given a dressing of manure as a mulch some time in April, and the others are given a light covering of peat. This seems to have prevented Black Spot, as previous to this treatment it was very difficult to control.

In addition, I prune according to the variety, the strong growers (such as Peace) being lightly pruned, but others a little more severely. After a few weeks of growth every bush is gone over and a certain number of inward-growing shoots removed, and a careful watch kept for any die-back. Disbudding is commenced as soon as side buds can be handled easily, and a preventive spray given against green and black fly and thrips. Early in June all roses known to be liable to Black Spot are given a spray of colloidal copper; this spray is repeated at about three-weekly intervals. All dead blooms are cut off daily, particular care being taken to see that the cut is made just above a leaf joint.

It is not usual for roses growing on this type of soil to need watering, but I have found it necessary in this exceptionally dry summer (1955). I do, however, make a habit of using liquid manure about ten days before a show, as this does seem to increase the size of the blooms.

Some time in November I go over all the bushes and shorten the longer growths in order to prevent the winter gales loosening them in the soil.

Many exhibitors use conical bloom-protectors before a show, but although I have a number of these they are rarely used. Exhibition blooms are always cut either the morning or evening of the day before a show. They are placed in deep water and stood in a cool room over-night. As I live only about seventeen miles from Vincent Square the roses are conveyed to the show in water. In conclusion, one word about tying blooms. I occasionally find it necessary to tie specimen roses, but never do this to decoratives.

A. A. NORTON
TORONTO, CANADA

THE growing of roses in our garden, situated in the northern part of metropolitan Toronto, presents an interesting challenge with regard to temperature and other natural hazards. Toronto is situated on a latitude similar to Marseilles, France, and summer temperatures frequently reach 95°F. or higher with winter lows of 10° to 20°F. below zero. We do have some tempering influence from the waters of Lake Ontario, but the varying periods of freezing and thawing do a great deal of damage in February and March.

The preparation and location of our garden followed established procedure when we moved to our present home in 1942, but as time progressed it was evident that drainage was not adequate, as the lower lying beds were quite wet for several weeks in April and May. We planned to widen the beds by adding an extra row to each, and it was decided to lay a tile drainage system at the same time. Accordingly, when preparing the additional space, the earth was excavated to a depth of thirty inches below the lawn level and four-inch weeping tile laid in the bottom and a sump constructed at the upper and lowest level into which the tile connected. An ordinary cistern pump suffices to remove the excess water in the spring from the lower sump and during dry weather in July and August underground irrigation is accomplished by letting the hose run into the upper sump for several hours once a week.

Winter protection is of prime importance and how to adequately protect the plants from the hazards of warm bright sunshine during the day and extreme freezing at night is quite a problem. The use of Fibreglas insulation during the last three winters has given splendid results, and it is our intention to continue with its use. Our method of applying the insulation is quite simple. First soil is mounded around the bushes to a height of six to eight inches, then the plants are pruned leaving about three inches of stem above the soil mounds. The Fibreglas is then placed over and around the canes and mounds. This is allowed to remain until the first week in April or later, according to the season. The canes will be found quite green with some shoots of two or three inches, whereas any unprotected canes will be destroyed at least to the level of the soil. The earth mounds are now removed and the pruning completed, leaving three to four buds on each cane, cutting out the weaker canes entirely. Climbers and floribundas are tied with twine, wrapped with Fibreglas and then covered with burlap. Since using Fibreglas, winter loss is quite small and the plants do show increased vitality.

Fertilizing is carried out with an application of cow manure every two years, followed by chemicals and lime. Care must be taken not to use an excess of lime, as this will produce an alkaline soil, which is not appreciated by the roses.

Black Spot and Mildew are both prevalent in season, but with regular spraying are kept under control. We mix our own spray formula, using lead arsenate, sulphur, lime sulphur and nicotine with Bentonite as a spreader and binder. Captan* has been added this year and so far results have been excellent, also a soluble fertilizer is added for foliage feeding and we feel it has considerable merit.

No mulches are added but the beds are cultivated each week and this, with the underground irrigation, maintains sufficient moisture during periods when rainfall is inadequate.

We do have considerable enjoyment and outdoor recreation in caring for our garden and it is always a pleasure to share our enjoyment with visitors.

Early in our rose growing, we became infected with the virus of Rose Shows and have received a fair share of awards and Show Day is the highlight of the rose season.

The beginning of the year we planned to take a British and European holiday and have it coincide with the National Rose Society Summer Show in London. Being still infected with the rose show virus, we hoped to take some roses to enter in the show, but unfortunately reservations had been made for our flight before we learned of the date, July 1st. We left Toronto on June 28th, but we were determined to take some roses with us, and the blooms were cut early in the morning and stored in cold water until packed for air transportation. The thorns and leaves were removed from the lower portion of the stems, which were wrapped with cellu-cotton and then placed in small plastic bags, which were filled with cold water and the bags tightly tied around the stems. The blooms were loosely covered with perforated plastic and

* Orthocide.

the roses then packed in a suitable container for carrying. We had no thought that our roses would win any award, but thought they would add some interest. Had the show been held in mid-June and we could have staged our entries within twenty-four hours after picking the blooms, I am sure our entries would have been more presentable, but our best blooms were over before our Canadian Rose Society Show on June 20th.

We did enjoy our visit to Britain and the National Rose Show and the Trial Grounds at St. Albans. The friendship and the hospitality of the British people were the highlights of a trip which will long be remembered. Some day we hope to again visit London at Rose Show time.

NIGEL RABAN
BRISTOL

SIX years ago I, too, was a happy man. Six years ago I grew my roses and enjoyed them and no thought of Shows had ever entered my mind. Black Spot was only a name and a bit of Mildew in the summer—well, what did that matter? Then, unfortunately, my wife and I went to a local show and, wishing to support the cause, we put up a dozen roses in a jam jar. That was the beginning. We were beaten right out of the race and at the end of the Show my wife said to me, "We ought to have been in the money there. You know, the trouble was that wretched jam jar." And that is how it all began.

Roses are probably the simplest of all garden plants to grow. They make very little demand upon the gardener and they are extraordinarily tolerant of a wide diversity of conditions. It is quite impossible to lay down definite rules of treatment, and the most that can be said is, that in your own experience on your own soil such a treatment is good, such a treatment is unsuccessful. To you, therefore, friend beginner, who are reading this article, I would say this; do not take anything written here as gospel. Use it as a guide to form your own opinions which can only be reliably made after some years of experience.

Running quickly over the main tasks of the Rose Year, it has always seemed to me that by far the most important is the preparation of the

'YELLOWHAMMER' (flor.)

Raised by Samuel McGredy & Son, Portadown, N. Ireland.
Trial Ground No. 762. Reg. No. 346. Trial Ground Certificate.
Gold Medal, Summer Show, 1954.
For description see page 144, "Rose Annual" 1955

beds in which the roses are to be planted. These beds must be deeply dug, with plenty of manure incorporated just below the top spit, and a heavy dressing of bonemeal, incorporating this with the top spit itself. The beds should be prepared some time before you actually plant the roses themselves. I like to prepare my beds about mid-September in readiness for November planting. In my experience the secret of successful planting is to plant really firmly, using the foot to stamp the soil down well round the rose. In addition to this, a few hand-fuls of a mixture of peat, bonemeal and coarse sand will help to produce those little fibrous roots which are so good for the well-being of the rose in its first year. After planting, leave your roses alone and don't touch them until the following spring when you carry out your pruning.

There is at the present time great argument going on, both as to the method of pruning and its date. I believe in moderate to hard pruning, carried out at the end of March and I am also sure that if you are clever with a knife, this implement is better than a pair of secateurs. If, how-ever, you are like me, a born fool with anything sharp, use a pair of secateurs, as nothing is worse than the jagged torn cuts of the un-successful knife addict. One point about pruning on which everybody seems to be in agreement is that maiden trees must be cut back hard the first year. Of the established plants, I am inclined to think every variety must be treated on its own merits. For example, I would always prune Charlotte Armstrong very hard to induce plenty of basal growth whereas Peace definitely resents such treatment and is best left fairly long. The date for pruning is also a variable one. In my case it is geared to the Summer Show and I keep a carefully tabulated list of the varieties grown, showing me the length of time that has to elapse between the pruning and the full flush of bloom given normal weather conditions. I do not therefore prune my roses on one particular day but over a whole period of four weeks starting with the slow varieties such as Glory of Rome or Peace, and finishing with the ones which come very quickly such as Mme Butterfly, The Doctor, and McGredy's Ivory: these latter varieties are rather a problem as they are not pruned until the 9th or 10th of April, and if the year is an early one there is always the danger of a certain amount of bleeding. This is one of those things which as an exhibitor you have to put up with.

Manuring and fertilizing is the next problem and as soon as I have pruned I like to give a good dressing of well rotted farmyard manure over all the beds except those which contain maiden cut-backs. In addition to this there is a dressing of an artificial fertilizer fairly early in May as this seems to give the plants that little added incentive to do their best for the Summer Show. Another dressing of this fertilizer is supplied in July which has the same effect for the autumn exhibitions. The inorganic fertilizer which I use is one made up to a recipe kindly given me by our worthy President, namely, eight parts of super-phosphate, three of sulphate of potash and two of sulphate of ammonia. Many other people have their own pet recipes, all of them, I am sure, are good.

From mid-April onwards you can expect to receive your first attacks of garden pests. The main problem is twofold; that is to say, greenfly and thrips. Greenfly are easily controlled by using some proprietary preparations such as Pyrethrex R. Thrips are more difficult and only appear to attack the pale pink varieties, particularly the Ophelia group. A dusting of D.D.T. in the early stage as soon as the sepals begin to turn back seems to be very effective. Later in the season will come the inevitable troubles of Mildew and Black Spot. If you are in an area where these fungi are very prevalent there is nothing for it but regular spraying at ten-day intervals with one of the satisfactory proprietary washes. Tulisan has always been very successful in my case but I am looking forward to trying the new wash publicized this year under the name of Orthocide. In addition to spraying it is of un-questionable benefit to apply grass clippings to the rose beds. Not only does this help to reduce the incidence of Black Spot to a very marked degree but it also acts as a first-class cool mulch to the plants themselves.

Do try your hand at showing, you will find it the most fascinating of all gardening occupations. Trying to put up the best possible bloom and thereby make some worth-while contribution to the Show, is the logical and most satisfying outcome of all the work which you have done during the year. If success comes your way be grateful, if it passes you by, do not despair or complain. Always remember that by putting up a vase or a bowl you have contributed to the overall picture of the Show itself.

In conclusion, may I warn beginners of two garden pests which cannot be treated with spray or nicotine dust as they are two-legged. Their names are "Theorist" and "Dogmatist". Watch out for them both and allow them no place in your Rose Garden. Theorist is the pest who walks round your garden and says: "Ah, I see you go on pruning in the old-fashioned way: of course you know, the right thing to do is to prune your roses with a razor blade on the second Sunday before Advent." "Dogmatist" is the man who walks round your garden and says: "Huh, I see you are growing so-and-so, you won't like it, it won't do here you know." Allow these pests to have no place in your garden. There is only one way of growing roses successfully in your soil and to your liking, that is by your own personal experiments, by your own hard work, by the sweat of your own brow. Good luck and go to it, friend! Hope to see you at the Show next year.

SAM CARSON
GOSFORTH, NEWCASTLE-UPON-TYNE

THE growing of roses in the north has always presented many difficulties over the years. How to maintain vigorous growth is always a problem. It is difficult to maintain a rose in health over a period of years, say twenty, but it can be done. A number of instances can be cited. When roses were comparatively cheap I bought and grew some hundreds of them. I still retain about 250 hybrid teas and hybrid perpetuals, very many ramblers and climbers and a fair number of the floribunda type, including the Poulsen group, Frensham, Fashion, Masquerade, etc.

It is my proud boast I have grown roses consistently well. How has this position been arrived at? The answer is in a few words—by giving constant attention to their welfare. To grow roses as many have said countless times, "one must love them". Successful growing necessitates certain conditions; selection of a suitable site where roses can grow without hindrance, and not handicapped by the shade of overhanging trees; preparation of the soil which includes manuring, proper attention to planting which should be firm at all times, and a keen interest in cultivation and the further development of the plants under our care. I have endeavoured faithfully to fulfil all the conditions for successful growth and I can claim a fair measure of success. I have consistently kept the roses apart from other subjects in the garden. It is a mistake to attempt to grow them in a mixed border of herbaceous, biennials or annuals. Such attempts can only meet with failure. You may have success for a time, but sooner or later plants will suffer from lack of light and air, a supreme necessity. You will find that roses are best segregated. A rose-garden should be our aim. It should be fenced off from the rest of the garden. A sketch of the selected area should be made, and each rose plant given a numbered position. I still retain the sketch I made nearly twenty years ago. If labels are lost, as they very often are, there are then no doubts as to identification of varieties. This is most important when it comes to "showing". Too little attention, I feel, is given to labels and consequently the public are often misled. It will save the exhibitor a great deal of worry and annoyance at Show times. Every effort should be made to keep the plants labelled.

After the planting of roses in November and early December, which I find the most suitable time, the most important operation is the pruning of the bushes. I prefer to do this in early spring, either at the beginning of April or towards the middle of the month. In northern districts the best hope of success during the growing years lies in rigid adherence to this rule. I find that the plants begin to show signs of deterioration if this operation is omitted.

I am constantly adding to my stock. Each year I add a few of the newer varieties. I will not deny that I have lost roses from various causes, mostly die-back. Diseases like Black Spot and Mildew are only rarely met with. The former is a trouble almost unknown in the north. Occasionally Mildew is a source of worry, but no serious damage to plants has resulted from attacks of this malady. The worst forms of the latter disease have been found in varieties like Night, Mrs. Henry Morse, George Dickson, and Christopher Stone. Proximity to hedges or cover is often a contributory cause of the disease.

It has often been said that it is harmful to manure rose-beds during the winter, but the fact remains that one of our most successful growers of exhibition roses practises this method each year. His plants are strong and vigorous, with fine blooms in prospect. After April pruning, the ground is forked over and manure dug in. Each year the fresh growth is almost certain to meet with set-backs in the shape of late frosts. Often I have had to cut back many damaged shoots to good wood. I consistently adhere to this plan. Rigorous pruning is a necessity. Each year I anxiously await the flowering stage. In the intervening period between pruning and flowering, constant attention must be given to the plants. They must be kept free from greenfly, maggots and caterpillars, their principal enemies. This can be done fairly successfully if the proper means are taken. Insecticides can be used, but these should be followed by personal attention. The "finger-and-thumb" method must be resorted to.

For many years I have confined my attention largely to the growing of exhibition roses. Twenty years ago there was little call for such exhibition roses as there were few facilities for showing. I was guided in my choice of varieties by the study of the lists appearing in the literature sent out by the Society. I aimed at growing all the varieties included in the lists and I almost succeeded in this aim. I have grown most varieties named in the official lists issued at regular intervals in recent years.

In the preparation of roses for the show-bench I have at various times improvised means of protection of a primitive nature. In recent years I have had recourse to the use of canvas or cardboard covers which have been sufficient to protect blooms from wind and weather. These are of standard type and can be bought in two sizes, seven-and-a-half inches or ten inches in diameter.

As attacks from Black Spot are a rare occurrence with us we do not find it necessary to mulch with lawn mowings to the extent practised in the south. Constant use of the hoe to provide proper aeration of the soil is desirable and it ensures freedom from weeds.

If the ground is sufficiently manured and well prepared before planting, little liquid manuring is necessary, as is the case with most crops in the garden, during the flowering season. Bonemeal will be found to be a great help in the formation of a good rooting system, essential for good growth and future development.

Selection of varieties must, of course, play an important part in the matter of success with exhibition roses. The old varieties are giving place to a new race of giant roses. Gone are the old favourites of say, twenty years ago. George Dickson and Lord Rossmore are perhaps the only ones still in favour. More attention is being given to recent introductions like Red Ensign, William Harvey, Karl Herbst, Symphonie, Show Girl and others.

ROSE NOTES FROM QUEENSLAND
AUSTRALIA

FRED ARMBRUST

To give some idea of the conditions under which we grow roses here in Queensland, I am starting with a short geographical survey.

Queensland is Australia's second largest state, with a little over half of its area in the tropics, and the rest in the warm temperate regions. Its greatest length from North to South is 1,300 miles, whilst its greatest width from East to West is 900 miles, and in actual area it is more than eleven times larger than England. Queensland is subject to very hot summers and very mild winters, with frost in South Queensland and on the tablelands. The rainfall ranges from under 10 inches in some parts to over 200 inches in other parts.

Roses are grown from Cairns in the tropic North (Cairns is our most northern city with a population of approximately 25,000) to the borders of New South Wales, and out on the great Western plains. Brisbane is Queensland's capital, with a population of over 500,000, and is naturally the centre of our National Rose Society's activities. In Queensland most types of roses will grow and grow really well, but there are a few that just will not thrive in our hot climate. They are the thin petalled roses of 25 petals and less which do not show up to advantage. Roses of many delicate hues and colours also fade a little under our hot sun. On the credit side, however, roses are never dormant and are always growing and flowering and we can pick rose blooms the whole year through. We can bud or hybridize whenever we wish, although some parts of the year are better than others for budding.

Pruning

To elaborate on our methods of cultivation and to start with pruning, we in Queensland light or high prune which, in effect, is simply the removal of dead and dying wood and spindly useless growth. Coupled with the foregoing "pruning" in May, June and July, we "Summer thin" as, for example, whenever my wife or I cut a spent bloom from a

106

bush, or cut blooms for indoor decoration, we always cut back to a good strong eye and this usually gives a stem to each bloom of an average length of twelve inches. This light pruning and thinning has paid handsome dividends in the shape of larger plants from which we always obtain plenty of bloom. For example, we get bushes of varieties such as Charlotte Armstrong in two years over six feet high, Rouge Meilland and Helen Traubel in two years over seven feet high and, in fact, I had one Charles Mallerin in two years over eight feet high. I find also that the larger the plant the larger number of quality blooms.

Last year, as an experiment, I tried heavy pruning on twelve of my plants with discouraging results. Every plant bled profusely and took a long time to recover, two died and two are still very weak. In very large gardens light pruning is also adopted, and at Brisbane's New Farm, a Rose Park of several thousand plants, the work is done in stages so that when the last section is pruned the first section is ready for summer thinning. A stem that is cut back to a good eye throws out laterals that are flowering within four to six weeks.

Making up the Soil

The method generally adopted is to thoroughly make up the soil beforehand with compost or well rotted animal manures which are fairly easy to obtain here. This thorough initial preparation is necessary owing to the trees never going dormant. I further supplement the food in the soil by top-dressings of well rotted stable and poultry manures every three months, starting six months after first planting.

Drought Conditions

Drought conditions are not uncommon out West where water is often at a premium. The dryness is overcome by mulching heavily and it is amazing how roses thrive on a minimum of water. When I first established my beds, I had no mulch and during our hot dry summers had to water heavily twice a week. In desperation, I hit on an idea which has cut my watering down from twice weekly to once a fortnight or once only every three weeks. There is a pine sawmill near by and one day, after a good watering, I put sawdust and shavings around each bush to a depth of six inches. Not only did the sawdust preserve the moisture in the ground but it also prevented most weeds from coming through. When watering, I do *not* remove the sawdust but water through it. Sawdust holds up to four times its weight in water. I must stress here that I do not mix the sawdust with the soil, I lay it on top only.

Diseases

Our main diseases are Mildew, Black Spot and White Scale. Black Spot is far less prevalent out in the dry West, but on the coast it can be very bad if untreated. Mildew and White Scale can be controlled by a white oil preparation, while Black Spot can be kept in check with copper oxychloride. I mix both white oil and copper oxychloride together and spray once a fortnight and find it very satisfactory.

Pests

Our main pests are aphides and thrips, and to control these I use a mixture of D.D.T. and nicotine sulphate and spray whenever the pests appear. Now and again there is a mild plague of caterpillars or green grasshoppers; a spray containing lead arsenate controls them.

Hybridizing

With regard to hybridizing, I follow the rules and regulations up to pollination except that, with the pollen parent, I invert and twirl it over the seed parent with the male stamens just touching the stigma of the seed parent. In this way, I make certain of a good dusting with the pollen. I pollinate during late October, November and December—sometimes in the afternoon and sometimes in the morning but either time gives similar results. December is the middle month of our summer here in Australia. I follow no set plan for my crosses, except that on each occasion I use exhibition blooms from strong-growing plants. Acting on the advice of my good friend Mr. Jack Bailey, the Curator of the Botanical Gardens of Brisbane, I gather the seed pods when yellow, open them immediately and plant the creamy-white seeds while they are still damp. The seeds are planted in six-inch flower pots in a finely sieved mixture of soil and peat moss—fifty per cent of each. Each flower pot is clearly labelled with the cross it contains. The seeds are saturated each day with water and from five weeks onwards the seedlings arrive.

Immediately the seedlings straighten up, and before they have time to send down any roots, I pot them in three-inch pots. Later the

'FIRECRACKER' (flor.)

Raised by E. S. Boerner, Jackson & Perkins, Newark, U.S.A.
Trial Ground No. 821. Reg. No. 364. Trial Ground Certificate.
Certificate of Merit, Summer Show, 1955.
For description see page 145

seedlings are transferred to six-inch pots, where they stay until buds are taken. They grow strongly in a mixture of soil and peat moss—seventy-five per cent soil and 25 per cent peat moss—if watered daily and given, once a week, a solution of liquid manure. The seedlings are sprayed regularly with white oil and nicotine sulphate and they usually survive with no losses at all. The pots containing seeds and those containing seedlings are always off the ground on an elevated platform about four feet high.

Planting the seeds immediately from the seed pods is apparently suited to Queensland's warm climate, because on four occasions I obtained 100 per cent success with germination. Rod Stillman × Bravo gave eleven seeds and eleven seedlings; Narzisse × Mme A. Meilland six seeds and six seedlings, Charlotte Armstrong × Rouge Meilland, Charlotte Armstrong × Narzisse and Rouge Meilland × Clg. Mme A. Meilland each gave five seedlings from five seeds. Other crosses were less successful. Two of my recent "babies" on their first flowering show promise for plants so young, both Narzisse crosses—one by Mme A. Meilland (Peace) and one Charlotte Armstrong. Rose growing is my hobby, and I find raising seedlings very fascinating. There are very few hybridists in Queensland to my knowledge. The others, like myself, are amateurs raising the seedlings in their back yards in their spare time.

ROSES IN REGENT'S PARK

LEONARD HOLLIS

THE Queen Mary's Rose Garden in the Inner Circle, Regent's Park, London, is without doubt one of the finest public mass displays of roses in the country and easily the most outstanding in the Home Counties, and enjoys the very real advantage, from the visitor's point of view, of being only a few minutes' walk from either Regent's Park or Baker Street underground stations.

Originally planned in 1931, the garden has since been extended by the cutting of many new beds in the lawns near the main gates, looking towards the tea-house. In its original conception as a means of publicising British-grown roses it has proved an outstanding success, besides giving great pleasure to the many thousands of visitors every year. Indeed, one has only to walk through the rose garden on any day between mid-June and the end of September to see numbers of admirers round the beds, often taking notes of those varieties having a special appeal. As a collection it is by no means comprehensive or even fully representative—rather does it illustrate the colourful displays to be achieved by mass plantings of roses, even in densely populated areas.

For those who have not yet visited these gardens, a description may be of some interest. Perhaps I should explain, at this stage, that my remarks are based, not on just a few visits each season, but on close observation of the beds on two or three occasions each week throughout the year. I am fortunately placed in this respect, as up to a recent date my office was only a few minutes' walk from the rose garden. The site is an open one, on naturally heavy clay soil, not too well drained, and includes no less than seventy formal beds, each devoted to one variety, and each containing between one hundred and fifty and two hundred trees, planted closely. In addition, however, there are very fine borders of the scarlet-crimson floribunda Frensham near the tea-house, and beds of Pinocchio, another fine floribunda, against the Chester Road gates, as well as deep mixed borders of hybrid perpetuals, hybrid teas, floribundas and polyantha pompons in bold groups, with the species and the old-fashioned roses at the back, behind the main garden. A further eighteen formal beds of hybrid teas are to be seen in the gardens behind St. John's Lodge, which are open to the public and only two minutes' walk away: these provide a very pleasant retreat for visitors requiring a peaceful hour or so away from the crowds. In all, including St. John's Lodge gardens, there must be something like seventeen thousand rose trees.

The focal point of the main rose garden is a large circle, bisected by a dry path, and enclosed by sixty-six massive wooden pillars, connected by ropes, on which a selection of the popular ramblers are trained. Albertine, Alberic Barbier, American Pillar and Crimson Conquest transform these pillars into objects of beauty in June and July, and beneath them seats are placed strategically for viewing the entire circle. Inside the enclosure is a central bed, from which radiate a further ten beds, forming an inner circle, and beyond these is an outer circle of another ten beds. There have been many changes in the varieties occupying these and other beds in the post-war years, as some roses never seem to settle down so close to the heart of the Metropolis. The old floribunda Salmon Spray is used as the centre-piece and while I admire the constitution of this Australian variety—it exceeds five feet without difficulty in my own garden—it is not a very distinct colour and the trees tend to look shabby. I feel that a wonderful opportunity has been lost for displaying the brilliance of one of the new floribundas in vermilion scarlet, if a floribunda is used at all here, especially as this bed was remade in 1955. The publicity value of this centre-piece is enormous.

In the inner circle are separate beds of Signora, Ena Harkness, Elizabeth of York, Mme Louise Laperrière, Prima Donna, Monique, Charles Gregory, The Doctor, Armagh, and Home Sweet Home. Of these, only Elizabeth of York and Home Sweet Home have been in residence for a large number of years, and the former, despite its magnificent constitution, is now beginning to show signs of age. Mme Louise Laperrière, a new crimson decorative, replaced Étoile de Hollande in 1955 and Monique, in rose-pink, was also a 1955 addition, in lieu of Betty Uprichard. Prima Donna makes a most attractive bed when in full bloom, the flowers being of a warm coppery orange-salmon shade, rather paler than those of Mrs. Sam McGredy, but with similar reddish-bronze young foliage and wood. Ena Harkness has made a good bed, but Charles Gregory, The Doctor and Armagh have not settled down, and while the first two produce a fair floral display, growth is poor. Armagh has suffered badly from mildew each year since it was planted; the trees have made little growth and I am afraid it is due for replacement.

In the outer circle are beds of Commonwealth (flor.), Sonata, Talisman, Dickson's Perfection, Eden Rose, McGredy's Salmon, Fantasia, Edith Nellie Perkins, Angels Mateu and Daphne Gandy (flor.). Commonwealth replaced Kirsten Poulsen Improved in 1955, while Sonata and Eden Rose were 1954 newcomers, in lieu of Margaret Amos and Margaret McGredy respectively. The extraordinary freedom of flowering and pleasing formation of Talisman are admirably displayed in a bed which has given excellent service for many years. The colourful combination of pink, scarlet and gold attracts many admirers and the bed is a favourite with the amateur photographer, as it is a riot of colour in full bloom. The perfume is really pronounced. Dickson's Perfection also does very well, both here and in another bed near the lake and, apart from the blooms being on the thin side, I have nothing but praise for this rose. The habit of growth, foliage and freedom of flowering are excellent, and there is a sweet fragrance, not usually found in this colour, which might be described as a glowing shrimp-pink and orange. It is seen at its best in cool weather and is a very fine autumnal. The bed of Daphne Gandy is really outstanding and although this bright scarlet-crimson is classified as a floribunda it is very close to the hybrid tea in the size of the blooms, which are borne in small clusters. The bud and young flower are shapely, but there is looseness in the expanded bloom. I have been favourably impressed by the freedom with which this variety breaks from the base, and by the general strong growth and healthy foliage support. It makes a very even bed. Eden Rose, while growing freely, has so far confirmed the impression that it is not free flowering or continuous enough, and there has been quite a lot of mildew on the trees. It is perhaps unfortunate that the new bed of Commonwealth should be next to Daphne Gandy, in a similar colour, as although they are separated by the main path, I cannot see the former gaining anything from this proximity.

Outside the main enclosure but on the same level are seven beds cut in the grass on the terrace. These comprise Sutter's Gold, Lady Belper, Mrs. Sam McGredy, Lucie Marie, Golden Revelry, McGredy's Yellow, and Grand'mère Jenny, in that order. There are, of course, too many roses of similar colouring here for maximum effect. The

'CLEOPATRA'

(Walter Bentley × Condesa de Sástago) × Spek's Yellow.
Raised by Wilhelm Kordes, Holstein, Germany.
Trial Ground No. 925. Reg. No. 367. Trial Ground Certificate.
Gold Medal, Summer Show, 1955.
For description see page 145

first and last named were new beds in 1954, having ousted Mrs. Wemyss Quin and Fortschritt (Progress) (flor.), respectively, and they did well in their first season. Grand'mère Jenny, in particular, came with very rich colouring and attracted a lot of attention. Indeed, the depth of colour obtained in most of the varieties in the garden is above average. Lady Belper, which replaced Emma Wright in 1953, has not made a lot of growth and confirms my own experience that it is not very free flowering, although the apricot-orange colouring is charming. The bed of Mrs. Sam McGredy was entirely remade and replanted in 1954 but it is evident that the constitution of this old favourite is not equal to the conditions in Regent's Park. It never was one of the strongest growers in town gardens, and I number myself among the ranks of those who, with reluctance have ceased to grow it, except in the climbing form. As it is, some replacements have to be made in the bed in Regent's Park each year, and even then growth is spindly.

Perhaps the strongest bed in the entire layout is that of Lucie Marie, a straw-yellow, deeper in the centre. It is also one of the longest established, and excellent photographs of the same bed appeared in *The Rose Annual* for 1941 and 1944. The flower is short petalled and therefore low centred, but as a hardy, free-flowering rose for display in town gardens it is first-class. The blooms have the unusual characteristic of intensifying in the centre with age, to a coppery-orange, which forms quite a contrast with the outer petals in certain conditions. Next to Lucie Marie is a bed of the new yellow, Golden Revelry, which was planted in 1953. Introduced as a very hardy and strong growing yellow rose, I have been very disappointed with its performance. Growth has been poor—not as strong as that we used to expect from the old favourite Christine, of which the medium-sized blooms are reminiscent. The yellow shade is not as intense as that of the old variety and there has been a lot of dead wood—practically the entire tree in many cases—following the winter of 1954-5.

On the lower level, immediately below the foregoing beds and near the lake, are beds of Spek's Yellow, Picture, Pinocchio (flor.), McGredy's Yellow, Pilar Landecho, Masquerade (flor.), Peace, and Mme Butterfly. All of these, with the exception of Picture (very poor growth) and McGredy's Yellow, are doing well, and Pilar Landecho, Peace, and Pinocchio are excellent. The juxtaposition of the beds of

Masquerade and Peace, in similar colourings of pink and gold, strikes me as a mistake, and really overwhelms the floribunda, which replaced Dusky Maiden in 1954. Indeed, if I may venture the criticism, the colour grouping in the layout as a whole offers ample scope for improvement. I am glad to see that less drastic pruning is now being practised on the bed of Peace.

On the opposite side of the main path and on the same level is a semicircular arrangement, consisting of beds of Sweetness, Mrs. T. B. Doxford, Senateur Potie, Opera, Talisman, and Symphonie. The first three varieties were never in the first flight, but are long-established beds. Opera was planted in 1954, and from my own experience of this gold medal introduction I looked forward to this being one of the best beds in the park. Unfortunately, the newly planted trees were crippled by severe weather and have not yet made the strong growth typical of the variety. Symphonie replaced McGredy's Sunset in 1955 and it is too early to say how it will fare. In the four years I have grown it, it has done well, and the only faults I can find are the rather harsh shade of carmine-pink in the older blooms and the somewhat globular formation, although it will produce specimen blooms, and is nicely scented.

Walking alongside the lake towards Bedford College one passes a long row of beds cut in the lawns on the left-hand side. There are also many pillars of climbing hybrid teas and other types, the growths being trained on three uprights. Among the beds of dwarf-types the intense coppery orange-scarlet blooms of Mary Wheatcroft attract a great deal of attention, and the reddish wood and young foliage are a pleasing background. Phyllis Gold still looks well, especially in the autumn when the richest golden tone is displayed. This bed seems to have taken a new lease of life since it received a top-dressing of fibrous loam two or three years ago. Vogue (flor.) is badly placed next to Hector Deane, and at a casual glance the colouring seems identical. It is a nice grower, and the flower is large for a floribunda. Karl Herbst, Alain, and Rosemary Gandy were planted as recently as 1955 and it is really too early to comment on them. Generally, the roses in this stretch have to compete with flowering cherries and other ornamental trees, the roots of which encroach on the rose beds. The plants of Violinista Costa are very stunted and give little idea of the strong, branching habit of this fine bedder when pruned less severely.

On the tea-house side of the York Road gates are further beds cut in the lawns. Fashion has done very well, making a very even bed in a most attractive orange-salmon colour, although it is not as continuous in bloom as many of the floribundas. Rubaiyat has a lovely perfume and long, elegant petals, and is a useful rose if you like the colour. This is a light red or deep carmine-pink, according to the weather and soil, reminiscent of the colour of the old favourite, General McArthur. Comtesse Vandal makes a very dwarf bed there and, as is her wont, shows mildew later in the season, but there is something very captivating in the long buds and young blooms, with coppery fire in the heart. While I appreciate the need to keep the trees compact in a public park I sometimes feel that the pruning methods followed in Regent's Park are too drastic, having regard to the somewhat meagre diet provided, as no animal manures are ever used except when making the beds.

The practice for many years, when remaking a bed, has been to replace the soil entirely with fresh loam to a depth of eighteen inches or so, and to plant the strongest trees of the variety replaced in bold groups in deep borders behind the rose garden proper. The result is a mass of colour—I cannot say how many varieties there are in these mixed borders—many have long since ceased to be catalogued, but they range from some of the old hybrid perpetuals, such as Fisher Holmes, Ulrich Brunner, Frau Karl Druschki, and Hugh Dickson, to such current favourites as Crimson Glory and Christopher Stone. The species, R. hugonis is very effective towards the back of the border early in the season, as are also the hybrid rugosas.

No rose-lover visiting the Queen Mary's Rose Garden should fail to inspect the rose garden behind St. John's Lodge, which lies next to the Institute of Archaeology and is little more than a stone's throw from the Chester Road gate to the main rose garden. It has a pleasant approach across a long lawn, flanked by deep herbaceous borders, and takes the form of two connected circular gardens. In the first, radiating from a centre-piece of a large fountain, complete with water lilies and fish, are eight large beds. Of these, Angèle Pernet, Shot Silk, and Dame Edith Helen are very long established, probably well over twenty years old, and still producing plenty of blooms. It is interesting to find Dame Edith Helen doing so well, as most of us find her unsuitable for general garden display. The bed of McGredy's Yellow is much superior to those in the main garden and gives a far better idea of the qualities of this fine pale yellow rose, while Duchess of Atholl, a fairly recent planting, is doing quite well in vivid russety-orange and old rose shades.

In the second circle there are nine beds of hybrid teas and there is a circular bed of that fine old ivory white decorative, Clarice Goodacre, cut in a small arbour at the extreme end of the garden. It says much for the constitution of this rose that it has flourished here for so long, as it is surrounded by lime-trees and does not get a lot of sun. Pillar roses also are featured in this attractive and secluded rose garden, notably Emily Gray, with buff-yellow blooms against highly varnished bronze foliage and reddish wood.

THE ROSARIAN'S BOOKSHELF

The Old Shrub Roses. By Graham Stuart Thomas, F.L.S. 224 pp., 18 plates in full colour and monochrome. (Phoenix House, 32s. 6d.)

To many of us Mr. G. S. Thomas's name is almost synonymous with "old roses", and his booklet *Roses as Flowering Shrubs* has been the only modern reference on the subject. Part of this new book, probably the most important to most gardeners, is an expansion of this list, sections in which all the old roses in cultivation today are catalogued and described. Origins and synonyms, beauties and peculiarities are all extremely well related. Such necessities as cultivation and pruning are also well done.

Another considerable section consists of the late Dr. C. C. Hurst's "Notes on the Origin and Evolution of our Garden Roses" and "Notes on the Origin of the Moss Rose", reprinted from the *R.H.S. Journal* for 1922. These form rather a heavy lump in the middle of the book, and because of it one seems to be continually jumping from one group of roses to the next and back. Might it not have been possible to integrate these "notes" into the main text? Perhaps I am carping; the material is very interesting and valuable for reference and will certainly come to far more general notice in its reprinting here.

The book on the whole is personal in its approach, and in part traces the rise of Mr. Thomas's own interest in the subject. It is a little sentimental too in style; and each chapter is prefaced by a line or two of verse, while there are chapters on "Old Roses in Pictures" and "Old Roses in the Garden".

There are twenty-one good monochrome pictures, many being close-up portraits and some of roses never illustrated before. There are also nine colour plates. The frontispiece, a reproduction of Redouté's Rosa Mundi, is excellent; but some of the photographs are very dark and lack lustre, while I feel we might have been spared the reproduction of a painting of the author's garden. I mention this because there is nothing more disappointing than poor colour reproductions, especially when they push up so much the price of what will certainly be a much sought-after book and a standard reference work on the subject.

A. J. HUXLEY

KEEPING CUT FLOWERS FRESH

I RECENTLY cut a dozen blooms of that fine new rose Margaret and it was interesting to observe how well they lasted in water, but on the fourth day they began to wilt so I tried the experiment of cutting the ends freshly on a slant, washing out the container and refilling it with water hot enough to comfortably bear the hand in it. In a few hours these roses had brightened up and were almost as good as freshly cut. Bacterial growth on dead cells at the cut is one of the causes of wilting, and slitting, or tearing the ends is a most undesirable practice. Smashing the ends with a hammer as commonly practised in florists' shops is the worst possible and certainly increases bacterial growth. Clean containers and water that has been boiled are the best means of keeping cut flowers fresh, and recutting the stems every day and fresh clean warm water in a clean container will increase their keeping qualities. Exhibitors should, however, be careful that warm water does not open their blooms too rapidly, if they are cut in right condition for showing them, as soon as they have had a long "drink" and are fully turgid, ice-cold water has in my experience kept them better for the show bench, but if they are "young" or slow in opening, warmth may finish them to the proper stage.

On this subject we reproduce below an interesting article by the Editor of the *American Rose Magazine*.

WARM OR COLD?

FRED J. NESBIT

IT's always confusing when one successful grower or exhibitor writes specific directions about how an operation must be handled and then another, equally successful, is equally certain that *his* way (the exact opposite) is best. Such a situation is all too common in the literature of rose culture.

How can such a state come about? Very probably because many

growers do not test several or all alternatives *under controlled conditions*; that is, with all other factors constant and only the contested factor differing. In lieu of this, most gardeners tend to say: "I did *this*, followed it with *that* and here are my results. The results *must* be the result of *this* and *that*."

Dr. Kenneth Post of Cornell University used to put this whole situation in proper perspective by saying: "Often plants live *in spite of* what we do, rather than because of our treatment."

All this is only by way of leading up to a point which puzzles many rose growers and exhibitors. When you cut your blooms should you put them in warm or cold water? What is more important, why?

Many exhibitors place their roses at once in cold water on being cut. A very successful man even boils the water and then refrigerates it before taking it into the garden to receive the blooms as they are cut.

If we look at the principles involved, however, you can see that there is much logic on the side of the opposite practice.

First, what are we trying to do? It is obvious that we want to so treat the cut bloom that it will keep in the best possible condition for the longest possible time.

How would you define good condition of a cut bloom? (*a*) It should not wilt; this must be the first consideration. (*b*) It should not open too rapidly. (*c*) Change of colour (such as unnatural blueing of reds) should be avoided or kept to a minimum.

The last factor is concerned more with air temperature relationships and varietal characteristics than with the subject now under consideration, so can be ruled out of this discussion.

Wilting is caused by the lessening of turgidity of the plant cells; in other words, the water level within the cells falls below the desirable point. Wilting is dependent upon two main factors: water intake and respiration. As water intake lessens and respiration increases, the water level in the plant or plant part is necessarily reduced. When this continues the firmness of the tissues involved decreases and the plant or flower "wilts".

Now the rate of both of these processes will vary directly with changes of temperature. Generally speaking the rate of both factors is low at low temperatures and increases as the temperature rises, within reasonable limits sufficient for this discussion. As we wish to raise the water level within the cut flower (bloom, stem and leaves) to the highest practical point it is evident that we must raise the water intake (gain) and reduce the transpiration (loss) at the same time.

How can this be done?

If we plunge the stem of a freshly cut rose in water at 100°F., the rate of intake will be greater than if the water is colder. The reasons are several: (*a*) there is an increased permeability of the cells to water; (*b*) a lower viscosity of protoplasm and colloidal gels in the cells (which increases the rapidity with which water is passed from cell to cell up the stem); and (*c*) a decrease in the viscosity of the water itself. All of these factors speed the flow of water into the plant cells. In this way, then, we tend to keep all the tissues turgid.

Even under such conditions, however, wilting can take place if respiration continues at a high rate. As increased air temperature, light (which increases leaf or petal-cell temperature) and air movement will increase respiration, it is evident that the cut blooms should be placed where the air is cool, the light dim (or non-existent) and the air is still.

When we have provided warm water about the stems and cool, still air and an absence of at least bright light to the top of the stem, foliage and flower we have satisfied all possible physiological factors necessary for delaying wilting.

Now how about the rapidity of opening of the flower? Not as much definite information is known about this factor. It is believed by physiologists, however, that very rapid opening (to shattering) of the bloom will be retarded if the cells are kept turgid and the air temperature kept low. As both of these factors have been taken care of above this is but another argument for those prescribed practices.

In the whole problem I can see *not one single argument* to support the view that cold water should be used for plunging cut blooms. If you have used cold water in the past, are you certain that your blooms lasted well *because* of this treatment, or might they have stood up well *in spite of it?*

THE SUMMER ROSE SHOW

A. G. L. HELLYER

IF I were asked to coin one phrase to describe the Summer Show, held in both R.H.S. halls on July 1 and 2, I should call it the "Ena Harkness Show". I should choose that description because I do not remember when I have seen this grand red rose shown in such fine shape in so many exhibits. If Ena Harkness had been a novelty instead of a rose in comfortable middle age, she would have been a sensation. It was no accident that the best bloom in the show exhibited by an amateur was Ena Harkness. Congratulations to Mr. G. D. Arthur for producing this massive yet perfectly formed flower. It completely outweighed his other two, very nice flowers though they were, and so he had to be satisfied with fourth place in Class 55, but I am sure the premier prize for the "best bloom" made ample amends. Incidentally the first place in this class was won by Mr. E. R. Kisch whose best bloom was also Ena Harkness, his other two being McGredy's Yellow and Show Girl.

The second remarkable thing about the Summer Show was the success of the amateurs. The classes were all exceptionally well filled and the standard of quality was as high as any we have ever seen. This quality was maintained right through from the big box classes down to the vases and it was, in fact, in a small vase class that Mr. Arthur scored his outstanding success.

Class 22 for the S. W. Burgess Memorial Cup is one of the big amateur events for it calls for six vases with from four to six stems in each—a lot of flowers for an amateur to find. Such a class tends to set the tone of a show, and a very high tone I discovered it to be when I examined Mr. Edgar M. Allen's winning exhibit of Ulster Monarch, Karl Herbst, Mrs. Charles Lamplough, Peace, Ethel Sanday, and Bacchus. The last, an exceptionally bright scarlet, was to be seen in a number of exhibits, always good, and always effective on account of its exceptionally brilliant colour.

The Edward Mawley Challenge Cup for twelve specimen blooms in a box (Class 23) was won by Mr. R. White. Here William Harvey was outstandingly good and there were also very fine blooms of Directeur Guèrin, Mirandy and McGredy's Ivory.

Even more remarkable was the set of twenty-four blooms in a box with which Mr. L. Kemp won Class 24. I could not find a bad bloom in the box and if I single out Ida McCracken, Red Ensign, Malar Ros and Coy Colleen for special mention, it is rather because their colour or their form particularly appealed to me than because they were the best judged solely by show standards. Coy Colleen, for example, is not perhaps really big enough to stand on its own, but is such a beautifully formed rose that it is a delight to see it in a collection. I noticed it again looking equally charming in the box of six blooms with which Mr. A. W. J. Green won the Brayfort Challenge Cup in Class 34. Some of Mr. Green's blooms looked a little tired, I thought, but not Coy Colleen.

All these classes are open to amateurs irrespective of the number of trees grown. But there are, of course, also large sections of the schedule confined to amateurs with limited numbers of trees—Classes 37 to 43 for those with not more than 500 rose-bushes, Classes 44 to 50 where the limit is 250, and Classes 51 to 56 where it comes down to 150. These were the sections that attracted the biggest entries of all—and some of the best blooms. After all, Mr. Arthur's champion Ena Harkness was in the 150 rose-tree section.

One of the most impressive sights I have ever seen at a rose show was the entry for Class 52 which is for six blooms in a box. They filled more than half of one of the long R.H.S. tables and the standard was so even that the judges must have had a stiff task to find the winner of the Charles Rigg Cup. They decided on Mr. H. E. Buxton who had McGredy's Ivory, Rex Anderson (easily his best flower), Directeur Guèrin, Madame Abel Chatenay and two blooms of Karl Herbst so very different in shade that at first I mistook them for distinct varieties.

Even better as a box of six was that with which Major-General R. F. B. Naylor won Class 58 and the Gardeners' Company Challenge Cup. Here it was really difficult to find a fault and though I decided that John Ellis was General Naylor's best bloom, his other five, Karl Herbst, Barbara Richards, Ena Harkness, McGredy's Ivory, and Crimson Glory were in the top class. Incidentally General Naylor had another success in Class 59, the Kathleen Louise Mahaffy Memorial Class, but his six specimen blooms in a vase, though good, were not as perfect as those in the box.

There were, of course, many other outstanding exhibits in the amateur classes but it would be boring to go through them in detail and I hope I have said enough to give an idea of the quality of the entries.

The late season had not suited the nurserymen nearly so well for they must always cut most of their flowers from maidens and these never flower quite as early as cut-backs. As a result some exhibits were not so well packed with bloom as usual and there were instances where I felt that a few more flowers would have been desirable if only to hide the "works". Wire stands and the other impedimenta of staging are not often very sightly objects and the less one sees of them the better.

No such criticism could be levelled at the beautifully staged exhibit with which Messrs. R. Harkness & Co. once again won the Queen Mary Challenge Cup and Championship Trophy in Class 1. Here were the great billowing masses of bloom to which we have been accustomed by this firm—a spectacular exhibit which seemed to contain nothing but good flowers. Josephine Bruce confirmed the favourable impression I had previously formed of this deep crimson rose and I was also much impressed by the weight and quality of the ivory Burnaby, a rose I had not previously seen.

Messrs. R. Tucker and Sons were second with an arrangement excellent in quality but lacking a little in density. It was a particularly happy thought to contrast the old purple gallica rose Tuscany with Golden Polyantha, and to place Spek's Yellow between Independence and Flaming Sunset.

Chaplin Bros., who were third, had a notable basket of Ena Harkness. There was no other light crimson in the Show to touch it for brilliance and sustained quality.

In Class 2 there were only two entries and Messrs. B. R. Cant and Sons won the Coronation Trophy. This class calls for an arrangement on an island table, always a difficult assignment, and if I say that I found Messrs. Cant's exhibit a trifle confused, I am not so much criticizing the exhibitor as emphasizing the problems of this kind of staging. Too few flowers will give a dreadfully thin appearance, but in a well packed exhibit such as Messrs. Cant's, it can be a bit difficult to sort out the individual varieties. Having said which, let me add that there were many flowers worth looking at in this exhibit—none better, perhaps, than those of Donald Prior, still one of the best crimson floribundas. Claude was another notable variety here. This hybrid tea has size as well as brilliance to commend it.

The second place in this class was taken by Messrs. W. Lowe & Sons, who used bowls on tall pillars for height and then filled in with more bowls at table level to give solidity. The coppery-pink shades were specially well represented here, Queen and Skylon being notable examples.

There were three entries in Class 3 which calls for an 18 ft. by 4 ft. exhibit against a background, but limits the number of varieties that can be shown to 24 and the number of stems to 24 of each variety. This calls for ingenuity in staging if a thin effect is to be avoided and I thought that Mr. F. Carter, who won the class and the China Trophy that goes with it, had not quite achieved this. But his blooms were good and clean, particularly so in the case of Flaming Sunset, Opera, Lady Belper, Grand'mère Jenny and Fashion.

The second prize in Class 3 was won by Mr. R. M. Cooke whose exhibit was even thinner than that of Mr. Carter. Here I was much impressed by the brilliance of Gertrude Westphal, a nearly single scarlet, close to Commonwealth in colour. Sultane was also startlingly bright; what strides have been made in recent years in the production of these striking bicolour roses.

Messrs. T. Townsend & Sons were third, and I thought their rather widely spaced bowls looked very well. This was one of the few exhibits in which Peace was shown well, but more impressive was Marcelle Gret, an uncommonly rich yellow rose in this as in numerous other exhibits.

Class 4 resembles Class 1 in every respect except size, that is to say it calls for a group of cut roses against a background with no limitations as to number of varieties or blooms. The size in Class 4 is 10 feet by 4 feet against the 20 feet by 4 feet demanded in Class 1. It should be a popular class but on this occasion it only produced two entries, the judges withholding the second prize and awarding a first to Mr. G. Cox and a third to Mr. Edwin Murrell. The former had a very nicely arranged and well filled exhibit in which Opera was outstanding. Mr. Murrell made the mistake, I think, of showing old-fashioned roses, for lovely though these are, they do not give the blaze of colour that seems to be essential to win prizes in a competitive class such as this. Personally I thought Mr. Murrell's bowls of Persian Yellow, Roger Lambelin, Jeanne de Montfort and other old varieties, were quite delightful and I am sure that many visitors to the Show would agree.

Messrs. Hilling & Co., and Messrs. Hillier & Sons were two other exhibitors who specialized in nineteenth-century roses. The former displayed these varieties particularly well, with great arching sprays of some of the more vigorous species to crown the exhibit. Here I stopped to admire the richly fragrant blooms of Charles de Mille and the intense purple colouring of Nuits de Young. In Messrs. Hillier's less imaginatively staged exhibit, William Lobb and Gipsy Boy reminded me once again how far behind the Victorians we still lag in the production of "blue" and purple roses. They are colours we must recapture soon.

A large circular table space in the centre of the hall was filled by Messrs. Wheatcroft Bros. with a non-competitive exhibit which included some of the more recent attempts to produce a blue rose. Of these I find Prelude one of the most satisfactory to date. In the right setting it can be delightful but the colour lacks the robustness achieved so gloriously in the best of the old roses. We get nearer to it in Magenta, the new hybrid musk rose which Wheatcrofts were also showing. This looks to be a very fine rose by any standards and one which I shall certainly try in my own garden.

And so to the newest of all the roses, those shown for the Gold Medals and Certificates of Merit given for the best seedlings. This year there were four Gold Medal Roses, 'Queen Elizabeth', Cleopatra, 'Sir Winston Churchill' and Circus.

The first two were shown by Messrs. Wheatcroft Bros. 'Queen Elizabeth' is a Lammerts seedling and Cleopatra was bred by Kordes. There is no doubt which was the favourite with the public for it was always difficult to get near 'Queen Elizabeth' because of the crowd milling around. It is, of course, a very striking rose, rather too big for a floribunda but yet not quite in the hybrid tea class, for which reason the Americans have suggested a new classification for it. The colour is first-rate, a clean, gleaming camellia pink that is never loud or vulgar and yet always attracts attention. The stems as shown were notably long but did not branch in the manner one expects from a floribunda.

Cleopatra is yet another of the bicolours—not, perhaps, one of the brightest but certainly one of the most striking in contrast, the inside of the petals being an intense cherry flame, and the outside rich golden yellow. The flowers are of good shape, medium size and fair fragrance. Judged solely on the cut flowers I thought it a very good rose.

'Sir Winston Churchill' was raised and shown by Messrs. Alex. Dickson. It is a full, shapely hybrid tea with high-pointed centre—a copybook rose one might say—and the colour is bright carmine rose with a touch of gold at the base. Of course we have seen roses of this style and colour before, but we can do with more of them and 'Sir Winston Churchill' looks to be a very useful addition.

I thought that Circus was a trifle lucky to get its Gold Medal on this occasion, not because I do not think it is a good rose, but because it was obviously not quite ready for the Show. It is one of the very free floribundas but really not much more than the crown buds were open at the time of judging, though there was ample promise of what was to come. Individually the flowers are unusually shapely for a floribunda and they shade from deep yellow (almost an apricot) in the centre, to coppery-red or cerise on the outside. Circus was shown by Messrs. R. Harkness & Co.

Messrs. Sam McGredy had a Certificate of Merit for Lilac Time, another of the "blue" hybrid teas. The colour is really a soft magenta rose with a bar of purple on the outside petals. It is a pleasant colour and one which I imagine would light up well. The flowers are shapely but not big and they carry a pleasant fragrance.

Beauté, another C. of M. rose, was raised by M. Charles Mallerin and shown by Messrs. Wheatcroft Bros. This is a hybrid tea with what seemed to me to be a tea fragrance. The colour is warm deep apricot and the shape of the half-opened flower is particularly attractive, tall and curving outwards at the top as in Autumn or President Hoover.

Messrs. Henry Morse & Sons had a Certificate of Merit for their yellow floribunda rose Sandringham. This is obviously very free flowering but as shown I did not think the colour sufficiently strong nor do the flowers carry many petals. But the judges had seen it in its garden trials and were, no doubt, influenced by its performance in these in making the award.

SUMMER SHOW PRIZE WINNERS 1955

PRIZE WINNERS 1955

Class

1. QUEEN MARY'S CHALLENGE CUP AND CHAMPIONSHIP TROPHY. A representative group 20 ft. × 4 ft. Trophy and Gold Medal, R. Harkness & Co. Ltd.; Gold Medal, R. Tucker & Sons and John Mattock; Silver Gilt Medal, Chaplin Bros.; Silver Medal, E. W. Stedman Ltd.
2. THE CORONATION TROPHY. Display of roses on island table 12 ft. × 8 ft. Silver Gilt Medal and Trophy; B. R. Cant & Sons Ltd.; Silver, W. Lowe & Son (Nurseries) Ltd.
3. THE CHINA TROPHY. Twenty-four distinct varieties, space 18 ft. × 4 ft. 1, F. Carter; 2, R. M. Tooke; 3, J. Townsend & Sons.
4. THE NORMAN ROGERS CHALLENGE CUP. A representative group of cut roses arranged for effect. Space 10 ft. × 4 ft. 1, G. Cox; (no 2nd prize); 3, H. Murrell Ltd.
5. BOWL OF ROSES, 30 stems. 1, R. Harkness & Co.; 2, F. Carter; 3, J. Townsend & Sons.
6. THE JOHN HART MEMORIAL CUP. Forty-eight blooms distinct varieties. 1, C. Longley (Roses) Ltd.; 2, R. Harkness & Co. Ltd.; 3, F. Cant & Co. Ltd.
7. THE KILBEE STUART MEMORIAL CUP. Twenty-four blooms, distinct varieties. 1, F. Carter; 2, C. Longley (Roses) Ltd.; 3, Jarman & Co.
8. TWELVE BLOOMS, distinct varieties. 1, R. Harkness & Co. Ltd.
9. THE LEWIS LEVY MEMORIAL CUP. Three baskets of floribunda roses. 1, F. Cant & Co. Ltd.; 2, J. Townsend & Sons.
10. TWO BASKETS OF POLY POMPON ROSES. 1, F. Cant & Co. Ltd.; 2, G. Longley & Sons.
11. THREE BASKETS OF H.T. CUT ROSES. 1, R. Harkness & Co. Ltd.
12. THE A. C. TURNER CHALLENGE CUP. Fifteen distinct varieties. 1, G. Cox; 2, J. Townsend & Sons.
13. DINNER TABLE DECORATION. 1, Mrs. W. E. Harkness; 2, Mrs. C. A. Tisdall; 3, Mrs. A. K. Wort.
14. DECORATIVE ARRANGEMENT. 1, Mrs. W. E. Harkness; 2, Mrs. C. A. Tisdall; 3, F. Carter.
15. VASE OF CUT ROSES LIGHTLY ARRANGED. 1, Mrs. C. A. Tisdall; (no second prize); 3, Mrs. A. K. Wort and F. Carter.

AMATEURS—OPEN CLASSES

18. BOWL OF DECORATIVE ROSES, 18 stems. 1, E. M. Allen; 2, R. White; 3, Miss H. M. Boyer.
19. BOWL OF DECORATIVE ROSES, 12 stems. 1, Maj.-Gen. R. F. B. Naylor; 2, A. N. Warren; 3, R. White.
20. THREE VASES OF FLORIBUNDA ROSES. 1, J. R. Colyer; 2, A. N. Warren.
21. ONE BOWL OF FLORIBUNDA ROSES. 1, A. N. Warren; 2, E. Royalton Kisch.
22. THE S. W. BURGESS MEMORIAL CUP. 1, E. M. Allen; 2, J. R. Colyer.
23. THE EDWARD MAWLEY CHALLENGE CUP. Box of 12 specimen blooms. 1, R. White; 2, E. Royalton Kisch.
24. BOX OF SIX SPECIMEN BLOOMS. 1, J. R. Colyer; 2, E. M. Allen; 3, A. N. Warren.
25. BOX OF SIX SPECIMEN BLOOMS, one variety. 1, R. White; 2, W. H. J. Sansum; 3, Mrs. W. A. Rapier.
26. VASE OF SIX SPECIMEN BLOOMS, two varieties. 1, E. M. Allen; 2, Maj.-Gen. R. F. B. Naylor; 3, A. N. Warren.
27. THE LINDSELL CUP. A box of twenty-four specimen blooms. 1, M. L. Kemp; 2, G. D. Burch.

Amateurs who grow and stage without assistance

28. ONE BOWL OF H.T. DECORATIVE ROSES. Not more than 18 stems. 1, A. W. J. Green; 2, Mrs. A. E. Griffith; 3, W. C. Thorn; 4, F. Fairbrother.
29. BOWL OF H.T. DECORATIVE ROSES, 12 stems. 1, A. Norman; 2, A. W. J. Green; 3, W. C. Thorn.
30. THREE VASES OF FLORIBUNDA ROSES, distinct varieties. 1, F. Fairbrother; 2, Lt.-Col. D. Pope; 3, L. P. Roberts.
31. BOWL OF FLORIBUNDA ROSES, 12 stems, one variety. 1, G. D. Burch; 2, H. N. Taylor; 3, W. J. Northfield; 4, L. P. Roberts.
32. THE H. R. DARLINGTON MEMORIAL CUP. Six vases of H.T. decorative roses. 1, F. Fairbrother; 2, M. L. Kemp; 3, A. Norman; 4, W. J. Northfield.
33. THE NICHOLSON CHALLENGE CUP. A box of 12 specimen blooms. 1, G. D. Burch; 2, W. J. Northfield; 3, M. L. Kemp.
34. THE BRAYFORT CHALLENGE CUP. A box of six specimen blooms. 1, A. W. J. Green; 2, E. R. Kisch; 3, W. J. Northfield; 4, F. Fairbrother.
35. BOX OF SIX SPECIMEN BLOOMS, one variety. 1, F. Fairbrother; 2, A. W. J. Green; 3, M. L. Kemp; 4, A. Norman.
36. VASE OF SIX SPECIMEN BLOOMS. 1, Mrs. J. C. Vernon Miller; 2, F. Fairbrother; 3, A. W. J. Green.

Restricted to growers of not more than 500 trees who grow and stage without assistance

37. ONE BOWL OF H.T. DECORATIVE ROSES, 12 stems. 1, H. N. Raban; 2, Mrs. J. C. Vernon Miller; 3, B. S. T. Wallace; 4, Mrs. E. Toogood.
38. ONE BOWL OF FLORIBUNDA ROSES, 9 stems. 1, C. E. Sansom; 2, Mrs. E. Toogood; 3, F. M. Bowen.
39. THE EDWARD J. HOLLAND MEMORIAL CUP. Four vases of H.T. decorative roses. 1, S. Phillips; 2, E. E. Gatward; 3, C. H. Clark; 4, H. N. Taylor.

Class

40. THE SAM MCGREDY CHALLENGE CUP. Box of 12 specimen blooms. 1, E. E. Gatward; 2, Mrs. A. C. Newman; 3, W. G. H. Cates.
41. BOX OF SIX SPECIMEN BLOOMS, not fewer than four varieties. 1, C. E. Samson; 2, F. M. Bowen; 3, A. E. Barton.
42. ONE VASE OF SIX SPECIMEN BLOOMS. 1, Mrs. J. C. Vernon Miller; 2, E. E. Gatward; 3, F. E. Timbrell; 4, D. Pettett.
43. ONE VASE OF SIX SPECIMEN BLOOMS, not fewer than four varieties. 1, H. N. Raban; 2, D. Pettett; 3, E. E. Garward; 4, F. M. Bowen.

Restricted to growers of not more than 250 trees who grow and stage without assistance

44. ONE BOWL OF DECORATIVE ROSES, 12 stems. 1, W. J. Widgery; 2, E. H. Lockton; 3, R. O. Samuel; 4, Mrs. J. C. Vernon Miller.
45. THE SLAUGHTER MEMORIAL CUP. Three vases of decorative roses. 1, B. W. W. Sampson; 2, Mrs. J. C. Vernon Miller; 3, B. Dennis; 4, W. G. H. Cates.
46. ONE BOWL OF FLORIBUNDA ROSES, 6 stems, one or more varieties. 1, R. O. Samuel; 2, C. M. Lister; 3, E. H. Lockton; 4, Miss H. I. Port.
47. BOWL OF FLORIBUNDA ROSES, 6 stems, one variety. 1, E. H. Lockton; 2, J. C. Alexander; 3, G. H. Swain.
48. BOX OF SIX SPECIMEN BLOOMS. 1, J. L. Garland; 2, W. G. H. Cates; 3, E. H. Lockton; 4, F. R. Willis.
49. ONE VASE OF THREE SPECIMEN BLOOMS, distinct. 1, W. J. Widgery; 2, H. Munro; 3, G. H. Swain; 4, W. G. H. Cates.
50. ONE VASE OF THREE SPECIMEN BLOOMS. 1, F. Willis; 2, P. McPhail; 3, J. R. Garland; 4, H. C. Wilson.
51. ONE VASE OF DECORATIVE ROSES, 6 stems. 1, A. W. Liquorish; 2, A. H. Arnold; 3, J. Wilson; 4, R. G. Conisbee.
52. THE CHARLES RIGG CUP. A box of six specimen blooms. 1, H. E. Buxton; 2, L. Brown; 3, J. Wilson; 4, Dr. T. A. L. Scott and A. E. Pinnock.
53. ONE VASE OF SIX SPECIMEN BLOOMS. 1, F. J. Alliker; 2, A. H. Arnold; 3, Dr. T. A. L. Scott.
54. ONE VASE OF THREE SPECIMEN BLOOMS, distinct. 1, F. J. Alliker; 2, Mrs. M. Pearce; 3, Lt.-Col. R. H. A. Lucas; 4, C. L. Magnus.
55. ONE VASE OF THREE SPECIMEN BLOOMS. 1, J. N. Kirsop; 2, A. E. Humber; 3, Mrs. F. E. Lister.
56. ONE VASE OF FLORIBUNDA, 4 stems. 1, Mrs. W. M. Hobby; 2, J. C. Alexander; 2, L. Brown.

METROPOLITAN CLASSES

57. ONE BOWL OF DECORATIVE ROSES, 12 stems. 1, L. Hollis; 2, B. Dennis; 3, Maj.-Gen. R. F. B. Naylor.
58. THE GARDENERS' COMPANY CHALLENGE CUP. A box of six specimen blooms. 1, Maj.-Gen. R. F. B. Naylor; 2, D. W. Chapman; 3, S. Phillips; 4, L. Hollis.
59. THE KATHLEEN LOUISE MAHAFFY MEMORIAL CUP. One vase of six specimen blooms. 1, Maj.-Gen. R. F. B. Naylor; 2, A. G. Hulf; 3, D. W. Chapman; 4, J. N. Harvie.

Restricted to amateurs who have never won a first prize at any exhibition of the Society

60. ONE VASE OF DECORATIVE ROSES, 6 stems. 1, A. G. Hulf; 2, G. W. C. Vincent; 3, H. Bennett; 4, L. Howell.
61. BOX OF SIX SPECIMEN BLOOMS. 1, M. W. Hammond; 2, J. H. Kirsop; 3, J. R. Hinton; 4, G. W. C. Vincent.
62. VASE OF FLORIBUNDA ROSES. 1, H. A. W. Arnold; 2, W. Birkbeck; 3, G. H. Swain; 4, J. B. Boland.
63. ONE VASE OF THREE SPECIMEN BLOOMS, distinct varieties. 1, D. Ball; 2, P. G. Phillips; 3, W. G. Gregory; 4, F. C. H. Witchell.
64. ONE VASE OF THREE SPECIMEN BLOOMS. 1, R. C. J. Richardson; 2, H. Bennett; 3, E. W. J. Wonnacott; 4, F. Kennett and E. Mc. P. Watts.

Restricted to amateurs who have never previously exhibited at any exhibition of the Society

65. ONE VASE OF SIX STEMS. 1, F. R. Arnold; 2, E. A. Brown; 3, D. S. Smith; 4, T. E. K. Molyneux.
66. ONE VASE OF SIX STEMS, ANY VARIETIES. 1, D. S. Smith; 2, Miss P. V. James; 3, R. C. T. Richardson; 4, F. R. Arnold.

Restricted to Provincial Members resident 100 miles or more from London

67. THE FRANKLIN DENNISON MEMORIAL BOWL. One vase, eight stems. 1, D. Pope; 2, J. E. Eld; 3, F. Fairbrother; 4, Col. W. B. Wright and W. H. J. Sansum.
68. THREE VASES OF DECORATIVE ROSES, 5 stems in each. 1, F. Fairbrother; 2, Lt.-Col. D. Pope and F. E. Timbrell.
69. VASE OF SIX SPECIMEN BLOOMS. 1, Col. W. B. Wright; 2, J. E. Eld; 3, H. Davies.

AFFILIATED SOCIETIES

70. THE FRANKLIN DENNISON MEMORIAL CUP. One bowl of floribunda roses and one bowl of H.T. type. 1, Eastcote Horticultural Society; 2, Ibis Horticultural Society; 3, Hoover Horticultural Society and Colchester Rose Society.

ARTISTIC CLASSES

Class
71. DINNER TABLE DECORATION. 1, Mrs. D. Thorn; 2, Mrs. A. Gotobed; 3, Mrs. G. E. Dalton; 4, Mrs. F. E. Barker.
72. ARRANGEMENT OF CUT ROSES. 1, Mrs. M. E. Barton; 2, Mrs. F. E. Baker; 3, Miss N. Watson; 4, Miss A. M. Aldous.
73. SIDEBOARD DECORATION. 1, Mrs. A. Gotobed; 2, Mrs. G. E. Dalton; 3, Miss N. Watson.

Restricted to amateurs who grow and stage without assistance
74. THE QUEEN ALEXANDRA PERPETUAL TROPHY. Dinner table decoration. 1, Mrs. H. G. Clacy; 2, Mrs. F. E. Barker; 3, Mrs. D. Thorn; 4, Mrs. M. E. Barton.
75. ARRANGEMENT OF CUT ROSES. 1, Miss E. Pickering; 2, Mrs. H. G. Clacy; 3, Mrs. A. E. Griffith.
76. ARRANGEMENT OF SEVEN BLOOMS. 1, Mrs. D. Thorn; 2, Mrs. E. H. Lockton; 3, Mrs. M. E. Barton; 4, Miss E. Pickering.
77. A SMALL ARRANGEMENT OF ROSES, not exceeding six in. overall. 1, Miss F. M. Perry; 2, Mrs. D. Thorn; 3, Mrs. A. Gotobed; 4, E. H. Lockton.

Restricted to exhibitors who have never won a first prize in the artistic classes at any exhibition of the Society
78. ARRANGEMENT OF CUT ROSES WITH FOLIAGE. 1, Mrs. N. Raban; 2, Miss H. I. Port; 3, Mrs. M. J. Heyes.

ORTHOCIDE AND KARATHANE

I experimented Orthocide Captan 50 per cent wettable for control of black spot with this spray, using a strength of 2 lb. per 100 gallons of water on a bed of 60 rose-trees containing such susceptible varieties as The Doctor, Julien Potin, Marcelle Gret, Sutter's Gold. In order to make the test as fairly as possible I did not spray the adjoining bed of 60 trees with any control. The unsprayed bed was very seriously attacked by black spot but the bed sprayed with Orthocide remained almost entirely free and The Doctor produced me some of the finest blooms I have ever had. I sprayed the bed twice only, once in early June and again in mid-July. The only criticism I have of this very effective fungicide is that in the dry summer we experienced the leaves remained spotted with white until sprayed thoroughly by overhead watering. It is dangerous to come to a conclusion on the evidence of one year but I am sufficiently confident in the value of the spray to use it again next summer.

It has the merit of being easy to prepare and it can be stored in galvanized containers. The mixture Captan, Karathane and Lindane for control of black spot, powdery mildew and aphids I found useful but not very effective against aphids.

Personally I prefer to spray quite early against greenfly and then use a separate control for black spot.

KARATHANE I found most effective for control of mildew both on rose-trees and on chrysanthemums and it should prove to be of benefit to those who suffer from mildew-infected plants. Out of doors I rarely get mildew but I did test Karathane on badly affected plants of Our Princess and it was most effective. I have never had such fine mildew-free blooms on this variety as I have this autumn.

There is no doubt in my mind that these new introductions will prove to be of enormous value to rose-growers.

F. FAIRBROTHER

'LILAC TIME'

Golden Dawn × Luis Brinas.
Raised by S. McGredy & Son, Portadown. N. Ireland.
Trial Ground No. 841. Reg. No. 363. Trial Ground Certificate.
Certificate of Merit, Summer Show, 1955.

THE DECORATIVE CLASSES
AT THE SUMMER SHOW

ARBEL M. ALDOUS

THERE was a new look in the Old Hall this year and the comments of the crowds showed that the visitors were interested in the innovations. To the right was Class 72: "An artistic arrangement of cut roses . . . to illustrate a theme." There were nine exhibits in alcoves and there was unanimity of opinion about the first prize. With a small reproduction of the well-known Dignity and Impudence Mrs. Barton had a dignified arrangement of Virgo in a large tortoise and an impudent replica of a white floribunda in a very little one. Mrs. Barker was second with Full Measure—a lovely study of purple Prelude overflowing from two pewter mugs on taffeta that brought out the colour of both. Third was Miss Watson's charming picture in gold and white which carried out a quotation from Swinburne by her emphasis on the thorns of *R. omeiensis* var. *pteracantha*. I liked The Midas Touch—though when I saw it after judging it looked very tumbled. Mrs. Gotobed's theme was most appropriate—The English Rose complete with Musical Accompaniment. I liked Mrs. Thorn's Invitation to the Waltz and Mrs. Dalton's Bridal Morn. I wonder if some of us missed the point of Mrs. Clacy's clever Interflora. Did we all realize that the containers were the actual baskets used when roses are sent by air? Last but not least, Miss Hambly-Parker gave us the problem picture. According to any reputable standard of Floral Art it was easily top of the class. A lump of wood, a few nondescript roses, a handful of pretty little shells scattered on sand. All very weird and wonderful and completely enigmatic. And the theme? "CONTEMPORA."

In Class 76: "An arrangement of not more than seven blooms . . ." Mrs. Thorn was first with seven perfect Peace, perfectly arranged. Mrs. Lockton was second with Sylvia. Mrs. Barton had a lovely picture with Cardinal Richelieu in a Venetian glass. A fourth in this large class went to Miss Pickering who had a creamy blend of Peace and others. Mrs. Gotobed had Dillys Allen on grey, and Mrs. J. F. Harkness's a study in pearly green; but I did not like (Sorry, Mrs. Heyes!) Karl Herbst on purple.

Next came Class 71: "An arrangement of cut Roses suitable for the centre of a dining table. Space allowed 3 ft. by 3 ft." There were nine entries, all good, all quite ordinary! Mrs. Thorn was first with a very "finished" centre-piece of Spek's Yellow, Mrs. Gotobed second, Mrs. Dalton third and Mrs. Barker fourth.

Then Class 75. "A bowl of Roses lightly arranged . . . in a $10\frac{1}{2}$ in. bowl." Those of the "old guard" remember the colossal effects of bygone days. And why not? This is the Summer Show of the National Rose Society. So let there be roses—yes, masses of them. This is one of the classes for the real enthusiast and it was disappointing to find so few. Those who did the bowl just put in all they had left, I surmise! By Miss Pickering's name in my notes I have written "Nice". Mrs. Clacy was second chiefly with a low arrangement of red floribundas. Mrs. Griffith was third with her well-known, well-grown, and well-shown Mrs. Henry Bowles. Miss Bairstone had a colourful group and about the other the less said the better.

Next the class for those "who have never won a first prize in the artistic classes at an exhibition of the N.R.S." Certainly this year's five entrants were not all "Novices"! Mrs. Raban from Bristol was first, but before the day was over her well-arranged bowl was in a sorry state. Miss Violet Stevenson, writing in last year's *Rose Annual*, ejaculated: "Why, oh why, must you touch the exhibits?" On good authority I was told that this bowl was tipped over by someone who wished to see if she had used the ubiquitous chicken wire! Miss Port was second, and I would hazard the guess that she belongs to a Flower Club. Mrs. Heyes had a garish combination of red and yellow. She likes colour!

Then we came to the corner. A positive scrum was milling round that corner! I tried several times to count the number of exhibits in Class 77: "A small arrangement of Roses not exceeding 6 in. overall." However, I did manage to see Miss Perry's delightful cluster of three Fashion buds which was first, and Mrs. Thorn's gay little Wedding Day which was second and Mrs. Gotobed's miniature which was third. There was probably a fourth, but, battered and bruised, I edged my way out of the mêlée, lucky to have lost only one button from my coat. I was told later that there were seven men in this large class.

Class 73 came next. It was a brain-wave (Whose?) to have raised the "sideboard" a few inches above the level of the staging; but would anyone really have all those yards of dust-collecting drapery on her sideboard? Or at such *odd* angles? Mrs. Gotobed was first, Mrs. Dalton second and Miss Watson third. I liked best Mrs. Colston-Hales's golden bowl. I was told it was "too large and ragged". I visualized it in the great hall at Longleat and certainly her taut brown satin gave the impression of polished oak. I liked Mrs. Barker's President Hoover. I was taken to look at it from another angle where there was a gap. But *why*, Mrs. B., those neatly fluted yards of two colours on a sideboard? And Miss Hambly-Parker would you *really* throw that marvellous shawl over your sideboard? It was very daring and thank you for doing it; for it gave the most jaded a jolt when it struck the eye.

And now at last and definitely least, we came to the seven poor, pathetic little tables. Shades of Eric Holroyd! Did he give the Queen Alexandra Perpetual Trophy for this! It is an obvious fact that the Show has outgrown the capacity of the Hall and "tables" take up a lot of room. But if we can imagine that a 3 ft. square represents the centre of a dinner-table as in Class 71, why should we not imagine that 6 ft. by 3 ft. represents something on a really large scale? Shouldn't we love to be asked to "do the flowers" for the Lord Mayor's Banquet? Or of a State Dinner at Buckingham Palace? If that American lady who, we are told, asked plaintively "must they all be alike?" came again, she might find them different indeed but still all alike. Gone are the large, but lovely, perfectly round centre-pieces with two "small arrangements" to carry on the middle decoration and/or four little corner pieces, often exquisitely done, or with just two or three perfect blooms to emphasize the unique charm of the rose used. Oh yes! The American lady may rest assured that she will not see this again. The judges won't have it. In fact at a recent show the judge wanted to mark down the best table because it had "four little corner vases". And yet we now have Class 77! At least Mrs. Clacy's table approached more nearly to the traditional standard than any of the others. So her name goes on THE CUP for a second time. Mrs. Barker was second with her meticulously perfect boat-shaped Lydia, Mrs. Thorn with Picture and the same technique, was third and Mrs. Barton fourth with a yellow medley of Masquerade and the same shape. Miss Bairstowe had a very cheerful mixture. There were some attempts to break away from monotony but the ideas were better than the execution.

THE BRISTOL GROUP OF THE NATIONAL ROSE SOCIETY

A. E. GRIFFITH

THE Eighth Annual Show of the Bristol Group of our Society took place at the Corn Exchange, Bristol, on Wednesday, July 6th, 1955, and it is pleasing to report the continued success of the Group with an increased number of exhibitors and an increasing improvement in the quality of blooms shown and in the general staging of them.

The best group by nurserymen was staged by Messrs. John Sanday (Roses) Limited, and won for them the Trade Challenge Cup and Gold Medal. Their exhibit of the new Ethel Sanday was outstanding. They also showed their new rose—Jane—which will be on the market in the autumn of 1956; a very attractive rose, not unlike Mrs. Sam McGredy in colour. A good group was also staged by Forest and Orchard Nurseries Ltd., for which they were deservedly awarded a Silver Gilt Medal. Non-Competitive groups were staged by Mr. Bertram Park and by Mr. Edgar Allen.

The Ladies' Decorative Classes here are always an attractive feature, Mrs. P. A. Blake winning the Flora Challenge Cup and Mrs. N. Raban the *Western Daily Press* Challenge Bowl. Other First Prize winners were Mrs. Barnard, Mrs. Parsons, and Mrs. Sanday.

In the Members' Section, Mr. E. R. C. Tizard put up four very good vases and won the Victor Osmond Challenge Bowl and Bronze Medal. The Davey Challenge Bowl for the best exhibit for growers of not more than 100 trees was well won by Mr. F. Wiltshire, whilst the N.R.S. Bronze Medal for the best exhibit by growers of not more than 250 trees deservedly went to Mr. G. C. Low. Other First Prize winners included Mrs. A. E. Griffith, Miss Joan Fulford, Messrs. Cottam, Phillips, Pinnock, Raban, Sansum, and E. T. Smith. The "best bloom" was won by Mrs. C. Vernon Miller with Ena Harkness.

There was a good entry for an excellent lunch, with commendably brief speeches. Mr. Oliver Mee, President, N.R.S., replied for the guests and Mrs. Edgar Allen on behalf of the Ladies. A noticeable feature of the Annual Show is the uncommonly pleasant atmosphere that prevails over the whole meeting. Congratulations and thanks to all those responsible.

THE PROVINCIAL ROSE SHOW, LEEDS

J. C. WATSON

THE best rose year many of us can remember, perfect weather, the ideal setting of Roundhay Park, completely efficient Show organization, all crowned by the visit of our Royal Patron, Her Royal Highness the Princess Royal, made this Show one to be remembered for many years to come. It was, indeed, a Royal occasion.

This year, the Society's Provincial Show was staged in conjunction with the Leeds Flower Show on the 19th and 20th July. It is twenty-nine years since the Society last visited Leeds. Two special marquees were provided to accommodate the entries for the Rose Show, which totalled 283 Trade and Amateur exhibits. After the bustle of the staging and the calm of the judging, the Roundhay (Leeds) Horticultural Society, under the Presidency of Mr. H. S. Wainwright, O.B.E., entertained the officials of the National Rose Society at a luncheon at which Sir James Croysdale, the Lord Mayor of Leeds, gave a cordial Yorkshire welcome to everyone. In responding, our President, Mr. Oliver Mee, O.B.E., struck a particularly happy note when he said that rose-growers made the best husbands, as their wives always knew where to find them.

In such a good year one expected to see blooms of exceptional quality, and one was not disappointed in either the Amateur or Professional tents. In the Open Amateur Classes, the First Prize Box of 12 Blooms, exhibited by Mr. J. H. Wilding, of Bolton, was the best that has been seen at Leeds in the last twenty-five years, to my own knowledge, and, I venture to say, has seldom been surpassed at any Show since the war. He had magnificent examples of Bacchus, Show Girl, Directeur Guèrin, Ethel Sanday and Sam McGredy included in this box. His First Prize Box of 6 Blooms was equally good. The Jubilee Trophy was won by Mr. F. A. Gibson, of Formby, who also was awarded the Society's medal for the best bloom in the whole Amateur section: an Eden Rose, as near perfection as surely it can possibly be grown. Whilst offering our congratulations to our Lancashire friends, we must not forget the charming exhibits in the Decorative Classes of Miss Aldous and Mrs. W. C. Thorn, of Colchester, who deserve our best thanks for coming so far to give so much pleasure and inspiration to less experienced exhibitors in these classes. The quality of blooms exhibited in the local classes was also of a very high standard, and it was gratifying to note exhibitors, famed for their prowess with the "lesser breeds", won over to our national flower.

As it would be impossible to describe with full detail the brilliant beauty of the Nurserymen's tent, one may only indicate what seemed to be the outstanding features. The Challenge Cup for the Best Exhibit was won by C. Gregory & Sons, Ltd., of Chilwell, whose bank of roses was a superb blaze of colour. It was pleasing to note Nurserymen using originality in their arrangements rather than the conventional massing of blooms. I liked very much indeed the stand exhibited by Messrs. McGredy, of Portadown. It was so arranged that one could appreciate the beauty of each variety. I wonder how many visitors noticed the magnificent bowl of Sam McGredy, in all their stateliness—an effect which would have been entirely lost in a more congested display. Messrs. Fryers, of Knutsford, also departed from the conventional massing of blooms, and tastefully used spacing and differing heights to gain effect. In the centre of their stand they were showing Eliane, a new rose from France which, as exhibited, is large, shapely, a deep pink and pleasantly scented. The Linwood Nurseries, of Swanland, East Yorks, staged a superb exhibit of which every bloom was a perfect specimen of its type. The rose that won the National Rose Society's medal for the best bloom in the Nurserymen's Section was a magnificent Brilliant, locally grown and exhibited by Messrs. Charles Kershaw, of Brighouse.

As this was the first Provincial Show to be held in Leeds since 1926, it was the first time that many of the visitors had seen new seedlings displayed. These proved to be of great interest. Only one Gold Medal was awarded, and that was to the hybrid polyantha Bonnie Maid, raised by Mr. E. B. Le Grice, of North Walsham. A pleasing floribunda, it has clusters of carmen rose, semi-double blooms; I thought it not very distinctive. There were several other good floribunda seedlings which gained Certificates of Merit. I was particularly impressed by Golden Delight, which is most appropriately named; by Sidney Peabody, a floribunda of a fascinating Tyrian rose colour; and by Sweet Repose, a most attractive variety which has flowers opening from pinkish buds into quite large apricot-coloured blooms. All these were displayed by Messrs. Gandy, of Rugby.

On the stand of Messrs. Wheatcroft, of Nottingham, I was particularly attracted by the new rose Magenta, a floribunda of deep, rich mauve, exquisitely scented. It was staged artistically. The effect of the new lavender roses has too often been spoilt by their being staged without regard to their subdued colouring. When placed alongside brilliantly coloured roses, they tend to add brilliance to their neighbours. When staged alone, or with pale-lemon and white roses, their own elegance is enhanced. Perhaps the rose that pleased me most was an unnamed seedling on the same stand, an exquisitely lovely milk-white flower with a clear cerise picotee edging; similar to Premier Bal, but a far more dainty and shapely bloom. The growing popularity of floribunda roses is not to be wondered at, as they are being developed continually and improved in size, shape, colour and fragrance. It may be that the truth of the modern tendency was summed up in the remark overheard at the Show: "I like to grow these roses because I just plant them, and they're no trouble"—obviously not an exhibitor!

One of the main objects of a Provincial Show is to stimulate interest in our national flower. This was certainly done at Leeds this year, not only among established gardening enthusiasts but also among the rising generation. On the Wednesday morning 1,400 senior schoolchildren were admitted to the Show free of charge. It was most encouraging to see the interest shown in the various exhibits by those whom we hope will become the rose-growers and exhibitors of the future.

One could not conclude without a special word of thanks to the officers of the Roundhay (Leeds) Horticultural Society; in this happy and successful Show we were particularly indebted to the President (Mr. H. S. Wainwright, O.B.E.), the Chairman (Mr. James M. Smedley) and the Secretary (Mr. W. L. Wood). Most of all, our thanks are due to Her Royal Highness for her gracious visit. It was indeed most gratifying to all concerned that there should be such an excellent Show upon the occasion of the visit of our Royal Patron.

THE AUTUMN SHOW

ROY HAY

WE shall remember 1955 with gratitude for the glorious weeks of sunshine which succeeded each other from April until the early days of October, but our felicitous memory will be tinged with remembrances of some gardening disappointments and not a little exasperation. The growth of most plants, roses not excepted, was good, clean and robust, and as far as my part of the world was concerned, the first blooming was all that could be desired. The autumn flowers, however, of many varieties did not live up to expectations, and with the single exception of that oddity among roses Masquerade, in the gardens around us in Surrey there were many disappointments.

It was, therefore, with no little anticipation that we repaired to the Royal Horticultural Society's halls on September 9th to see how the growers, large and small, had fared. All seemed to have found the season difficult at the end, for the entries in the Amateurs' Classes were by no means as numerous as usual, nor was the quality that which we have come to expect. The Nurserymen's Groups and Classes contained, of course, many beautiful roses, but I notice from my lists of those varieties which showed up well there were some changes from a year ago. There was also a much greater disparity in the quality of blooms from different nurserymen than we are accustomed to see at shows but all attempts to draw any morals as regards the parts of the country that had stood up to the unusual weather conditions better than others proved fruitless. We thought, however, that the exhibit of James Cocker & Sons, which had come from Scotland, contained blooms of outstanding freshness and quality; good though they were, they took second place to the magnificent exhibit from R. Harkness & Co. They were, however, among the Gold Medal winners. Once more I carried out the exercise which I find so interesting at rose shows, namely, a careful examination of all the trade groups, to note down the roses which really stand out, and again it was noticeable that the same varieties impress themselves upon one, no matter by whom they are shown. Those that impressed me most were Spek's Yellow, Karl Herbst, Monique, Moulin Rouge, Frensham, Lady Belper, Peace,

'SANDRINGHAM' (flor.)

Raised by Wilhelm Kordes, Holstein, Germany.
Trial Ground No. 851. Reg. No. 369. Trial Ground Certificate.
Certificate of Merit, Summer Show, 1955.
For description see page 147

Sutter's Gold, Flaming Sunset, Picture, Independence, Helen Traubel, Ena Harkness and Masquerade. Of all these it is probably true to say that Ena Harkness surpassed them all, but Masquerade and Monique I see are marked in my notebook with three stars.

We do not go to the Autumn Rose Show with quite the same feeling of anticipation of seeing outstanding novelties that we get at the Summer Show. Nevertheless, there is always the excitement attending the award of the President's International Trophy. I suppose that had we thought about it much in advance we should have expected 'Queen Elizabeth' to qualify for this blue ribbon of the rose world, and none of us were very surprised when we saw the award list. From all accounts it is going to be a very popular rose, and unless Harry Wheatcroft is exaggerating it may well prove to be the greatest rose since Peace. Certainly the vista of a series of varieties carrying flowers almost as good as the hybrid tea varieties on branching stems after the form of the floribunda is an exciting one, because we shall not only be able to cut good bowls of flowers from these newcomers but they are most effective *en masse* in the beds and borders. Improved bedding roses are coming into their own at just the right time, because many of us are beginning to fear for the traditional bedding out schemes, and even for the time honoured herbaceous border in these days of high maintenance costs, labour shortage, and a general tightening up of the money bags. It may well be that the new floribunda varieties will replace many a bedding out scheme in the gardens of the future.

The other floribunda varieties of note, People and Sweet Repose, the former from Wheatcroft Bros. Ltd., and the latter from Gandy's Roses Ltd., have the appearance of being worthy newcomers, but, of course, neither is so effective as a cut flower as is 'Queen Elizabeth'. Incidentally a bowl of 'Queen Elizabeth' on the new rose tables which had been cut on the previous Monday had stood for two days in the R.H.S. Show on the Tuesday and Wednesday, and after another day in one of the back rooms was brought forth still very fresh and beautiful for the Rose Show on the Friday.

C. Gregory & Son Ltd. in their island table display which won them the De Escofet Memorial Cup showed a number of varieties which were out of the common run—Gay Crusader and the orange-salmon Chief Seattle were particularly good while in the A. C. Turner Cup Class for fifteen varieties Messrs. George Longley & Sons included the little known Marie Cassant, Norah Longley, Alice Amos, and Teschendorf Jubilee Rose. Sparrieshoop, Britannia, Siren and Elmshorn were also included in this collection, which apparently indicated that prizes are to be won by breaking away from the old favourites.

In the Amateurs' Classes I suppose we must give great credit to those who exhibited for being able to exhibit at all, and if the quality throughout was a good deal lower than we have seen in previous years, at least, it was pretty much of a level from all parts of the country.

I have never been to Formby, but it must be quite a horticultural paradise if one can judge by the number of flower specialists who descend upon London to romp away with prizes at the National specialist shows. Mr. F. A. Gibson again won the first prize for a box of 12 specimen blooms—Dorothy Anderson, Eden Rose, Fred Howard, Gordon Eddie, Dr. F. Debat, Peace, Barbara Richards, Margot Anstiss, Symphonie, Show Girl, Opera and Margaret—all post-war varieties. His six specimen blooms—Peace, Opera and Margaret, were also well in advance of their nearest competitor.

Edgar M. Allen of Bideford always manages to reach the metropolis with praiseworthy blooms, and his entry in the six vases of H.T. decorative roses class contained very good blooms of Dorothy Anderson, Karl Herbst and Verschuren's Pink. I thought W. C. Thorn's bowl of 18 roses exceptionally good and there was no doubt that J. H. Wilding in the N.R.S. Challenge Cup for 12 specimen blooms put up a great effort. Again all the varieties shown were post-war introductions, and among them Karl Herbst and Opera were outstanding. It was the first time I have seen Ethel Sanday in a prize winning set, but it showed up well, as did Brilliant, Red Ensign, Peace, Volcano and the ubiquitous Ena Harkness. One does not think of Bolton as a paradise for roses, but Mr. Wilding certainly produced some excellent blooms, and in his entry in the three distinct varieties class 6 specimen blooms, he chose all red varieties—Red Ensign, William Harvey, and Karl Herbst. H. C. Wilson of Chessington walked away with the first prize for floribunda roses using the tried and trusty friend Frensham. It will be interesting to see how the variety stands up to competition from some of the newer and larger floribunda varieties that are now coming to the fore. A very nice entry came from F. R. Willis of Orpington—6 specimen blooms included Poinsettia, Symphonie and Lady Trent, the latter a variety not often seen on the show benches. The metropolitan classes were neither better nor worse than usual. F. A. Gibson's box of 6 blooms was a mixture of old and new with Phyllis Gold, Tallyho, Frau Karl Druschki, Show Girl, and Mrs. A. R. Barraclough looking very attractive. Major-General R. F. B. Naylor of Barnet, a fairly regular winner in this section, had good blooms of Peace, Fred Howard and Anne Letts, in his vase of 6 roses.

If anything I thought the novices showed up better than usual and Mr. T. E. K. Molyneux of Chaldon and Mr. K. B. Ewart of Reading had every reason to be proud of their exhibits. In the latter exhibit Peace and Confidence were outstanding and M. Beresford of Harlow had an excellent bloom of Pink Spiral in his fine set, which included The Doctor, Karl Herbst, William Harvey and Crimson Glory.

There were some changes in the provincial section prize winners. F. A. Gibson continued his successes in other sections by winning two first prizes and Miss J. E. Fulford of Northam was equally at home here as in the unaided amateurs' section.

Now we come to the decorative classes. Although the Society still sticks rigidly to its rule that only roses may be used in the artistic classes, I do not propose to waste your time or mine by repeating my plea for a wider and more imaginative ruling for these classes. I still think that the best interests of the rose are not being served by excluding other flowers from artistic arrangements—at least, I would have thought one class might have been included in which other flowers might be used to offset the beauty of the rose. However, this principle seems to be so deeply ingrained among rosarians that it was a signal step forward to see Class 4 "An Artistic Arrangement for Cut Roses (no other flowers) with any foliage and/or decoration" to illustrate a theme. Let it be said at once that such interpretative arrangements that I have seen at other exhibitions have left me quite cold. Of course, if an exhibitor is attempting to illustrate a theme by a floral arrangement, one expects first of all competence in arrangement and originality in the presentation! Limiting the choice of flowers to one genus must obviously make the game more difficult. That is probably why most of the efforts appeared to me a trifle childish. The class was almost a monopoly of the ladies from Colchester, who are very good at this sort of thing, and Miss A. M. Aldous from that fair town arranged a very nice large single yellow rose in a pleasant setting. Mrs. F. E. Barker, arranging blooms of Peace with a globe and entitling it "The Hope of the World", also did a workmanlike job which was quite attractive, but of the others I think the less said the better.

The decorated dinner tables were well enough, and again Mrs. F. E. Barker arranged a very charming table. But one wonders whether after all these years when we must have seen hundreds of tables' each looking very much like its neighbour, and each very much like those we saw last year and the year before, has the time not come when artistic arrangement of roses might take on a new look? It should be possible to gather together a few ladies or gentlemen skilled in the art of flower arrangement, pool their ideas and present the visiting public with inspirations which would quicken interest in the rose as a cut flower. Especially would I like to see a class for arrangements of a mere half dozen roses. Practically anybody with a reasonably nimble set of fingers can make an attractive bowl if they can go out into the rose garden and cut to their heart's content. To make an attractive arrangement with the dozen or half dozen blooms, which is almost all people can afford to buy from a florist's shop, is something quite different.

The National Rose Society, I regret to have to say, is lagging behind the specialist societies in its approach to floral arrangements. Every year we see more and better examples of floral art at the big specialist shows—not only at the big shows but at the smaller shows up and down the country, but of all the local shows I have seen this past twelve months I cannot recollect any that were distinguished for the outstanding rose arrangements. Maybe, the rose is a difficult flower to arrange, perhaps it does not lend itself as well as some other flowers to a multiplicity of arrangements. I have heard it said by skilled arrangers that this is so and I would think that this is an added reason for a more catholic approach to the problem by admitting other flowers in the arrangements.

AUTUMN SHOW 1955

PRIZE WINNERS

Class
1. THE AUTUMN ROSES CHALLENGE CUP. A representative group. Challenge Cup and Gold Medal, R. Harkness & Co. Ltd.; Gold Medal, F. Carter and J. Cocker & Sons; Silver Gilt, Frank Cant & Co. and E. W. Stedman Ltd.; Silver, Chaplin Bros.
2. THE DE ESCOFET MEMORIAL CUP. Display of roses on island site. Gold Medal and Cup, C. Gregory & Sons Ltd.; Silver, B. R. Cant & Sons Ltd.
3. A REPRESENTATIVE GROUP, 10 ft. × 4 ft. 1, R. M. Tooke; 2, P. Alpnenaar.

Class
4. THE A. C. TURNER CHALLENGE CUP. Fifteen distinct varieties. 1, G. Longley & Sons.
5. TWO BASKETS OF FLORIBUNDA ROSES. 1, H. Morse & Sons.
6. TWO BASKETS OF POLY POMPON ROSES. No entries.
7. ONE BASKET OF H.T. CUT ROSES. No entries.
8. SPECIMEN BLOOMS IN BOXES. 1, G. Longley & Sons; 2, Clifford Longley (Roses) Ltd.
9. TWELVE BLOOMS IN BOXES. 1, G. Longley & Sons; 2, Clifford Longley (Roses) Ltd.
10. DINNER TABLE DECORATION. 1, Mrs. A. K. Wort; 2, Mrs. C. A. Tisdall.
11. BOWL OF ROSES. 1, Mrs. C. A. Tisdall; 2, Mrs. A. K. Wort.
13. BOWL OF ROSES, 18 stems. 1, J. Clarke; 2, E. M. Allen; 3, F. A. Gibson.
14. BOWL OF FLORIBUNDA ROSES, 12 stems. 1, J. Clarke; 2, Maj.-Gen. R. F. B. Naylor.
15. SIX VASES OF ROSES. 1, E. M. Allen; 2, F. A. Gibson.
16. THE N.R.S. CHALLENGE CUP. Box of twelve specimen blooms, distinct. 1, F. A. Gibson; 2, M. L. Kemp.
17. BOX OF SIX SPECIMEN BLOOMS. 1, F. A. Gibson; 2, J. Clarke.
18. VASE OF SIX SPECIMEN BLOOMS. 1, E. M. Allen; 2, F. A. Gibson; 3, C. C. Williamson.
19. BOWL OF ROSES, 18 stems. 1, W. C. Thorn; 2, Miss H. Boyer; 3, W. J. Northfield.
20. BOWL OF ROSES, 12 stems. 1, E. Royalton Kisch; 2, F. Fairbrother; 3, A. Norman.
21. BOWL OF FLORIBUNDA ROSES, 12 stems. 1, F. Fairbrother; 2, J. H. Wilding; 3, A. Norman.
22. FOUR VASES, distinct varieties. 1, A. Norman; 2, W. J. D. Northfield.
23. THE N.R.S. CHALLENGE CUP. Box of twelve specimen blooms, distinct varieties. 1, J. H. Wilding; 2, A. Norman; 3, W. J. Northfield.
24. BOX OF SIX SPECIMEN BLOOMS. 1, J. H. Wilding; 2, W. J. Northfield.
25. BOX OF SIX SPECIMEN BLOOMS, four varieties. 1, Miss J. E. Fulford; 2, E. Royalton Kisch; 3, J. H. Wilding.
26. VASE OF SIX SPECIMEN BLOOMS. 1, W. J. Northfield.
27. ONE VASE OF FOUR SPECIMEN BLOOMS, distinct varieties. 1, Miss J. E. Fulford; 2, L. P. Roberts; 3, J. H. Wilding.
28. BOWL OF ROSES, 12 stems. 1, G. Walters; 2, B. W. Sampson; 3, J. E. Wiseman.
29. BOWL OF FLORIBUNDA ROSES, 9 stems. 1, Mrs. E. Toogood; 2, Lt.-Col. D. Pope; 3, F. M. Bowen.
30. FOUR VASES DISTINCT VARIETIES. 1, S. Phillips; 2, A. E. Buzza.
31. BOX OF SIX SPECIMEN BLOOMS, four varieties. 1, C. F. Warren; 2, J. R. Hayley; 3, A. E. Buzza.
32. ONE VASE OF THREE SPECIMEN BLOOMS, distinct varieties. 1, G. Walters; 2, N. A. Gibson; 3, Col. W. B. Wright.
33. VASE OF SIX SPECIMEN BLOOMS, four varieties. 1, J. E. Wiseman; 2, N. A. Gibson; 3, C. F. Warren.
34. THREE VASES OF DECORATIVE ROSES, 4 stems. 1, B. W. W. Sampson; 2, C. M. Lister; 3, L. Brown.
35. ONE BOWL OF FLORIBUNDA ROSES, 6 stems. 1, H. C. Wilson; 2, C. M. Lister; 3, H. E. Buxton; 4, E. H. Lockton.
36. ONE BOWL OF FLORIBUNDA ROSES, 6 stems. 1, H. C. Wilson; 2, C. E. Newman; 3, E. H Lockton.
37. BOX OF SIX SPECIMEN BLOOMS. 1, F. R. Willis; 2, W. H. King; 3, L. Brown.
38. VASE OF THREE SPECIMEN BLOOMS, distinct varieties. 1, W. G. H. Cates; 2, C. M. Lister; 3, F. R. Willis.
39. ONE VASE OF THREE SPECIMEN BLOOMS. 1, W. G. H. Cates; 2, B. W. W. Sampson; 3, L. Brown.
40. ONE BOWL OF DECORATIVE ROSES, 12 stems. 1, N. A. Gibson; 2, L. Hollis; 3, Maj.-Gen. R. F. B. Naylor.
41. BOX OF SIX SPECIMEN BLOOMS, distinct varieties. 1, N. A. Gibson; 2, D. W. Chapman.
42. VASE OF SIX SPECIMEN BLOOMS. 1, Maj.-Gen. R. F. B. Naylor; 2, D. W. Chapman; 3, N. A. Gibson.
43. VASE OF DECORATIVE ROSES, 6 stems. 1, T. E. K. Molyneux; 2, J. R. Hinton; 3, W. H. King.
44. BOX OF SIX SPECIMEN BLOOMS, four varieties. 1, M. Beresford; 2, J. T. Watts; 3, Mrs. B. I. Cross.
45. VASE OF SIX SPECIMEN BLOOMS. 1, E. W. J. Wonnacott.
46. VASE OF THREE SPECIMEN BLOOMS, distinct varieties. 1, M. Beresford; 2, E. W. J. Wonnacott; 3, J. T. Watts; 4, Miss I. G. Reynolds.
47. VASE OF THREE SPECIMEN BLOOMS. 1, E. W. J. Wonnacott; 2, H. Bennett; 3, M. Beresford.
48. VASE OF ROSES, 6 stems, distinct varieties. No 1st or 2nd prize; 3, C. F. Dale.
49. VASE OF ROSES, 6 stems. 1, K. B. Ewart; 2, Mrs. B. I. Cross; 3, G. L'E. Wallace.
50. BOWL OF DECORATIVE ROSES, 6 stems. 1, Miss J. E. Fulford; 2, Col. W. B. Wright; 3, F. A. Gibson.
51. THREE VASES OF DECORATIVE ROSES, 4 stems. 1, F. A. Gibson; 2, Lt.-Col. D. Pope.
52. VASE OF SIX SPECIMEN BLOOMS. 1, F. A. Gibson; No second; 3, Lt.-Col. D. Pope.
53. DINNER TABLE DECORATION. 1, Mrs. F. E. Barker; 2, Miss A. M. Aldous; 3, Mrs. M. E. Barton; 4, Mrs. D. Thorn.
54. ARRANGEMENT TO ILLUSTRATE A THEME. 1, Mrs. F. E. Barker; 2, Mrs. M. E. Barton; 3, Miss A. M. Aldous; 4, Mrs. D. Thorn.
55. DECORATION FOR A DINNER TABLE. 1, Mrs. C. Walters; 2, Mrs. H. G. Clacy; 3, Mrs. D. Thorn.
56. ONE BOWL OF MIXED ROSES. 1, Mrs. H. G. Clacy; 2, Mrs. A. E. Griffith; 3, Miss A. M. Aldous.
57. BOWL OF MIXED ROSES, 7 blooms. 1, Miss A. M. Aldous; 2, Mrs. M. E. Barton; 3, Mrs. A. E. Griffith.
58. BOWL OF MIXED ROSES. 1, Mrs. B. I. Cross; 2, L. Howell; 3, C. F. Dale.

THE TRIAL GROUND IN 1955

H. EDLAND

THE glorious weather of 1955 will live, I imagine, for a long time in our memories and be referred to with nostalgia when in the future we suffer our normal summers. If, however, the roses could speak, their comments on 1955 would be far from favourable as for them it was one of the most difficult seasons in memory. In the early months they had to endure the most bitter weather and later suffer severely from heat and drought, which was accompanied by an absolute plague of thrips which sucked at what little moisture remained in their foliage.

It would be more pleasing in writing this report to eulogise over outstanding successes but, alas, truth must out. On four nights in succession in February the temperature at the Trial Ground dropped to zero, and it was heartbreaking when pruning to find good stout stems of two or three years old frosted right back. A peculiar feature of the frost perhaps worth recording, is that whilst the old stems were damaged, the new growth of the previous summer was often damaged less severely. The only explanation I can think of for this was that the heavy frosts were on the ground and not in the air. It was a pity it was not the reverse, as in the circumstances the trees had to be pruned back to within a few inches of the soil. This fortunately did not apply to all varieties; many of the floribundas stood up to the weather well, as did the hardy pillar roses from Herr Kordes. The trees affected worst were the old ramblers on tripods grown simply for decoration of the garden, and their recovery will not be complete until all the old wood is replaced with new. The damage did not prevent them flowering, but after so doing one stem after another collapsed, and the rose foreman was constantly cutting the plants back.

The overall picture of 1955, however, had its bright side, in the remarkable way in which the roses recovered after their hard pruning. Our Hon. Editor asserts that the recovery was due to the good root systems possessed by the plants as a result of the moderate pruning which they had hitherto received, and pointed to the lightly pruned trees in the pruning trials which, although cut down hard of necessity this year, recovered better than those which had been hard pruned previously. In other words, that the root system is controlled by the complementary top growth, the more top growth the more root, and vice versa.

To get back to the trials, the first flowering was good and up to usual standard, and although late, but not so late as in 1954, the trees were in full bloom by the second and third weeks in July.

Looking for further bright spots, I think we can take comfort from the fact that though the Trial Ground is so bleak, it is all to the advantage of members. Roses which do well at St. Albans should do even better in more sheltered situations, and the fact that the roses now on trial have had so searching a test must be an added advantage.

The floribundas are still dominating the awards—I would say unfortunately as my personal taste leans towards the shapely hybrid teas, although perhaps others will disagree with me. In any event the floribundas are fulfilling the popular demand for hardy, free flowering plants, and in 'Queen Elizabeth' we have a variety with the characteristics of the floribunda—i.e. flowering in clusters—as well as the unusual habit of producing some single blooms on individual stems. This variety was a worthy winner of the President's International Trophy awarded for the best new rose of the year. People, Circus, Golden Fleece, Jiminy Cricket and Sweet Repose were other outstanding floribundas which are likely to be in high demand in the next few years.

Of the hybrid teas, Cleopatra is a very attractive shapely bicolour, and one which I am sure will appeal to all for its brightness, and in particular to the ladies for cutting purposes. The ladies will also like Lilac Time for its unusual colour. Chief Seattle is a very full petalled rose with a lovely fragrance, whilst the orange-red blooms of Mojave will make tremendous appeal.

Another item of interest is that the Trial Ground is being extended to take in the front portion of the ground hitherto reserved by The Hertfordshire Institute for fruit trials. This additional land has been included in a new lease to cover a period of twenty-one years. With the increase in the trials, the Council decided the time was ripe to engage an assistant rose foreman, and L. G. Thompson commenced work with the Society on the 4th June last; accommodation has been provided for him. Finally, for the greater security of the roses on trial, a chain link fence along the frontage of the Trial Ground has been erected.

Mr. Lugg, Superintendent of The Hertfordshire Institute, has continued to be a true friend of the Society during the past year and the Committee is sure that it has gained another friend in the new Principal, Mr. Pelham, to whom all good wishes are extended. Our appreciation is again expressed to Mr. Baines for the conscientious way in which he carries out his duties.

For the benefit of new members, it should be explained that the roses on trial are judged under the following headings:

1. Growth (vigour, habit and foliage); 2. Freedom from disease; 3. Beauty of form, or formation of truss and colour; 4. Freedom of flowering; 5. General effect; 6. Fragrance.

Twenty points are given for the first four and ten each for the remaining two items. To get an award a variety must receive a total of seventy points, and not fewer than half marks under the first four headings. This is to ensure that any one outstanding characteristic shall not unduly influence the result.

LIST OF TRIAL GROUND AWARDS 1955
(To which is appended the Show Awards in 1955)

BLOSSOM HILL (flori.) Trial Ground No. 852. Reg. No. 388. *Raiser:* W. Kordes, Germany. *Distributors:* Henry Morse & Sons, Norwich. Growth vigorous and upright, foliage dark green, glossy and plentiful, *16.* Freedom from disease, *17.* Blooms semi-double, 10 petals, 2½ inches across when open. Cream, edges very pale pink. Pretty in bud stage, *16.* Freedom of flowering, *16.* General effect, *5.* Fragrance nil. A variety which if lightly pruned will make a good hedge rose.

BUCCANEER (H.T.). Trial Ground No. 882. Reg. U.S.A. Golden Rapture × unnamed seedling. *Raiser:* H. Swim, Armstrong Nurseries, California. *Distributors:* R. Harkness & Co., Hitchin. Tall upright, very vigorous growth with large dark green foliage, *16.* Freedom from disease, *18.* Blooms large, 5 inches across when fully open. 30–36 petals, centre petals small. Colour, deep brilliant yellow, *15.* Freedom of flowering, *12.* General effect, *5.* Tea fragrance, *6.* This variety may be grown as a shrub rose.

BURNING LOVE (flori.). Trial Ground No. 948. Reg. No. 384. Fanal × Crimson Glory. *Raiser:* M. Tantau, Germany. *Distributors:* Wheatcroft Bros. Ltd., Nottingham. Bushy uniform habit of growth; foliage medium green and plentiful, *15*. Freedom from disease, *17*. Colour a pleasing bright rich scarlet, with 3–5 blooms per truss well spaced; blooms of 22 petals, 4 inches across when open, *17*. Freedom of flowering, *12*. General effect, *6*. Moderate fragrance, *5*.

CIRCUS (flori.). Trial Ground No. 975. Reg. U.S.A. Fandango × Pinocchio. *Raiser:* H. Swim, Armstrong Nurseries, California. *Distributors:* R. Harkness & Co. Ltd., Hitchin. Bushy compact habit of growth; foliage dark green and plants well furnished, *15*. Freedom from disease, *15*. The blooms are very double and multicoloured and have an unusual colour progression; they are first yellow with markings of pink and salmon, changing entirely to pink and salmon in the older blooms; the blooms have 33 petals and are produced in well spaced trusses, *17*. Freedom from disease, *15*. General effect, *6*. Fragrance, *7*. Gold Medal Summer Show 1955.

CLEOPATRA (H.T.). Trial Ground No. 925. Reg. No. 367. (Walter Bentley × Condesa de Sástago) × Spek's Yellow. *Raiser:* W. Kordes, Germany. *Distributors:* Wheatcroft Bros. Ltd., Nottingham. Habit of growth, dwarf, bushy and compact; foliage a glossy light green, *15*. Freedom from disease, *16*. Blooms shapely with 45 medium sized petals, borne singly on stiff stems; bicolour of glowing rich scarlet with old gold reverse; very bright and attractive, *18*. Freedom of flowering, *16*. General effect, *8*. Moderate fragrance, *5*. This should prove an excellent bedding rose. Gold Medal Summer Show 1955.

COUNTESS OF DALKEITH (flori.). Trial Ground No. 867. Reg. No. 383. Sport of Fashion. *Distributors:* Dobbie & Co., Edinburgh. This variety resembles the parent plant in every respect except colour. This is outstanding, a brilliant vermilion flushed with orange. It received for growth, *15*. Freedom from disease, *10*. Colour and form, *16*. Freedom of flowering, *15*. General effect, *8*. Fragrance, *2*.

FIRECRACKER (flori.). Trial Ground No. 821. Reg. No. 364. *Raiser:* E. S. Boerner, Jackson & Perkins Co., New York. *Distributors:* S. McGredy & Son, Portadown. Habit of growth, dwarf and bushy; foliage medium green and abundant, *18*. Freedom from disease, *17*. Blooms orange-scarlet with gold at base, 4½ inches across when opened, produced in even trusses, 12 petals, *17*. Freedom of flowering, *18*. General effect, *8*. Fragrance, *4*. Certificate of Merit Autumn Show 1955.

GARDEN DELIGHT (Hy. Poly.). Trial Ground No. 876. Reg. No. 391. *Raiser:* A. Norman, Guildford. *Distributors:* R. Harkness & Co., Hitchin. Growth vigorous and branching. Foliage medium green and abundant, *15*. Freedom from disease, *15*. Blooms of rosette type 3½ to 4 inches when open, 34 petals. Colour deep rose pink, *14*. Freedom of flowering, *15*. General effect, *5*. Fragrance, *6*.

GOLDEN DELIGHT (flori.). Trial Ground No. 837. Reg. No. 350. Goldilocks × Ellinor Le Grice. *Raiser and Distributor:* E. B. Le Grice, North Walsham. Habit of growth, dwarf and bushy; well furnished with small medium green foliage, *16*. Freedom from disease, *14*. Blooms deep clear yellow, 58 small petals, open 3 inches across; produced in well spaced trusses, *14*. Freedom of flowering, *15*. General effect, *7*. Moderate fragrance, *5*. Certificate of Merit Provincial Show 1955. This may prove to be a very good yellow dwarf floribunda.

GOLDEN FLEECE (flori.). Trial Ground No. 968. Reg. U.S.A. Diamond Jubilee × Yellow Sweetheart. *Raiser:* E. S. Boerner, Jackson & Perkins Co., New York. *Distributors:* S. McGredy & Son, Portadown. Growth uniform and bushy; foliage medium green and plentiful, *15*. Freedom from disease, *15*. Blooms large and full, 26 petals, 4 inches across when open, in clusters; pale yellow which fades with age, but very pleasingly, *15*. Freedom of flowering, *15*. General effect, *6*. Fruity fragrance, *4*. Certificate of Merit Autumn Show 1955.

HENRI MALLERIN (H.T.). Trial Ground No. 665. Reg. France. *Raiser:* Charles Mallerin. Upright and uniform habit of growth, medium green foliage, *15*. Freedom from disease, *17*. Blooms well formed, 48 petals, 4 inches across when open, bright buttercup yellow, *15*. Freedom of flowering, *15*. General effect, *7*. Fragrance, *6*.

JIMINY CRICKET (flori.). Trial Ground No. 923. Reg. U.S.A. Goldilocks × Geranium Red. *Raiser:* E. S. Boerner, Jackson & Perkins Co., New York. *Distributors:* Alex. Dickson & Sons, Ltd., Newtownards, and S. McGredy & Son, Portadown. Habit of growth good, bushy and branching, dark green, rather small foliage, *15*. Freedom from disease, *15*. Blooms coppery-salmon, 3½ inches across when open, 24 petals; produced on well spaced trusses, *13*. Freedom of flowering, *15*. General effect, *6*. Sweet fragrance, *7*. Certificate of Merit Provincial Show 1955.

KATHLEEN FERRIER (flori.). Trial Ground No. 634. Reg. No. 382. Gartenstolz × Shot Silk. *Raisers:* G. A. H. Buisman & Son, Holland. Habit of growth very vigorous and bushy; foliage dark green and glossy, *20*. Freedom from disease, *18*. Blooms deep salmon-pink with lighter shades at base, 18 petals 2½ inches across when open, produced in small clusters on very erect stems, *12*. Freedom of flowering, *15*. General effect, *5*. Sweet fragrance, *6*. A variety which if pruned lightly will be suitable for a hedge.

LA JOLLA (H.T.). Trial Ground No. 808. Reg. U.S.A. Charlotte Armstrong × Contrast. *Raiser:* H. Swim, Armstrong Nurseries, California. *Distributors:* R. Harkness & Co., Hitchin. Habit of growth, vigorous and upright; foliage dark glossy green, *14*. Freedom from disease, *15*. Bud long pointed, producing well formed blooms, 40–45 petals, 5 inches across when open; colour shades of pink, yellow and rose, on long stems, *16*. Freedom of flowering, *12*. General effect, *6*. Fragrance, *7*.

LILAC TIME (H.T.). Trial Ground No. 841. Reg. No. 363. Golden Dawn ×
Luis Brinas. *Raisers and Distributors:* S. McGredy & Son, Portadown. Habit of
growth moderately vigorous and upright; foliage medium green, rather small,
14. Freedom from disease, *12*. Colour, lavender and probably the best yet in
this range; blooms shapely, 30–36 petals and when fully open 3½ inches across,
17. Freedom of flowering, *15*. General effect, *5*. Sweet fragrance, *7*. Certificate
of Merit Summer Show 1955.

MOJAVE (H.T.). Trial Ground No. 877. Reg. U.S.A. Charlotte Armstrong
× Signora. *Raiser:* H. Swim. Armstrong Nurseries, California. *Distributors.*
R. Harkness & Co., Hitchin. Habit of growth, vigorous upright and uniform.
Leathery light green foliage, *15*. Freedom from disease, *15*. Buds pointed,
orange-red, opening to glowing copper, 5 inches across, 22 petals; a very
decorative variety, *17*. Freedom of flowering, *12*. General effect, *7*. Fragrance, *4*.

MONTEZUMA (H.T.). Trial Ground No. 978. Reg. U.S.A. Fandango ×
Floradora. *Raiser:* H. Swim, Armstrong Nurseries, California. *Distributors:*
R. Harkness & Co., Hitchin. Habit of growth vigorous and upright; dark green
leathery foliage, plentifully produced, *18*. Freedom from disease, *18*. Blooms
well formed and large, 5 inches across when open, 33 petals; colour, deep
orange-salmon, *15*. Freedom of flowering, *14*. General effect, *6*. Fragrance, *4*.
It promises to be a good garden and exhibition variety.

PASSION (flori.). Trial Ground No. 731. Reg. No. 381. *Raiser:* J. Gaujard,
France. Vigorous and upright growth with dark green foliage, *16*. Freedom
from disease, *16*. Blooms 4 inches across when open, 36 petals; colour scarlet-
cerise, *12*. Freedom of flowering, *14*. General effect, *7*. Fragrance, *5*.

'QUEEN ELIZABETH' (flori.). Trial Ground No. 971. Reg. U.S.A. Charlotte
Armstrong × Floradora. *Raiser:* W. Lammerts, Los Angeles, U.S.A. *Distributors:* Wheatcroft Bros. Ltd., Nottingham. Habit of growth very vigorous,
bushy and upright; foliage dark green and abundant, *20*. Freedom from disease,
18. Blooms a warm pink freely produced in well spaced trusses also individually
on long stems, 32 petals, blooms 4 inches across when open, *15*. Freedom of
flowering, *18*. General effect, *7*. Fragrance, *4*. Gold Medal Summer Show, and
winner of the President's International Trophy as the best new rose of the year.

ROUNDELAY (H.T.). Trial Ground No. 880. Reg. U.S.A. Charlotte
Armstrong × Floradora. *Raiser:* H. Swim, Armstrong Nurseries, California.
Distributors: R. Harkness & Co., Hitchin. Habit vigorous and upright; dark
green leathery foliage, *16*. Freedom from disease, *14*. Blooms rosette shaped of
65 petals, those in centre very small, 4 inches when open; crimson, *14*. Freedom
of flowering, *14*. General effect, *5*. Fragrance, *7*.

SANDRINGHAM (flori.). Trial Ground No. 851. Reg. No. 369. *Raiser:*
W. Kordes, Germany. *Distributors:* H. Morse & Sons, Norwich. Growth
vigorous and upright, with abundant medium green foliage, *16*. Freedom from

disease, *15*. Blooms creamy-yellow in early stage, 2½ inches across, 30 petals, *12*. Freedom of flowering, *16*. General effect, *5*. Fragrance, *6*. Certificate of Merit Summer Show 1955.

SIDNEY PEABODY (flori.). Trial Ground No. 324. Reg. No. 379. Glory of Rome × poly. seedling. *Raiser:* G. de Ruiter, Holland. *Distributors:* Gandy's Roses Ltd., Rugby. Habit of growth bushy and vigorous; foliage dark green and plentiful, *20*. Freedom from disease, *18*. Blooms cerise, produced in trusses; size when open 3½ inches, 36 petals, *10*. Freedom of flowering, *15*. General effect, *5*. Slight fragrance, *3*.

'SIR WINSTON CHURCHILL' (H.T.). Trial Ground No. 868. Reg. No. 368. *Raisers and Distributors:* Alex. Dickson & Sons Ltd., Newtownards. An excellent growing variety with upright habit; plentiful dark green foliage, *16*. Freedom from disease, *15*. Blooms, pink with salmon shadings of good shape and size, 48 petals, when open 5 inches across, *15*. Freedom of flowering, *15*. General effect, *5*. Fragrance, *5*. Gold Medal Summer Show 1955.

SWEET REPOSE (flori.). Trial Ground No. 323. Reg. No. 376. Geheimrat Duisberg × poly. seedling. *Raiser:* G. de Ruiter, Holland. *Distributors:* Gandy's Roses Ltd., Rugby. A very vigorous growing variety, with dark green foliage freely produced, *16*. Freedom from disease, *15*. Blooms, pink and gold in bud to paler shades with age, producing a pleasing mottled effect. 3 inches across, 27 petals, flowering freely in clusters, *15*. Freedom of flowering, *16*. General effect, *6*. Good fragrance, *7*. Gold Medal Autumn Show 1955.

TONGA (H.T.). Trial Ground No. 903. Reg. No. 312. *Raisers and Distributors:* W. Lowe & Son (Nurseries) Ltd., Beeston. Vigorous and upright habit of growth; foliage dark green and leathery, *16*. Freedom from disease, *14*. Blooms of good form and size, 45 petals and 5 inches across when open; deep golden yellow with outer petals tinged scarlet to pink tones. Very pretty in the bud form, *15*. Freedom of flowering, *14*. General effect, *5*. Good fragrance, *6*.

VILLE DE GAND (H.T.). Trial Ground No. 723. Reg. U.S.A. Georges Chesnel × seedling, × Mme Joseph Perruad × seedling. *Raiser:* J. Gaujard, France. Vigorous, upright, compact habit of growth; bronze-green foliage, *17*. Freedom from disease, *12*. Blooms, a brilliant red which hold their colour well, 25 petals 3½ inches across when open, *16*. Freedom of flowering, *14*. General effect, *6*. Fragrance, *5*.

WILDFIRE (flori.). Trial Ground No. 976. Reg. U.S.A. Minna Kordes × Pinocchio. *Raiser:* H. Swim. Armstrong Nurseries, California. *Distributors:* R. Harkness & Co., Hitchin. Vigorous, well branched and compact habit; plants well clothed with dark green foliage, *16*. Freedom from disease, *15*. Bright scarlet blooms, 12 petals which open to 3 inches across freely produced in large clusters. *15*. Freedom of flowering, *15*. General effect, *7*. Fragrance very slight, *2*.

SHOW AWARDS, 1955

Gold Medals were awarded to:—

BONNIE MAID (flori.). *Raiser and Exhibitor:* E. B. Le Grice, North Walsham. This variety has given an excellent display for the last four years in the Trial Ground, where it received a Certificate in 1952. The blooms are semi-double and 3 inches across when open. The colour is silvery-pink with a deep pink reverse. It is a vigorous growing and attractive variety free of disease. Trial Ground No. 616.

CIRCUS (flori.). *For description see Trial Ground Awards.*

CLEOPATRA (H.T.). *For description see Trial Ground Awards.*

PEOPLE (flori.). Tantau's Triumph × (Käthe Duvigneau × Tantau's Triumph). *Raiser:* M. Tantau, Germany. Exhibited by Wheatcroft Bros. Ltd., Nottingham. An unusual colour. It may be best described as crimson shaded pink, with dark shadings on the curves of the petals. The habit of growth of the plant is bushy and vigorous, and free from disease. The blooms when open are 3 inches across with 26 petals, and are produced in large trusses. Awarded a Trial Ground Certificate and Certificate of Merit in 1954 and this year went on to receive the higher award. Trial Ground No. 686.

QUEEN ELIZABETH' (flori.). *For description see Trial Ground Awards.*

'SIR WINSTON CHURCHILL' (H.T.). *For description see Trial Ground Awards.*

SWEET REPOSE (flori.). *For description see Trial Ground Awards.*

Certificates of Merit were awarded to:

ARDELLE (H.T.). *Raiser:* H. M. Eddie & Sons, Canada. *Exhibitors:* C. Gregory & Son, Chilwell; R. Harkness & Co., Hitchin. A strong growing garden variety which produces blooms of perfect form and of exhibition size. Colour cream with slight tinge of pink, 72 petals. Awarded a Trial Ground Certificate in 1954.

FIRECRACKER (flori.). *For description see Trial Ground Awards.*

GOLDEN DELIGHT (flori.). *For description see Trial Ground Awards.*

GOLDEN FLEECE (flori.). *For description see Trial Ground Awards.*

JIMINY CRICKET (flori.). *For description see Trial Ground Awards.*

LILAC TIME (H.T.) *For description see Trial Ground Awards.*

SANDRINGHAM (flori.). *For description see Trial Ground Awards.*

INTERNATIONAL AWARDS, 1955

ROME
Floribundas. GOLD MEDAL—Fanfare. *Armstrong Nurseries.*
FIRST CERTIFICATE—Circus. *Armstrong Nurseries.*
Climbers. GOLD MEDAL—Grand'mère Jenny. *Francis Meilland.*
Hybrid tea type. FIRST CERTIFICATE—Montezuma. *Armstrong Nurseries.*

BAGATELLE, PARIS
GOLD MEDAL—Golden Fleece (flori.). *E. S. Boerner, Jackson & Perkins.*
FIRST CERTIFICATE—Circus. (flori.). *Armstrong Nurseries.*
SECOND CERTIFICATE—Montezuma. (H.T.). *Armstrong Nurseries.*
THIRD CERTIFICATE—Soraya. (H.T.). *Francis Meilland.*
DECORATIVES CERTIFICATE—Fanfare (flori.). *Armstrong Nurseries.*

GENEVA
GOLD MEDAL (H.T. type)—Montezuma. *Armstrong Nurseries.*
SILVER MEDAL (H.T. type)—Cote Rotie. *Chabert.*
CERTIFICATES (H.T. type)—Impeccable. *Chabert.* Soraya. *Francis Meilland.*
GOLD MEDAL (flori.)—Circus. *Armstrong Nurseries.*
SILVER MEDAL (flori.)—Fanfare. *Armstrong Nurseries.*
CERTIFICATE (flori.)—Golden Fleece. *E. S. Boerner, Jackson & Perkins.*

LYONS
GOLD MEDAL (H.T. type)—Soraya. *Francis Meilland.*
SILVER GILT MEDAL (H.T. type)—Miss France. *Jean Gaujard.*
FIRST CERTIFICATE (H.T. type)—Impeccable. *Chabert.*
CERTIFICATES—Mme Camille Laurens. *Dorieux.* Message. *Francis Meilland.*

TOKIO
PRIZE OF HONOUR. Eve. *Jean Gaujard.*

BADEN BADEN
PRIZE OF HONOUR—Irma (H.T.). *W. Kordes.*
SILVER MEDAL—Goldbusch (H.T.) *W. Kordes.*
BRONZE MEDALS—Hamburger Phoenix. (Kordesii perp. cl.). *W. Kordes.*
Zweibrucken. (Kordesii perp. cl.). *W. Kordes.* Coral Dawn. (Perp. cl.).
E. S. Boerner, Jackson & Perkins. Leverkusen. (Kordesii). *W. Kordes.*
CERTIFICATES OF MERIT—Dortmund. (Kordesii perp. cl.). *W. Kordes.* Pink
Cloud. (Perp. cl.). *E. S. Boerner, Jackson & Perkins.*

Floribunda awards
GOLD MEDAL—Buisman's Triumph. *Buisman.*
SILVER MEDAL—Circus. *Armstrong Nurseries.*
BRONZE MEDALS—Fanfare. *Armstrong Nurseries.* Ama. *W. Kordes.*
Morgensonne. *W. Kordes.*
CERTIFICATES OF MERIT—Red Cap. *Armstrong Nurseries.* Kathleen Ferrier.
Buisman. Korona. *W. Kordes.*

A number of other awards were made to unnamed varieties by Tantau,
Meilland, Kordes, Gaujard and Jackson & Perkins.

THE ROSE ANALYSIS

H. EDLAND

IN the past, it has been customary to give in the respective tables the total number of points scored by each variety. These have now been omitted, as it is felt that owing to the great disparity in the pointings between the variety at the top of the table and that at the bottom, a false impression of the merits of the respective varieties is created. In last year's table for "varieties producing large specimen blooms suitable for exhibition", the variety Peace received 492 votes against 65 by Golden Melody, and to take another example, in the table for "Roses for General Garden Cultivation" Ena Harkness received 443 against 60 for Rubaiyat. Now both Peace and Ena Harkness are exceptional varieties, but when one considers how the performance of all roses varies according to soil conditions and other factors, it is perhaps misleading to indicate differences so marked. Perhaps the fault lies in the method employed for pointing, yet I do not know a fairer way of assessing merit in a table when 24 varieties are listed, than to give 24 points to the rose at the top of each voter's list and one point to the last variety mentioned. At any rate this method has again been adopted to arrive at the results, while suppressing the actual points received by each. Any suggestions from members to improve on this method will be most welcome, as the problem is a difficult one.

In other respects the Analysis follows on similar lines to last year, and we are again indebted to a large number of enthusiasts for their help. Before listing their names, however, perhaps a comment on the tables will not be out of place. My first thought was one of surprise that in a very difficult year with conditions very much different from normal, there were not more changes in the lists, but on second thoughts realized it would have been folly on the part of the voters to have abandoned established favourites which have proved their worth over a period of years. This mitigates of course against inclusion of the new varieties, which perhaps is advisable until they have thoroughly proved themselves, yet when one is impressed by a particular variety, it is a little disappointing to find it omitted from the tables, or placed very low down. I suppose everyone studying the lists will have their own opinions of the voting and it would be a sad look-out if there were not disagreement over the inclusion of some varieties to the exclusion of others. In this respect I think that Ethel Sanday should be much higher than twenty-fourth in the list of Roses for General Garden Cultivation (South), that Anne Letts should be included, and that The Doctor is much too highly placed in the respective lists. I could go on but such thoughts are purely personal and arise out of my own experience of particular varieties. If members care to send in similar criticisms then I will know the Analysis is of interest!

The names of the voters were:

Miss A. M. Aldous (Essex), J. H. Alexander (Midlothian), E. M. Allen (Devon), L. A. Anstiss (Middx.), Miss M. Bairstow (Herts.), Mrs. M. E. Barton (Essex), Messrs. Bees Ltd. (Cheshire), A. D. Bide (Surrey), G. D. Burch (Bucks.), S. Carson (Northumberland), F. Carter (Berks.), G. W. Chadwick (Yorks.), Mrs. H. G. Clacy (Surrey), H. G. Clacy (Surrey), L. W. Condliffe (Midlothian), Messrs. D. & W. Croll (Angus), Mrs. G. E. Dalton (Surrey), A. Dickson (N. Ireland), J. E. Eld (Somerset), F. Fairbrother (Devon), A. Fryer (Cheshire), G. Geary (Leics.), F. A. Gibson (Lancs.), Mrs. L. A. Gotobed (Middx.), A. W. J. Green (Bucks.), Mrs. A. E. Griffith (Finchley), Mrs. W. E. Harkness (Herts.), J. N. Hart (Middx.), N. P. Harvey (Kent), G. L. Hey (Beds.), F. H. Hicks (Berks.), L. Hollis (Surrey), Mrs. M. Johnson (Flintshire), M. L. Kemp (Essex), Mrs. M. S. Latimer (Bucks.), A. W. Lowe (Notts.), J. W. Mattock (Oxford), S. McGredy (N. Ireland), Oliver Mee (Cheshire), A. J. Merryweather (Notts.), E. H. Morse (Norfolk), Maj.-Gen. R. F. B. Naylor (Herts.), A. E. Nevard (Essex), A. Norman (Surrey), Miss E. H. Parker (Herts.), Mrs. M. Pearce (Bucks.), Miss E. Pickering (Herts.), Lt.-Col. D. Pope (Somerset), C. F. Roberts (Essex), Leonard P. Roberts (Surrey), J. Roscoe (Lancs.), W. J. W. Sanday (Somerset), H. W. Stedman (Northants), W. H. Sumpster (Sussex), G. S. Thomas (Surrey), Mrs. W. C. Thorn (Essex), W. C. Thorn (Essex), F. E. Timbrell (Somerset), Mrs. Tisdall (Essex), C. C. Townsend (Worcs.), C. F. Warren (Cheshire), Miss N. Watson (Yorks.), J. C. Watson (Yorks.), Mrs. Wheatcroft (Notts.), Mrs. R. White (Bucks.), R. White (Bucks.), Mrs. M. Wilding (Lancs.), J. H. Wilding (Lancs.), Mrs. F. Wort (Surrey).

'PEOPLE' (flor.)

Tantau's Triumph × (Käthe Duvigneau × Tantau's Triumph.)
Raised by Math. Tantau, Holstein, Germany.
Trial Ground No. 686. Reg. No. 354. Trial Ground Certificate.
Certificate of Merit, Autumn Show, 1954.
For description see page 144, "Rose Annual", 1955

South

Position	NAME	Introduced	COLOUR
1	†Peace	1942	Golden yellow, edged pink
2	Karl Herbst	1950	Scarlet
3	★William Harvey	1948	Dusky scarlet red
4	Show Girl	1949	Deep pink
5	★†Ena Harkness	1946	Rich glowing red
6	★†The Doctor	1936	Bright silvery rose
7	★Red Ensign	1948	Deep crimson
8	Dorothy Anderson	1949	Bright rose pink
9	Eden Rose	1950	Carmine pink
10	Sam McGredy	1937	Buff shaded cream
11	McGredy's Ivory	1929	Creamy white shaded yellow
12	Ethel Sanday	1952	Yellow flushed apricot
13	†McGredy's Yellow	1929	Yellow
14	Gordon Eddie	1949	Buff orange
15	★†Crimson Glory	1935	Deep velvety crimson
16	Rex Anderson	1937	Cream shaded gold
17	Directeur Guèrin	1935	Creamy yellow
17	★Barbara Richards	1930	Maize yellow, flushed rose
17	Ulster Monarch	1951	Buff
20	†Phyllis Gold	1934	Golden yellow
21	Glory of Rome	1937	Reddish pink
22	★Golden Melody	1934	Chamois yellow
23	Charles Lamplough	1920	Lemon white
24	J. H. Ellis	1948	Deep pink

North

Position	NAME	Introduced	COLOUR
1	†Peace	1942	Golden yellow, edged pink
2	Karl Herbst	1950	Scarlet
3	Eden Rose	1950	Bright madder pink
4	Show Girl	1949	Deep pink
5	★†The Doctor	1936	Bright silvery rose
6	★Wm. Harvey	1948	Dusky scarlet red
7	★Red Ensign	1948	Deep crimson
8	★†Ena Harkness	1946	Rich glowing red
9	★Barbara Richards	1930	Maize yellow, flushed rose
10	Brilliant	1952	Deep scarlet
11	Opera	1949	Coppery orange red
12	★Golden Melody	1934	Pale golden yellow
13	Symphonie	1948	Carmine
14	Dorothy Anderson	1949	Bright rose pink
15	McGredy's Ivory	1929	Creamy white, shaded yellow
15	†McGredy's Yellow	1933	Yellow
17	Gordon Eddie	1949	Buff orange
18	Glory of Rome	1937	Reddish pink
18	Margaret	1954	Bright pink
20	Bacchus	1951	Bright scarlet
21	Ethel Sanday	1952	Yellow flushed apricot
22	†Grand'mère Jenny	1950	Peach outer petals shaded pink
22	★†Crimson Glory	1935	Deep velvet crimson
24	Rex Anderson	1937	Cream shaded gold

★ Most fragrant.   † Most suitable for standards.

South

Position	NAME	Introduced	COLOUR
1	†Peace	1942	Golden yellow, edged pink
2	*†Ena Harkness	1946	Rich glowing red
3	Karl Herbst	1950	Scarlet
4	†Spek's Yellow	1947	Golden yellow
5	†McGredy's Yellow	1933	Pale yellow
6	Lady Belper	1948	Bronze orange
7	†Grand'mère Jenny	1950	Peach, outer petals shaded pink
8	Picture	1932	Clear rose pink
9	*†Crimson Glory	1935	Deep velvety crimson
10	Eden Rose	1950	Deep pink
11	†Mrs. Sam McGredy	1929	Coppery orange, splashed red
12	†President Hoover	1930	Orange and red
13	*†Lady Sylvia	1927	Flesh pink, yellow base
14	Violinista Costa	1937	Orange scarlet, strawberry
15	Opera	1949	Coppery orange red
16	*Golden Melody	1934	Buff yellow
17	*†The Doctor	1936	Bright silvery rose
18	Sutter's Gold	1950	Golden yellow
19	Show Girl	1949	Deep pink
20	Virgo	1947	White
21	*†Golden Dawn	1929	Pale lemon yellow
22	Josephine Bruce	1953	Velvety crimson
23	Rubaiyat	1949	Deep cerise
24	Ethel Sanday	1952	Yellow–flushed apricot

North

Position	NAME	Introduced	COLOUR
1	†Peace	1942	Golden yellow, edged pink
2	*†Ena Harkness	1946	Rich glowing red
3	Opera	1949	Coppery orange red
4	†Grand'mère Jenny	1950	Peach, outer petals shaded pink
5	†McGredy's Yellow	1933	Pale yellow
6	†Spek's Yellow	1947	Golden yellow
7	Picture	1932	Clear rose pink
8	Lady Belper	1948	Bronze orange
9	†Mrs. Sam McGredy	1929	Coppery orange, splashed red
10	Virgo	1947	White
11	Sutter's Gold	1950	Golden yellow
12	Eden Rose	1950	Deep pink
13	Karl Herbst	1950	Scarlet
14	*†Crimson Glory	1935	Deep velvety crimson
15	*Golden Melody	1934	Buff yellow
16	*†Lady Sylvia	1927	Flesh pink, yellow base
17	*†The Doctor	1936	Bright silvery rose
18	*†Shot Silk	1924	Pink and salmon
19	Monique	1949	Silvery pink
20	Barbara Richards	1930	Maize yellow, flushed rose
21	*Hector Deane	1938	Brilliant salmon cerise
22	†Phyllis Gold	1934	Golden yellow
23	Independence	1950	Pure orange scarlet
24	Michèle Meilland	1945	Soft salmon pink

* Most fragrant. † Most suitable for standards.

ROSES SUITABLE FOR GARDEN PURPOSES

And which will also give large specimen blooms for exhibition

Position	NAME	Introduced	COLOUR
1	*Peace*	1942	Golden yellow, edged pink
2	*Ena Harkness*	1946	Rich glowing red
3	*Karl Herbst*	1950	Scarlet
4	*McGredy's Yellow*	1933	Pale yellow
5	*Crimson Glory*	1935	Deep velvety crimson
6	*The Doctor*	1936	Bright silvery rose
7	*Opera*	1949	Deep orange carmine
8	*Show Girl*	1949	Deep pink
9	*Red Ensign*	1948	Deep crimson
10	*William Harvey*	1948	Dusky scarlet red
11	*Grand'mère Jenny*	1950	Yellow, shaded pink
12	*Golden Melody*	1934	Buff yellow
13	*Phyllis Gold*	1934	Golden yellow
14	*Ethel Sanday*	1954	Yellow, flushed apricot
15	*McGredy's Ivory*	1929	Creamy white, shaded yellow
16	*Mrs. Sam McGredy*	1929	Coppery orange, splashed red
17	*Barbara Richards*	1930	Maize yellow, flushed rose
18	*Symphonie*	1948	Carmine
19	*Margaret*	1954	Rose pink
20	*Golden Dawn*	1929	Pale lemon yellow
21	*Gordon Eddie*	1949	Buff orange
22	*Dorothy Anderson*	1949	Bright rose pink
23	*Glory of Rome*	1937	Reddish pink
24	*Lady Belper*	1948	Bronze orange

CLIMBERS AND RAMBLERS, SUMMER FLOWERING ONLY

Position	NAME	Introduced	COLOUR
1	*Albertine*	1921	Coppery chamois to salmon
2	*Paul's Scarlet*	1916	Scarlet
3	*Chaplin's Pink*	1929	Warm pink
4	*Emily Gray*	1916	Golden yellow
5	*Dr. Van Fleet*	1910	Soft blush
6	*Crimson Conquest*	1931	Scarlet
7	*Excelsa*	1909	Bright rose to crimson red
8	*American Pillar*	1902	Clear rose, pink eye
9	*Alberic Barbier*	1900	Yellow bud to cream white
10	*Crimson Shower*	1951	Crimson
11	*Dorothy Perkins*	1901	Rose pink
12	*Easlea's Golden Rambler*	1932	Golden yellow

FLORIBUNDA ROSES

Position	NAME	Introduced	COLOUR
1	Frensham	1946	Deep scarlet
2	Masquerade	1950	Yellow, pink and red
3	Fashion	1947	Coral peach
4	Alain	1946	Bright carmine red
5	Dainty Maid	1938	Carmine, shaded pink
6	Orange Triumph	1938	Orange scarlet
7	Donald Prior	1934	Scarlet, flush pink
8	Vogue	1949	Rose dove pink
9	Border King	1950	Brilliant strawberry red
10	Goldilocks	1945	Deep yellow
11	Red Favourite	1951	Dark glowing crimson
12	Border Queen	1949	Salmon pink to orange red
13	Dusky Maiden	1947	Deep crimson
14	Moulin Rouge	1952	Glowing scarlet
15	Karen Poulsen	1933	Intense scarlet
16	United Nations	1947	Pink shaded gold
17	Cocorico	1950	Geranium red, edged darker
18	De Ruiter's Herald	1948	Orange scarlet
19	Anne Poulsen	1935	Crimson red
20	Concerto	1953	Cinnebar red
21	Else Poulsen	1924	Bright rose pink
22	Poulsen's Bedder	1949	Rosy pink
23	Mary	1947	Orange cerise
24	Ma Perkins	1952	Pale pink, edged deeper

LARGE FLOWERED CLIMBERS AND CLIMBING SPORTS

Position	NAME	Introduced	COLOUR
1	Lemon Pillar	1915	Pale sulphur yellow
2	Cl. Etoile de Hollande	1932	Bright dark red
3	Cl. Mrs. Sam McGredy	1938	Coppery orange scarlet
4	Cl. Crimson Glory	1941	Deep velvet crimson
5	Mermaid	1917	Pale sulphur yellow
6	Cl. Shot Silk	1937	Cerise shaded orange salmon
7	Cl. Madame Butterfly	1925	Pink shaded apricot
8	Cl. Golden Dawn	1935	Pale lemon yellow
9	Cl. Madame Edouard Herriot	1921	Coral red shaded yellow
10	Allen Chandler	1924	Vivid scarlet
11	Cl. Lady Sylvia	1933	Light pink, yellow base
12	Cl. Madame Caroline Testout	1902	Bright warm pink

PERPETUAL OR REPEAT FLOWERING CLIMBERS

Position	NAME	Introduced	COLOUR
1	Mermaid	1917	Pale sulphur yellow
2	Zephirine Drouhin	1868	Bright carmine pink
3	New Dawn	1930	Blush pink
4	Elegance	1938	Spectrum yellow
5	Cl. Goldilocks	1952	Citron yellow
6	Guinée	1937	Blackish garnet, mottled scarlet
7	High Noon	1946	Deep yellow
8	Danse du Feu	1954	Orange cinnabar
9	Meg	1954	Shell pink tinged apricot
10	Phyllis Bide	1923	Pale gold, shaded carmine pink
11	Coral Dawn	1953	Rose pink
12	Aloha	1949	Buff pink, deeper pink reverse

DWARF POLYANTHA ROSES

Position	NAME	Introduced	COLOUR
1	Paul Crampel	1930	Deep orange red
2	Cameo	1932	Flesh pink
3	Golden Salmon Superior	1926	Vivid golden salmon
4	Coral Cluster	1920	Pale coral pink
5	Gloria Mundi	1929	Glowing orange
6	Little Dorritt	1930	Coral salmon
7	Ellen Poulsen	1912	Bright cherry red
8	Edith Cavell	1918	Bright crimson, white eye
9	Ideal	1921	Dark scarlet
10	Gloire du Midi	1932	Brilliant orange scarlet

ROSES FOR HEDGES

This table includes varieties suitable for hedges 4–5 ft. high without support

Position	NAME	Introduced	COLOUR
1	Frensham	1946	Deep scarlet
2	Dainty Maid	1938	Carmine shaded pink
3	'Queen Elizabeth'	1955	Pink
4	Penelope	1924	Pink, shaded salmon
5	Orange Triumph	1938	Orange scarlet
6	Peace	1942	Yellow, flushed pink
7	Elmshorn	1950	Bright crimson
8	Salmon Spray	1937	Salmon pink shaded carmine
9	Kirsten Poulsen	1925	Bright cherry red
10	Cornelia	1925	Apricot, flushed pink
11	Berlin	1950	Bright red
12	Elmshorn	1950	Light crimson

ROSES FOR HEDGES

This table includes varieties suitable for hedges over 5 ft. excluding ramblers and climbers

Position	NAME	Introduced	COLOUR
1	R. moyesii	1894	Dusky scarlet
2	Conrad F. Meyer	1899	Silvery pink
3	Bonn	1949	Bright orange scarlet
4	Blanc Double de Coubert	1892	White
5	Zephirine Drouhin	1868	Bright carmine pink
6	Berlin	1949	Bright red
7	Wilhelm	1934	Dark red
8	Penelope	1924	Pink shaded salmon
9	Prosperity	1919	White
10	Felicia	1928	Salmon pink, shaded yellow
11	Roseraie de l'Häy	1901	Magenta
12	Nevada	1927	White

SHRUB ROSES — PERPETUAL OR REPEAT FLOWERING

Position	NAME	COLOUR	Height in feet
1	Wilhelm (hyb. mosc.)	Dark red	6
2	Elmshorn (hyb. mosc.)	Bright crimson	5
3	Bonn (hyb. mosc.)	Orange scarlet	6
4	Penelope (hyb. mosc.)	Pink, shaded salmon	5
5	Zephirine Drouhin (bourbon)	Bright carmine pink	5
6	Prosperity (hyb. mosc.)	White	5
7	Cornelia (hyb. mosc.)	Apricot flushed pink	5–6
8	Berlin (hyb. mosc.)	Bright red	5–6
9	Felicia (hyb. mosc.)	Salmon pink, shaded yellow	6
10	Pax (hyb. mosc.)	White	6
11	Nevada	Milky white	6
12	Schneezwerg (hyb. rugosa)	White	5
13	Roseraie de l'Häy (hyb. rugosa)	Magenta	6
14	Vanity (hyb. mosc.)	Crimson	6–9
15	R. rugosa var. typica	Deep rose	4–5
16	Stanwell Perpetual (hyb. spin.)	White	5–6
17	Eva (hyb. mosc.)	Carmine red	4–5
18	Grandmaster (hyb. mosc.)	Buff pink	4

SHRUB ROSES—SUMMER FLOWERING ONLY

Position	NAME	COLOUR	Height in feet
1	R. moyesii	Dusky scarlet, brilliant red heps	8–10
2	R. hugonis	Yellow	7
3	Maiden's Blush (alba)	Warm pink	6–8
4	Celestial (alba)	Light blush	5–6
5	R. gallica var. versicolor	Light red with white stripes and blotches	4
6	R. gallica var. officinalis	Light red	4
7	R. gallica var. complicala	Pink	5
8	R. cantabrigiensis	Yellow	8
9	R. rubrifolia	Deep pink with greyish-purple foliage	6
10	R. alba	White	8
11	R. spinosirsima var. altaica	Cream white	6
12	Frühlingsanfang (hyb. spin.)	Pale yellow	8
13	R. xanthina	Yellow	8
14	Fruhlingsgold (hyb. spin.)	Yellow	9
15	Variegata di Bologna (bourbon)	White striped, deep pink	4
16	Fantin Latour (centi.)	Blush pink	4
17	Koenigin van Danemark (alba)	Deep pink	5
18	Mme Hardy (damas.)	White	4
19	R. willmottiae	Deep pink	9
20	R. omeiensis var. pteracantha	White	12

ROSES WITH LONG STEMS FOR INDOOR DECORATION

Position	NAME	Introduced	COLOUR
1	Ena Harkness	1946	Rich glowing red
2	Spek's Yellow	1948	Golden yellow
3	Picture	1932	Clear rose pink
4	Mrs. Sam McGredy	1929	Coppery orange, splashed red
5	Lady Sylvia	1927	Flesh pink, yellow base
6	President Herbert Hoover	1930	Orange and red
7	Peace	1942	Golden yellow edged pink
8	Virgo	1947	White
9	Sutter's Gold	1950	Yellow and pink
10	First Love	1952	Light salmon
11	McGredy's Yellow	1933	Pale yellow
12	Mme Butterfly	1920	Pink, shaded apricot
13	Comtesse Vandal	1932	Reddish copper, to pink
14	Michèle Meilland	1945	Soft salmon pink
15	Grand'mère Jenny	1950	Peach outer petals shaded pink

MINIATURE ROSES

Posi-tion	NAME	COLOUR
1	*Josephine Wheatcroft (Rosina)*	Pure yellow
2	*Pour Toi*	White
3	*Perle de Montserrat*	Pink
3	*Perle d' Alcanada (Baby Crimson)*	Crimson
5	*Maid Marion*	Rich velvet red
6	*Sweet Fairy*	Apple blossom pink
7	*Humpty Dumpty*	Carmine pink
8	*Prince Charming*	Crimson scarlet
9	*Cinderella*	White tinted pink
10	*R. rouletti*	Rose pink
11	*Peon (Tom Thumb)*	Crimson with white eye
12	*Little Princess*	White

AUDIT OF NEWER ROSES

This table includes only roses introduced in this country since January 1st, 1951

Posi-tion	NAME	Intro-duced	COLOUR
1	*Ethel Sanday (H.T.)*	1952	Yellow flushed apricot
2	*Margaret (H.T.)*	1954	Bright pink
3	*Josephine Bruce (H.T.)*	1953	Velvet crimson
4	*Bacchus (H.T.)*	1951	Bright scarlet
5	*First Love (H.T.)*	1952	Pale pink
6	*Moulin Rouge (flori.)*	1952	Glowing scarlet
7	*Pink Spiral (H.T.)*	1952	Rose pink
8	*Chrysler Imperial (H.T.)*	1952	Maroon red
9	*Brilliant (H.T.)*	1952	Deep scarlet
10	*Red Favourite (flori.)*	1951	Glowing dark crimson
11	*Concerto (flori.)*	1953	Bright glowing scarlet
12	*Tzigane (H.T.)*	1951	Vermilion red, reverse chrome yellow
13	*Korona (flori.)*	1953	Orange scarlet
14	*Golden Masterpiece (H.T.)*	1953	Deep lemon yellow
15	*Queen Elizabeth (flori.)*	1955	Clear self pink
16	*Royalist (H.T.)*	1953	Bright deep cerise pink
17	*Bridal Robe (H.T.)*	1953	Ivory white
18	*Helen Traubel (H.T.)*	1953	Pale salmon pink

PRESIDENTS AND DEAN HOLE MEDALLISTS
OF THE NATIONAL ROSE SOCIETY

1877–1904   The Very Rev. DEAN HOLE, V.M.H.

1905–06   CHARLES E. SHEA
1907–08   E. B. LINDSELL
1909–10   Rev. F. PAGE-ROBERTS
1911–12   Rev. J. H. PEMBERTON
1913–14   CHARLES E. SHEA
1915–16   EDWARD MAWLEY, V.M.H.
1917–18   Sir EDWARD HOLLAND
1919–20   H. E. DARLINGTON, V.M.H.
1921–22   Sir EDWARD HOLLAND
1923–24   SYDNEY F. JACKSON
1925–26   C. C. WILLIAMSON
1927–28   H. R. DARLINGTON, V.M.H.
1929–30   ARTHUR JOHNSON
1931–32   HERBERT OPPENHEIMER
1933–34   Dr. A. H. WILLIAMS
1935–36   Major A. D. G. SHELLEY, R.E.
1937–38   HERBERT OPPENHEIMER
1939–40   JOHN N. HART
1941–42   CHARLES H. RIGG
1943–44   HERBERT OPPENHEIMER
1945–46   A. NORMAN ROGERS
1947–48   A. E. GRIFFITH
1949–50   E. J. BALDWIN
1951–52   D. L. FLEXMAN
1953–54   WILLIAM E. MOORE
1955–56   OLIVER MEE, O.B.E.

DEAN HOLE MEDALLISTS
(In addition to the Presidents above)

1912   GEORGE DICKSON, V.M.H.
1919   GEORGE PAUL
1921   S. McGREDY
1923   Miss E. WILLMOTT, F.L.S.
1925   COURTNEY PAGE
1930   Dr. J. CAMPBELL HALL
1930   WILLIAM E. NICKERSON
1935   WALTER EASLEA
1936   ALISTER CLARK
1942   Dr. HORACE J. McFARLAND
1945   Dr. H. V. TAYLOR, O.B.E.
1948   Dr. G. E. DEACON
1950   JOHN RAMSBOTTOM, O.B.E., D.Sc., M.A.
1940   F. S. HARVEY-CANT, M.B.E.
1952   BERTRAM PARK, O.B.E., Ch. Merite Agricole
1952   Dr. A. S. THOMAS
1954   W. E. HARKNESS

REVENUE ACCOUNT FOR THE YEAR ENDED 31st DECEMBER, 1955

1954 £		£	£	£
	PUBLICATIONS			
9,602	Expenditure	9,504		
1,000	Addition to Reserve for new Editions	1,000		
10,602		10,504		
309	Less Sales	271		
1,050	Advertising Revenue	1,203		
		1,474		
9,243			9,030	
	SHOWS			
1,386	Prize Monies, Medals and Plate	1,364		
600	Expenses	1,093		
1,986		2,457		
406	Less Proceeds	370		
1,580			2,087	
1,071	**TRIAL GROUND** Expenditure		1,559	
	SECRETARIAL AND OFFICE EXPENSES			
3,158	Salaries, Pensions and Assistance	3,940		
619	Rent, etc.	629		
982	Printing and Stationery	1,280		
2,139	Postages, Telephone, Hire of Rooms, etc.	2,440		
282	Repairs, Renewals and Alterations to Office	5		
105	Auditors' Fees	105		
7,285			8,399	
837	**ADVERTISING AND PUBLICITY**		1,000	
	DONATION			
—	Gardeners' Royal Benevolent Institution		250	
	PRESENTATION			
	Rose Gardens at Buckingham Palace and Harewood House		152	
			247	
200	**OFFICE EQUIPMENT**—Amount written off		200	
20,216			22,724	
	BALANCE			
5,027	Excess of Revenue over Expenditure for the year		4,823	
25,243			27,547	

1954 £		£	£
	SUBSCRIPTIONS AND AFFILIATION FEES		
23,330	Subscriptions	25,490	
426	Affiliation Fees	477	
23,756		25,967	
250	**LEGACY**		—
	INCOME FROM INVESTMENTS, ETC.		
1,189	Gross		1,538
48	**PROFIT ON SALE OF BADGES**		42
25,243			27,547

162

BALANCE SHEET, 31st DECEMBER, 1955

Liabilities

1954 £		£	£
	SURPLUS		
33,954	Balance 1st January, 1955	33,954	
	Add Excess of Revenue over Expenditure for the year ended 31st December, 1955	4,823	
	Proceeds of Realisation of Louisiana Power & Light Co. and Standard Gas & Electric Light Co. Shares	646	
33,954			39,423
	SPECIAL FUNDS		
	P. P. Gaskell Prize Fund	100	
	L. Hewlett Prize Fund	100	
200			200
	RESERVE FOR NEW EDITIONS OF PUBLICATIONS		
	Balance 1st January, 1955	3,000	
	Add Charge against Revenue Account for the year	1,000	
3,000			4,000
	CURRENT LIABILITIES		
391	Sundry Creditors	283	
3,792	Subscriptions received in advance (excluding Life Members)	3,639	
3,792			3,922
41,337			**47,545**

AUDITORS' REPORT

To the Members, National Rose Society,

We have audited the above Balance Sheet dated 31st December, 1955, and the Revenue Account for the year ended on that date, and have obtained all the information and explanations we have required. In our opinion such Balance Sheet and Revenue Account are properly drawn up so as to exhibit a true and correct view of the state of the Society's affairs according to the best of our information and explanations given us and as shown by the Books of the Society. We have verified the Securities representing the Investments of your Society at 31st December, 1955, and have found the same to be in order.

BRANNAN, WHITE AND CHARLTON,
Chartered Accountants, Auditors.

23 LAWRENCE LANE, LONDON, E.C.2.
10th January, 1956.

Assets

1954 £		£	£	£
	FIXED ASSETS			
	Freehold Houses at Cost			
	23 Orchard Close, St. Albans		2,028	
	36 Hazelwood Drive, St. Albans		2,537	
2,028				4,565
	Office Equipment, etc.			
	Balance 1st January, 1955		800	
	Additions at Cost		247	
			1,047	
	Less Amount written off		247	
800				800
125	Library as valued by the Secretary			125
2,953				5,490
	INVESTMENTS at Cost			
	£3,400 0 0 Conversion Stock 3¼% 1961 or after		2,582	
	£4,887 18 9 British Transport 3% Guaranteed Stock 1978/88		3,617	
	£1,500 0 0 Mersey Docks and Harbour Board 3½% Debenture Stock 1970/80		1,084	
	£300 0 0 Metropolitan Water "B" 3% Stock		195	
	£2,000 0 0 2½% Defence Bonds		2,000	
	£1,000 0 0 Savings Bonds 3% 1955/65		1,000	
	£2,000 0 0 Savings Bonds 3% 1960/70		1,968	
	£3,486 1 6 Savings Bonds 2½% 1964/67		3,547	
	£500 0 0 2½% National War Bonds "A"		500	
	£20,911 0 0 4% Consolidated Stock		19,243	
33,744				35,736
(35,748)	(Market Value 31st December, 1955, £33,245)			
	INVESTMENTS PRESENTED TO THE SOCIETY (not valued) 27 New England Electric System Common Shares			
	CURRENT ASSETS			
2,075	Stock of Publications and Badges as valued by the Secretary		1,098	
2,315	Cash at Bankers on Deposit and Current Account and in Hand		4,404	
250	Income Tax Recoverable		817	
				6,319
41,337				**47,545**

163

REPORT OF THE COUNCIL
FOR THE YEAR ENDED 31st DECEMBER, 1955

HER MAJESTY THE QUEEN

Her Majesty The Queen has honoured the Society by graciously accepting a number of trees for the new rose beds being constructed at Buckingham Palace.

ROYAL PATRON

The Council is pleased to report that our Patron, H.R.H. The Princess Royal, honoured the Society by a visit to the Provincial Show at Leeds and received a great welcome. Her Royal Highness has further honoured the Society by accepting a number of rose trees of modern varieties for her gardens at Harewood.

MEMBERSHIP

The membership, which started to grow rapidly from the end of the war, continued its upward progress in 1955. 7,789 new members were enrolled against losses 4,781 from resignations and deaths. The net gain over the year of 3,008 now gives a total membership of 43,808. The Council hopes that improvements in *The Rose Annual* proposed for 1956, together with the revival of the Spring Show, of which more details are given under the appropriate headings, will tend to increase interest and enthusiasm. Meanwhile the Council expresses thanks to all members who have helped in furthering the interests of the Society, making its grateful acknowledgment of the very considerable help in this respect given by members of the trade.

FINANCE

The Revenue Account for the year shows an excess of Revenue over Expenditure of £4,823 after providing a further £1,000 to be added to the Reserve for New Editions of Publications which now stands at £4,000. During the year £1,684 was spent on a new edition of *Roses: A Select List and Guide to Pruning*.

From the balance at the bank, the sum of £2,000 was invested in 4 per cent Consols, and a further £2,537 spent in the purchase of a property at St. Albans to house the new assistant foreman of the Trial Ground.

PUBLICATIONS

The Rose Annual for 1955 was sent to all members in March last, practically a month earlier than usual. Members were appreciative of this early delivery, and were also congratulatory regarding the new format of the publication, in particular the four additional colour illustrations. During the year the Council has given further consideration to *The Rose Annual* and propose still more improvements for 1956, which include a stouter cover, better paper, eight additional pages, and an increase to sixteen colour illustrations.

The new edition of *Roses: A Select List and Guide to Pruning* was issued in July to all who had made application for the publication. The Council wishes it to be known it is not too late for any member to apply for a free copy.

THE TRIAL GROUND

Despite a most difficult season, the trials of the new roses continued satisfactorily in 1955, a record number of 234 varieties having been received.

The severe frosts of the winter necessitated the trees being very hard pruned, but they recovered well, and there appeared little amiss by the time of the first flowering in July. The drought later affected the quality of the subsequent crops but at all times the Trial Ground was a blaze of colour.

Half of the new ground taken over was cleared and seeded down to grass and it is proposed next Autumn to cut therefrom a number of new trial beds. By then it is hoped to have the remainder of the new ground prepared.

The Council is further pleased to report that a new permanent assistant to the rose foreman has been engaged.

SHOWS

The Summer Show was held in the Royal Horticultural Society's Halls on July 1st and 2nd. As last year, the lateness of the season was unfavourable to the Nurserymen who exhibit from maiden plants, on the other hand the Amateurs' Section of the Show was undoubtedly the finest staged since the war, both in quality and quantity. The position was reversed at the Provincial Show held in conjunction with The Roundhay (Leeds) Horticultural Society at Roundhay Park, Leeds, on July 19th and 20th. The Nurserymen's exhibits were magnificent whereas the Amateurs' exhibits, though of good quality, were not up to expectations in numbers. The organization of the Show reflected the greatest credit on the Committee of the Roundhay (Leeds) Horticultural Society, to whom the Council expresses thanks for all the courtesies extended to officers and members of our Society.

The Autumn Show was held in the Royal Horticultural Halls on September 9th. In view of the long drought which preceded the Show the exhibits from both Amateurs and Nurserymen were remarkably good.

Arrangements have been completed for a Spring Amateur Competition in 1956, mention of which was made in last year's report. The Royal Horticultural Society at its Fortnightly Show on May 1st and 2nd has undertaken to put space at the Society's disposal and, furthermore, has agreed to allow free entry to members of the N.R.S. to the whole of the Show which will be in both Halls. The Council would like to place on record its appreciation of this kindly co-operation. A schedule of Classes is available on application to the Secretary, National Rose Society, 117 Victoria Street, S.W.1.

The Organizers of various leading Shows throughout the country again included some N.R.S. Classes in their schedules, the purpose of which is to provide opportunities of exhibiting to N.R.S. members who are unable to get to the Society's other Shows. Several, in addition, admitted members of the N.R.S. to their Shows free of charge on production of the N.R.S. Membership Card. The Council tenders thanks to all concerned for these concessions which were appreciated by members.

INFORMATION AND ADVICE BUREAUX

As usual, bureaux were established at the Exhibitions of the Society, also at Bristol, Chelsea and Olympia. They fulfil the purpose for which they are intended which is to give advice to non-members, and for the enrolment of new members. In 1956 it is hoped to establish a bureau at a Northern Show.

ADVICE TO MEMBERS : LIBRARY : LANTERN SLIDES : FILM

With the increasing membership the requests for the above likewise continue to rise and every effort is made to assist members promptly.

The Council would once again ask the indulgence of members respecting the condition of some of the books which through continuous use are rather worn. Unfortunately, as the majority are now out of print it is not possible to replace them. The gift of any books on roses for the library would be appreciated.

There are now four sets of lantern slides in use, two the standard size $3\frac{1}{4} \times 3\frac{1}{4}$, and two on Kodachrome 35 mm. film, mounted 2×2 in. The bookings for these are very heavy and would-be borrowers are requested to make their applications well in advance of when wanted.

The lecturing material has been increased this year by a rose film kindly made and presented to the Society by Mr. E. M. Allen, C.M.G., in conjunction with Mr. Joliffe. The film is in 16 mm. Kodachrome and takes one hour to show. No charge is made for the use of this film, although the borrower is requested to indemnify the Society against damage.

IN CONCLUSION

In conclusion the Council tenders its thanks to the Staffs, both at 117 Victoria Street and at Oaklands, St. Albans, for their loyal and excellent work during the year, also to members who do so much in spreading the advantages of membership. It is hoped all members will endeavour to obtain new members during 1956 and so enable the scope of the Society's activities to be extended still further.

By Order of the Council,

OLIVER MEE, *President*

31st December, 1955.

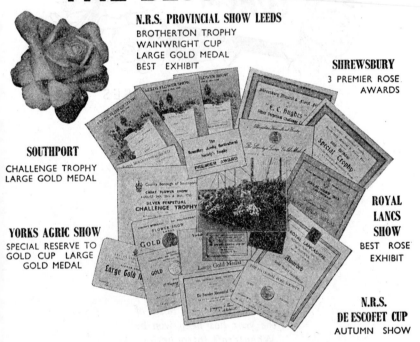

167

THE **NAME** IN ROSES

Three times in the last four years the President's Trophy for the best new Rose of the year has been won by Wheatcroft Introductions

WHEATCROFT BROS. LTD., Ruddington, NOTTINGHAM

COLLINS GUIDE TO

ROSES

FOR THE MODERN GARDEN

Bertram Park, O.B.E.

EDITOR OF THE ROSE ANNUAL

The most complete and up-to-date book on roses and their culture, enriched with both paintings of roses by eminent artists *and* by magnificent photographs. Here is a book that all rose lovers will need and cherish.

BRIEF DETAILS

● Introduction, preparation of soil, planning and planting, raise your own roses, budding, pests, principles of pruning.

● Lists of roses divided into: Hybrid Tea, Floribunda, Climbing, Species and Rose Shrubs, Polyantha, Pom-Poms, etc., each with an introductory section.

● Roses for specific purposes: hedges, exhibition, decoration, pot-pourri. The great Rose Societies.

● Illustrations include pictures of some 140 different roses, all in colour including the 16 pages of paintings. There are also pages in black-and-white.

Publication Summer, 1956, about 25s.

This is the forerunner of a new series (similar in scope to the now famous ' Garden in Colour ' series by the late T. C. Mansfield), and other books are planned to cover bulbs, hardy plants, etc.

COLLINS

Mc Gredy's Roses

1956 NOVELTIES

CAFÉ (floribunda). A complete colour break in roses. This *café-au-lait* coloured floribunda is a must for your garden. When we say that it was raised by W. Kordes of Germany, need we add that the plant has great vigour and really tough foliage.

COLUMBINE (floribunda). Best described as a miniature "Peace". The perfectly formed yellow flowers with a pink tinge at the edge of the petals are produced in open clusters on a plant of great vitality. This is a Frensham × Danish Gold seedling raised by Svend Poulsen of Copenhagen. Awarded Gold Medal, Newcastle.

FIRECRACKER (floribunda). A bright cherry pink floribunda from E. S. Boerner, U.S.A. This novelty has received very high Trial Ground pointings from the National Rose Society as it is always in flower and has a grand bedding habit. Trial Ground Certificate and Certificate of Merit N.R.S. and Shrewsbury.

GOLDEN FLEECE (floribunda). A new unfading straw yellow novelty bred from Diamond Jubilee. Another "always in flower" Boerner special from the U.S.A. Awarded Gold Medal, Bagatelle, Paris. Trial Ground Certificate N.R.S. and Certificates of Merit N.R.S. and Geneva, Switzerland.

LILAC TIME (H.T.). This much publicised rose, bred in our own nursery, is by far the best of any of the new lilac H.T.'s seen to date. Great vigour and lots of healthy dark green foliage make this an ideal bedding rose. Trial Ground Certificate and Certificate of Merit, N.R.S.

MAHAGONA (H.T.). A lovely mahogany coloured bedding rose raised by Wilhelm Kordes of Germany. It has been outstanding in all weather showing to advantage both in heavy rain and hot sunshine.

TWILIGHT (H.T.). A lavender and silver bicolour with a big reputation in the U.S.A. The plant is large and healthy with particularly fine foliage. An E. S. Boerner origination.

YELLOWHAMMER (floribunda). Undoubtedly the best deep unfading yellow floribunda to date. In fact, in really hot weather it deepens to an almost bronzy shade. Look at these awards—Trial Ground Certificate N.R.S.; Gold Medals N.R.S. and Newcastle; Certificate of Merit, Shrewsbury; first prize for best new floribunda Ghent Floralies, Belgium. Raised by S. McGredy and Son.

Bush Trees of above varieties	10/6 each
Standards (except Mahagona)	15/- each

OUR 1955 INTRODUCTIONS

SPARTAN (floribunda). President's Trophy winner. Salmon-orange. 10/6 each. Standards. 15/- each.

ROYAL TAN (H.T.). Light violet and tan.

RED WONDER (floribunda). Deep scarlet. Certificate of Merit.

TIVOLI (floribunda). Warm rose pink. Certificate of Merit.

BRIDAL ROBE (H.T.). Exhibition white. Clay Cup and Gold Medal.

ORANGE SWEETHEART (floribunda). Lovely orange cut flower.

PARADE (Climber). Perpetual flowering pink. 10/6 each.

Bush Trees (except Spartan and Parade)	7/6 each
Standards (except Spartan and Parade)	13/6 each

Illustrated Rose Catalogue Post Free on Request.
Many new beautiful colour blocks.

Samuel McGredy & Son
ROYAL NURSERIES, PORTADOWN, N. IRELAND

E. B. LeGRICE

ROSELAND NURSERIES
NORTH WALSHAM NORFOLK

◆

NEW ROSE INTRODUCTIONS IN 1956

Three new floribundas of merit and distinction
All 10/6 each, 120/- doz.

ALLGOLD: Brilliant unfading buttercup yellow. The colour is retained in sun and rain. The petals fall cleanly but still remain deep yellow. The blooms are three inches across, of about fifteen petals and are carried singly and in large trusses. The foliage is small, glossy, green and abundant. A healthy plant, about 2½ feet high.
This rose has attracted much attention at the Nursery, where its brilliant colour can be seen a long way off. An undoubted advance both in colour and growth. A worthy companion to the "Maid" series.

COPPER DELIGHT: A very pleasing flower of distinct soft clear orange. The blooms are up to 4 in. across when open and are freely produced on large well-spaced clusters. The growth is upright, robust and healthy. This new shade will add variety to the limited range of colours. Height 2½ feet. Semi-double.

LAVENDER LADY: Pure pastel mauve, deepening as the buds expand to 3 in. flowers. The bush is sturdy and the growth healthy. Flowers are freely produced in clusters. Scented. Height 2½ feet.

Raiser of Dainty Maid, Dusky Maiden, Ellinor and Marjorie Le Grice, Wellworth, Charming Maid, Kingcup, Prince Damask, Soldier Boy, Gipsy Maid, Posy, Honeyglow, etc.

BONNIE MAID (Floribunda) Gold Medal 1955, see page 149.

GOLDEN DELIGHT (Floribunda) Certificate of Merit 1955, see page 146.

For full descriptions and prices of these and all popular varieties,
write for free Catalogue "Roses to Grow", the candid catalogue
based on personal experience

My Roses are grown on virgin rose soil and are budded on selected seedling briar

FOR ROSES OF QUALITY

OUR 1956 INTRODUCTION

HESSIE LOWE

Lovely shade of peach-pink, shading to deeper pink on the outside petals. The blooms are moderately full and develop into beautifully high-centred well-shaped flowers. The growth is strong, exceptionally free flowering, with medium-green disease-resistant foliage. This rose has an exceptionally strong perfume and is in our opinion one of the best roses we have so far had the pleasure of introducing.

★　　★　　★

TONGA

Awarded N.R.S. Trial Ground Certificate. Deep golden orange-yellow, with outer petals heavily veined bronze and scarlet. The flowers are moderately large and elegantly shaped, with pointed petals—having an exquisite perfume. Foliage medium dark green and disease resisting.

★　　★　　★

THE QUEEN

Our Coronation Year introduction has been very popular and is in ever-increasing demand. The colour is burnt orange suffused salmon; it is a vigorous grower, with medium dark green disease-resisting foliage, the flowers are medium size—an ideal bedding variety.

★　　★　　★

SKYLON

N.R.S. Certificate of Merit. R.H.S. Award of Merit. The colour is deep glowing peach suffused pale vermilion, veined and splashed with scarlet; the buds are long and pointed, of perfect shape, and the habit of growth is strong and vigorous with large mildew-proof foliage.

★　　★　　★

OTHER INTRODUCTIONS. Yellowhammer, orange-yellow (floribunda); Spartan, orange-flame (floribunda); Tivoli, rose-pink (floribunda); Bridal Robe, ivory-white (H.T.); Delicado, shell-pink shaded peach (H.T.).

WILLIAM LOWE & SON (NURSERIES) LTD

THE NURSERIES, DERBY ROAD, BEESTON, NOTTINGHAM *Established 1875*

Fryer's *of KNUTSFORD*

Phone: KNUTSFORD 250

OUR EXCITING
NEW
ASSORTMENT
OF ROSES

NEW ROSES
OF ENTIRELY
DIFFERENT
SHADES
BRILLIANT
AND

Acres
of
Roses
Come
and see
them
in
BLOOM

Outstanding in Profusion

Our Catalogue is available at the end of June

MAY WE SEND YOU A COPY

A QUARTERLY JOURNAL FOR ALL ROSE LOVERS

THE ROSE

To many thousands of Rose lovers "The Rose" is almost indispensable. Every three months the reader can find, within its pages, instructions on what to do in every phase of Rose culture, together with seasonal hints on exhibiting, selection, planting, propagating, disease and pest control, soil preparation and pruning.

And, of course, there are the regular full colour plates which are acknowledged to be among the best and most faithful reproductions of Roses ever to appear in a horticultural journal. In short—a journal of news and views of the queen of flowers from every quarter of the globe.

"The Rose" is published four times a year—on the 20th January, April, July and October. The cost is 2s. per copy or 8s. 6d. per year posted regularly to your address.

KINDLY WRITE TO THE PUBLISHERS FOR A COMPLIMENTARY COPY

Managing Editor H. P. Champneys

PUBLISHERS

The Whitefriars Press Ltd, 26 Bloomsbury Way, London, W.C.1

A Famous Name wherever Good Roses are grown

*A*mong the trade names mentioned wherever rosarians foregather, that of Bees Ltd. is an oft-recurring and honoured name.

For generations Bees' Roses have made a rich contribution to the glory of many famous gardens and, indeed, in hundreds of thousands of less imposing yet well-loved gardens throughout the country.

Your garden deserves *good* Roses, well and strongly rooted, full of vigour and vitality, and we invite your valued enquiries.

Bees' catalogues are good companions for garden lovers, and a copy of our Planters' Guide to Rose bushes, Fruit trees, Plants and Shrubs, will gladly be sent on request. Autumn Guide ready September, 1956

BEES LTD., HEAD OFFICE, MILL ST., LIVERPOOL
Nurseries and Trial Grounds (1000 *Acres*). *Sealand, Chester*

189

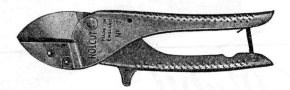

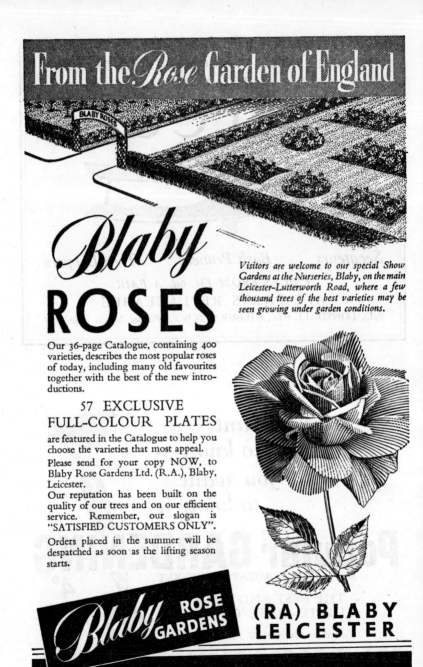

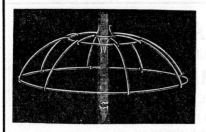

FOR PERFECT PRUNING
USE

FELCO SECATEURS

Accurate setting

THE CHOICE OF EXPERIENCED GARDENERS EVERYWHERE

Roses particularly demand careful pruning, and FELCO Secateurs are the very best for this purpose and for all other pruning requirements. Recommended by schools and centres of arboriculture, viticulture and horticulture.

★ Light, handy and sturdy!
★ Highest quality blades!
★ Handles in light unbreakable metal!

FULLY GUARANTEED

Price 30/-

From all good Ironmongers and Seedsmen, or write direct.

Write *now* for illustrated literature.

A RECENT TESTIMONIAL

"We recommend Felco Secateurs as by far the best we have ever used. We think any Rose grower would be delighted with them."

R. HARKNESS & CO. LTD.
*The Rose Gardens,
Hitchin, Herts.*

EDOUARD DUBIED & CO. LTD., NORTHAMPTON ST., LEICESTER
Tel: LEICESTER **65187-8**

195

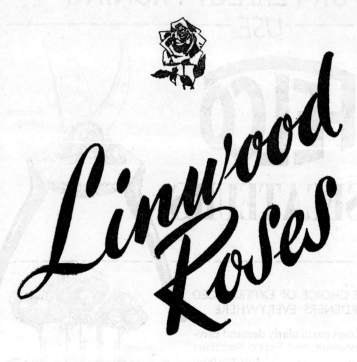

Linwood Roses

CATALOGUE FREE
ON REQUEST

LINWOOD NURSERIES

TRANBY LANE, SWANLAND, E. YORKS

Telephone FERRIBY 96Y

Hawlmark

Roses

OF WORLD-WIDE REPUTATION

INTRODUCTIONS FOR 1956

'SIR WINSTON CHURCHILL' (H.T.) *by Dicksons of Hawlmark*
Glowing rich pink deeply shaded and veined orange. Erect vigorous growth. We are proud to introduce this splendid rose which we are privileged to name after our greatest statesman. Awarded Gold Medal N.R.S. First Class Trial Grounds Certificate; Award of Merit R.H.S.
PRICE: 10s. 6d. each.

FIRECRACKER (floribunda) *by Jackson & Perkins*
Cerise-scarlet with yellow base. Large semi-double. One of the finest free growing varieties yet introduced. First Class Trial Grounds Certificate and Certificate of Merit N.R.S.
PRICE 10s. 6d. each.

GOLDEN FLEECE (floribunda) *by Jackson & Perkins*
Rich buff yellow. Clusters of large semi-double flowers. A very welcome colour addition. Awarded Gold Medal Bagatelle; First Class Trial Grounds Certificate N.R.S.
PRICE: 10s. 6d.

CAFÉ (floribunda) *by W. Kordes*
Café-au-lait colour. A completely new break.
PRICE: 10s. 6d.

Write for our 1956 catalogue of superior quality roses

DICKSONS OF HAWLMARK

Incorporated by Alex. Dickson & Sons, Ltd.

NEWTOWNARDS   Nr. BELFAST

ESTABLISHED 1836

BRANCH ROSE GARDENS

By Appointment   STOKE GOLDINGTON   BUCKS.

NEW ROSES FOR 1956

CIRCUS

A brilliant Floribunda Rose, yellow with lovely orange and orange-red shading. The flowers are double, a pretty shape, and the habit ideal for bedding. This excellent variety is the first Polyantha approaching the "flame" shades, and should find a place in bedding schemes with all but the tallest varieties. The best variety we have distributed since Ena Harkness and Frensham. Raised by H. C. Swim for Armstrong Nurseries. Gold Medal, Trial Ground Certificate, All-America Rose Selection. 10s. 6d. each; 120s. per dozen.

EDDIE'S CREAM POLYANTHA

A very fine variety, which we think is the best of its colour, and has the virtues one expects of a Floribunda. The flowers are double, with a pleasing apricot scent. While the more brilliant colours are always in greater demand, we think this variety has just the right shade to set them off. 7s. 6d. each; 84s. per dozen.

ARDELLE

An Exhibitor's Rose, producing very large flowers on extra strong plants. The colour is cream, sometimes pearly white. It is certainly remarkable for vigour and for the size of its flowers, which are of very lovely form. 7s. 6d. each; 84s. per dozen.

'SIR WINSTON CHURCHILL'

By courtesy of Messrs. Alex. Dickson & Son we can offer plants of this Hybrid Tea, which we, in company with many other members of the N.R.S., first saw on their stand of New Roses at the Summer Show. Gold Medal, Trial Ground Certificate. 10s. 6d. each; 120s. per dozen.

Our 1956 Catalogue would be gladly sent on request; among other varieties described will be the outstanding new Rose, 'Queen Elizabeth'.

R. HARKNESS & CO. LTD
THE ROSE GARDENS
HITCHIN HERTFORDSHIRE

Printed by Jarrold & Sons Ltd., Norwich